IEC

全球能源互联网报告

（中英文对照）

国际电工委员会（IEC） 著

国家电网有限公司国际合作部 译
中国电力科学研究院有限公司

中国电力出版社
CHINA ELECTRIC POWER PRESS

U0680783

图书在版编目（CIP）数据

IEC 全球能源互联网报告：汉英对照 / 国际电工委员会（IEC）著；国家电网有限公司国际合作部，中国电力科学研究院有限公司译. —北京：中国电力出版社，2018.11

ISBN 978-7-5198-2624-6

Ⅰ. ①I… Ⅱ. ①国… ②国… ③中… Ⅲ. ①互联网络－应用－能源发展－研究报告－世界－汉、英 Ⅳ. ①F416.2－39

中国版本图书馆 CIP 数据核字（2018）第 258541 号

审图号：GS（2019）735 号

此版本为 IEC 白皮书官方版本的中文译本。IEC 对中文译本不负责。如有不一致之处，应参阅英文原文。

出版发行：中国电力出版社
地　　址：北京市东城区北京站西街 19 号（邮政编码 100005）
网　　址：http://www.cepp.sgcc.com.cn
责任编辑：翟巧珍（010-63412351）　王　南（010-63412876）
责任校对：黄　蓓　朱丽芳
装帧设计：张俊霞
责任印制：石　雷

印　　刷：北京盛通印刷股份有限公司
版　　次：2018 年 11 月第一版
印　　次：2018 年 11 月北京第一次印刷
开　　本：880 毫米×1230 毫米　16 开本
印　　张：10.5
字　　数：166 千字
定　　价：120.00 元

编 译 组

主 审 舒印彪

翻 译 张佩佩　胡　浩　邢　璐　马文媛　王莹莹

审 校 范建斌　胡学浩　王晓刚　张占奎　王　真

　　　　　王　琳　孙冠中

执行摘要

全球能源互联网（GEI）是实现更大范围电力系统互联互通的最终演化趋势，体现了能量流、信息流、业务流的高度融合，是保障全球能源安全的智能化、自动化和基于网络的系统。

在全球经济发展的推动下，世界能源消费总量从 1965 年的 54 亿 t 标准煤增加到 2014 年的 185 亿 t 标准煤。化石能源占比超过 85%。未来世界能源消费仍将保持增长态势。长期形成的能源高消耗模式难以逆转。

为了应对这种趋势，全球能源互联网将构建以特高压电网为骨干网架，以输送大容量可再生能源为主的目标，实现跨国、跨洲，包含不同技术领域和层级，涵盖设备全寿命周期，且具有高度互操作性的泛在智能电网。

建设全球能源互联网是具有高度战略意义的，其关键技术条件已基本具备。另外，实现大范围跨洲或全球能源互联的技术难点在于前所未有的系统融合程度。为解决这一挑战，通用的国际标准和技术规范是不可或缺的，基于它们才得以构建具体的解决方案。尤其是系统层级的标准，有助于促进国内和国际共识的达成，因此已成为开展科研活动的前提，进而获得真正的市场商机。

本报告分析了全球能源互联网潜在市场的成熟度、相关技术和经济发展趋势，高度评估了其对能源、环境、技术和政策的影响。

实现全球能源互联网这一宏大的愿景，需要在标准化领域开展大量的工作，包括制定多系统互操作标准。因此，本报告旨在阐述全球能源互联网概念，为识别和确定实现大规模跨洲和全球能源互联的标准化需求奠定基础。

致　　谢

本报告由国际电工委员会（IEC）市场战略局（MSB）全球能源互联网项目组起草，国际能源署（IEA）作为合作方、国家电网有限公司（SGCC）作为项目牵头单位给予了特别贡献。项目组共召开三次面对面会议，分别为 2016 年 1 月（中国北京），2016 年 3 月（中国北京），2016 年 6 月（法国巴黎）。项目组成员如下：

舒印彪博士，国家电网有限公司，IEC 副主席，市场战略局召集人，项目负责人

Luis Munuera 博士，IEA，项目合作方

于军博士，国家电网有限公司，项目执行负责人

范建斌博士，国家电网有限公司

梁才浩博士，中国电力科学研究院有限公司

耿丹博士，气候议会

王伟博士，国家电网有限公司

邢璐博士（女），国网能源研究院有限公司

Richard Schomberg 先生，法国电力公司

Dongil Lee 博士，韩国电力公司

Jae Young Yoon 博士，韩国电气研究院

Chan-Ki Kim 博士，韩国电力公司

Ho-Keun Kim 博士，韩国电力公司

Stefan Engelhardt 博士，瑞典 SAP 公司

Alexander Rentschler 博士，德国西门子股份有限公司

Shinichi Suganuma 先生，东京电力公司

戴承伟先生，中国大唐集团

闫秦先生，中国大唐集团

胡浩博士，国家电网有限公司

Peter Lanctot 先生，IEC，MSB 秘书

目 录

缩略语表

技术和科学术语

AC	alternating current，交流	
AC	advisory committee（of the IEC），IEC 咨询委员会	
AIN	asset intelligence network，资产智能网络	
BI	business intelligence，商业智能	
BOS	balance of system，系统平衡	
CBA	cost-benefit analysis，成本效益分析	
COP	conference of the parties，缔约方大会	
CRM	customer relationship management，客户关系管理	
CSC	current source converter，电流源换流器	
CSP	concentrated solar power，聚光太阳能发电	
DC	direct current，直流	
DMS	document management system，文件管理系统	
DNI	direct normal irradiance，通常年太阳直射辐射度	
EAM	environmental assessment and management，环境评估和管理	
EDI	electronic data interchange，电子数据交换	
EES	electrical energy storage，电能存储	
EPC	engineering，procurement and construction（company），工程、采购与建设（公司）	
ERP	enterprise resource planning，企业资源计划	
FACTS	flexible AC transmission system，灵活交流输电系统	
FCF	frequency converter facility，变频器设备	
FMEA	failure mode and effects analysis，故障模式和影响分析	
FTU	field terminal unit，场监控单元	
GDP	gross domestic product，国内生产总值	
GEI	global energy interconnection，全球能源互联网	

GHG	greenhouse gas，温室气体	
GIS	geographical information system，地理信息系统	
HES	head-end system，前端系统	
HTS	high-temperature superconducting，高温超导	
HVAC	high-voltage alternating current，高压交流	
HVDC	high-voltage direct current，高压直流	
HWACT	half-wavelength AC transmission，半波长交流输电	
ICT	information and communication technology，信息与通信技术	
IEA-OES	Ocean Energy Systems Technology Collaboration Programme of the IEA，国际能源署海洋能系统技术合作项目	
IOT	Internet of Things，物联网	
IT	information technology，信息技术	
LCC	line-commutated converter，线换相换流器	
LCOE	levelized cost of energy，平准化能源成本	
MDM	meter data management，计量数据管理	
MTDC	multi-terminal direct current，多端直流	
OEM	original equipment manufacturer，原始设备制造商	
OLTP	online transaction processing，线上交易处理	
OT	operational technology，经营技术	
PMU	phaser measurement unit，相角测量单元	
PV	photovoltaic，光伏	
RE	renewable energy，可再生能源	
SC	subcommittee（of the IEC），分技术委员会	
SCADA/EMS	supervisory control and data acquisition/energy management system，数据采集与监控系统/能量管理系统	
SDO	standards developing organization，标准制定组织	
STE	solar thermal energy，太阳热能	
SyC	systems committee（of the IEC），系统委员会	
TC	technical committee（of the IEC），技术委员会	
TSO	transmission system operator，输电系统运营商	

UHV	ultra-high voltage，特高压	
UHVAC	ultra-high-voltage alternating current，特高压交流	
UHVDC	ultra-high-voltage direct current，特高压直流	
VSC	voltage source converter，电压源换流器	
WAMS	wide area monitoring system，广域测量系统	

组织、机构和公司名称缩写

ASEAN	Association of Southeast Asian Nations，东南亚国家联盟
ASG	Asian Super Grid，亚洲超级电网
ATSOI	Association of the Transmission System Operators of Ireland，爱尔兰输电系统运营商协会
BALTSO	Baltic Transmission System Operators，波罗的海输电系统运营商
CEPRI	China Electric Power Research Institute，中国电力科学研究院有限公司
CIGRE	International council on large electric systems，国际大电网会议组织
COP21	21st Conference of the Parties，2015 United Nations Climate Change Conference，联合国气候变化会议缔约国组织第 21 次会议
CSPG	China Southern Power Grid，中国南方电网
EDF	Electricité de France，法国电力集团
ENTSO-E	European Network of Transmission System Operators for Electricity，欧洲输电运营商联盟
EPRI	Electric Power Research Institute，美国电力科学研究院
ERCOT	Electric Reliability Council of Texas，德克萨斯州电力可靠性委员会
ETSO	European Transmission System Operators，欧洲输电系统运营商
EU	European Union，欧盟

HAPUA	Heads of ASEAN Power Utilities/Authorities，亚洲电力公司/负责人
IEA	International Energy Agency，国际能源署
IEC	International Electrotechnical Commission，国际电工委员会
IPCC	Intergovernmental Panel on Climate Change，政府间气候变化专门委员会
IPS/UPS	Integrated Power System/Unified Power System，集成电力系统/统一电力系统
ISO	International Organization for Standardization，国际标准化组织
KEPCO	Korea Electric Power Corporation，韩国电力公司
KERI	Korea Electrotechnology Research Institute，韩国电工技术研究院
MSB	Market Strategy Board，市场战略局
NEC	National Electrotechnical Committee，国家电工委员会
NERC	Northern American Electric Reliability Corporation，北美电力可靠性委员会
NGET	National Grid Electricity Transmission，英国国家电网
OECD	Organisation for Economic Co-operation and Development，经济合作与发展组织
SAPP	Southern African Power Pool，南部非洲电力联营集团
SE4ALL	United Nations Sustainable Energy for All initiative，联合国"人人享有可持续能源"倡议
SGCC	State Grid Corporation of China，国家电网有限公司
SMB	Standardization Management Board（of the IEC），标准管理局
TEPCO	Tokyo Electric Power Company，东京电力公司
TüV	technischer überwachungsverein（technical inspection association），德国技术检验协会
UCTE	Union for the Coordination of the Transmission of Electricity，

输电协调联盟

UKTSOA   United Kingdom Transmission System Operators Association，
英国输电系统运营商联盟

UN   United Nations，联合国

UNFCCC   United Nations Framework Convention on Climate Change，
联合国气候变化框架公约

专业术语

资产智能网络（asset intelligence network，AIN）

云中枢，其作用是促进资产协同管理并使企业充分利用物联网（IoT）。

背靠背系统（back-to-back system）

两个独立的相邻系统，具有不同且不相容的电气参数（频率/电压/短路容量），并通过一个直流环节进行连接。

注：高压直流（HVDC）输电系统通过一个直流环节连接两个独立的高压交流系统。HVDC 输电系统运行的基本原理是基于通过换流阀将交流电变换成直流电，反之亦然。换流阀是换流站的核心。

平衡系统（balance of system，BOS）

除光伏板外的光伏系统所有组件。

注：包括布线、开关、支架系统、一个或多个太阳能逆变器、电池组和电池充电器。

缔约国大会（conference of the parties，COP）

国际公约的理事机构。

注：最著名的联合国缔约国大会涉及签署了"联合国气候变化框架公约"（UNFCCC）的所有国家，该公约于 1992 年在巴西里约热内卢举行的地球高峰会议上通过。2015 年联合国气候变化大会（COP21）于 2015 年 11 月 30 日至 12 月 12 日在法国巴黎举行。这次会议是 UNFCCC 签署以来的第 21 届会议，因此称为 COP21。

艾焦（exajoule，EJ）

能量单位，1EJ 等于 10^{18}J。

注：在描述国家或全球能源预算时，通常使用基于焦耳的大型单位：$1EJ = 10^{18}$J。焦耳是功或能量的国际单位，等于 1N 的力使其作用点在力的作用方向上移动 1m 所做的功，相当于 1Wh 的 1/3600。

变频器设施（frequency converter facility，FCF）

电子或机电设备将一个频率的交流电变换为另一个频率的交流电的设施。

全球能源强度（global energy intensity）

以市场汇率计算生产 1 单位 GDP 所需要的能量。

能源的平准化成本（LCOE）

电源指标，用于在一个可比较的基础上对不同发电方法进行比较。

太阳热能（solar thermal energy，STE）

利用太阳能来产生热能或电能的能量和技术形式。

太瓦（terawatt，TW）

电力单位，1TW 等于 10^{12}W。

技术检验协会（technischer überwachungsverein，technical inspection association，TüV）

一个德国组织，致力于验证各种产品的安全性，以保护人类和环境免受危害。

特高压（ultra-high voltage，UHV）

电压等级超过 800kV。

第 1 章

引 言

可持续、负担得起、安全的能源供给是长期以来国家和国际能源政策的目标。实现能源系统可持续目标的核心问题是气候变化带来的挑战，其重要性在巴黎协定（Paris accords）后尤为凸显。电力能源具有质量高、用途广的特性。电能作为主要能源载体，成为实现低碳化能源供应的核心媒介。可再生能源，尤其是风能和太阳能，成本的大幅下降在全球范围内引发了应用热潮。如何实现大范围可再生能源接入成为人们关注的焦点。对于那些依赖化石燃料的能源终端用户，通过电力来替代其能源输入的方式（例如，交通运输中的电动汽车或电力工业过程电气化），来降低对化石燃料的依赖度，这样做仅仅增加了总的用电量而已。同时，世界上还有大量的无电人口。随着电力系统不断进步，发电量和电力需求不断增长，电网将会越来越多地在跨国和跨区域层面上进行互联。这一点也在近年来全球能源互联网这一理念引入中得以体现。

全球能源互联网是电网朝向更大范围互联这一发展过程的终极阶段，由跨国跨洲高压和特高压骨干网架形成的全球能源网络和涵盖互联各国各电压等级电网（输电网、配电网）的智能电网构成。全球能源互联网将各大洲的电网联结在一起，发挥不同时区和季节差异性优势，支持所有互联国家电力供应的平衡。

作为参与联合国"人人享有可持续能源"倡议（SE4ALL）的国际组织之一，IEC 及其制定的国际标准在应对基本的能源挑战中发挥着重要作用。IEC 编写本报告旨在阐述全球能源互联网概念，为识别和确定实现大规模、跨洲和全球能源互联的标准化需求奠定基础。

1. 本报告的主要目标

（1）对全球能源互联网在全球范围内的潜在需求、效益和条件提出高层次的评估。

（2）检验支持全球能源互联网实

施所需技术的潜在市场的成熟度。

（3）识别相关技术的技术和经济发展趋势。

（4）在高层次上评估其对能源、环境、技术、政策和相关标准的影响。

（5）提供如何在高层次上开展标准化工作的框架，为利益相关方参与标准化工作提出建议。

2. 本报告的主要范围

本报告从全球能源互联网的视角评估全球范围内工业和商业应用需求，能源资源的分布、开发和利用情况，以及潜在利益。通过收集多个国际组织的相关数据，采用情景比对法，对若干个全球输电方案进行了讨论和分析。

本报告分析了全球能源互联网潜在市场的成熟度。基于输电系统运营商和供应商的设备和技术现状，对一些相关领域的技术、商业发展趋势（即经济方面）和挑战进行了识别，这些相关领域包括清洁能源、特高压、智能电网、储能和电网控制。报告还阐述了全球能源互联网对环境方面带来的影响，如碳减排、输电线路影响等。

最后，报告探讨了全球能源互联网对现有能源系统标准的影响，重点提出了标准化工作的需求。

第 2 章

GEI 愿景

2.1 全球能源挑战

全球一次能源供给在过去 100 年里增长了 10 倍，在最近 40 年里增长了两倍多。2006 年，发展中国家，即非经济合作与发展组织（OECD）成员国的能源使用份额首次超过了发达国家，这一比例在 2013 年时达到了 61:39。传统的能源消费中心转移到中国、印度和南亚，这一现象与全球变化趋势密切相关：① 中国在过去 10 年内是一次能源需求和二氧化碳排放量增长最多的国家，然而由于可再生能源快速发展和能源强度改善，其二氧化碳年排放增量成功降到了 2004 年之前的水平，并出现了脱钩迹象。② 2000 年以来，印度的能源需求增量几乎占据了全球能源需求增长的 10%，而印度尼西亚则是全球范围内煤炭消费增长最多的国家。③ 欧洲通过设置排放上限、降低经济活动水平和快速发展可再生能源，显著改变了

其能源现状。④ 非传统油气技术的不断发展和应用，正在极大改变美国的能源前景和能源进口国定位。2014 年，全球清洁能源新增发电装机容量第一次超过了其他电源类型的总和。

尽管有以上这些进步，但全球人类活动引起的与能源相关的二氧化碳排放量仍创下了新纪录，2012 年排放量达到 316 亿 t，全球气温与前工业时代相比上升了 1℃。同时，全球仍有 13 亿人无法获得清洁能源。目前全球亟需安全、廉价、清洁的能源供应，同时面临着前所未有的一系列挑战以及迅速的技术变革，形势比以往更加严峻。

2.1.1 能源安全

在全球经济增长推动下，世界能源消耗从 1965 年的 54 亿 t 标准煤上升到了 2014 年的 185 亿 t 标准煤。其中，化石能源占比超过了消耗总量的 85%，而且由于长期以来形成的能源密集型消费模式较难逆转，因此世界

能源消耗在未来一段时间还会继续上升。

能源安全可以理解为"源源不断地以可负担的价格获得能源"。能源安全有很多维度，长期能源安全主要是指根据经济发展和环境可持续发展的要求及时地投资能源供应，短期能源安全则重在关注能源体系并及时应对能源供需突变状况的能力。

在网络与体系必须保持持续性平衡的能源市场，对于无法实时获得能源实物供给的担忧极为普遍，例如电力，某种程度上天然气也如此。在一些容量有限的市场，或者短期内价格无法调节供需平衡的市场中，尤为如此。

地球上有充足的能源资源，如化石能源。然而从长远来看，化石类的能源终将枯竭，并且受地域限制较大。化石能源开发的状况变化不定，其影响因素包括地缘政治、不断变化的经济前景、投资状况、快速变革的技术等。同时，地球上可再生能源资源十分丰富（见图 2-1），若这些资源的技术可开发潜力得到充分发掘，将能超过许多倍地满足世界能源需求。

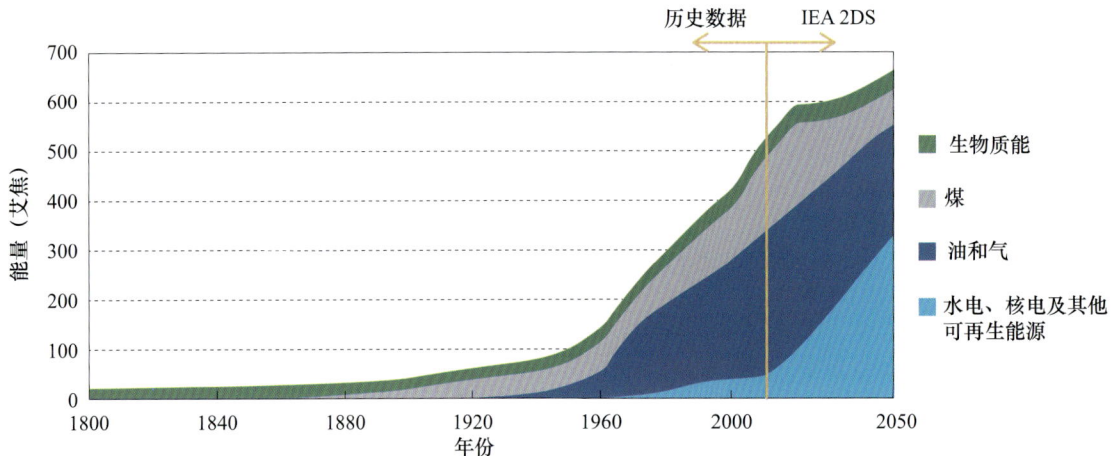

图 2-1　1800～2013 年主要能源供应来源及国际能源署 2013～2050 年展望

2.1.2　气候变化

政府间气候变化专门委员会一致认为，若不采取充分负责的、及时的行动，气候变化可能会给全世界造成不可逆的严重后果。要遏制危险的气候变化及其所带来的环境后果，需要我们不断减少温室气体排放。

能源生产与使用的温室气体排放量占到了人类活动温室气体排放总量的 2/3，因此能源领域的改革对于应对气候变化至关重要。在过去的 30 年中，尽管世界能源体系在脱碳方面做了很多努力，但成效微弱，2013 年化石燃料总量占全球能源供应量约 81%。在过去 40 年中，煤电仍然是能源结构中排放占比最大的类型。

自工业革命以来，每年燃料燃烧排放的温室气体从接近为零增加到 2013 年的 320 亿 t 二氧化碳当量，而且自 20 世纪 90 年代初至今，能源供应的碳排放强度（单位能源消耗的碳排放量）几乎没有改变（见图 2-2）。1990～2013 年期间，居高不下的碳排放强度，加上人口的增加（35%）以及人均国内生产总值的增加（60%），使得全球温室气体排放量急剧增加了近 60%。2014 年，全球温室气体浓度稳步增长至 445μL/L 二氧化碳当量。

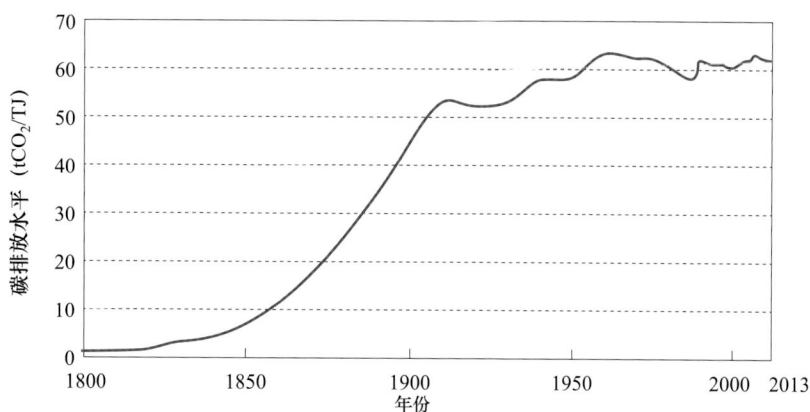

图 2-2　1800～2013 年全球能源供应的碳排放水平（IEA）

全球能源系统正处在应对气候变化的重大抉择关头，近期的联合国气候峰会对此挑战也做出了前所未有的响应。世界各国齐聚巴黎召开气候变化第 21 次缔约方会议，会议讨论了签署国际协约，确定了未来 10 年乃至更长时间应对气候变化的方向，旨在尽快达到全球温室气体排放峰值，并控制全球平均温度上升低于 2℃，努力将气温上升控制在 1.5℃ 以内。要实现这一温升目标，全球需要大量并持续减少全球温室气体排放。

温室气体会在大气中停留很多年，影响气候变化的是温室气体在一定时期内累积的浓度。据估计，截止到 2014 年全球已经排放了 19 700 亿 t 二氧化碳。政府间气候变化专门委员会预计，1991～2100 年累计排放的二氧化碳总量必须低于约 30 000 亿 t，只有 50% 的可能将全球温度上升控制在 2℃ 以内。考虑到非能源领域排放的温室气体，从现在到 2100 年，能源领域可排放量约为 8800 亿～11 800 亿 t，约占 20 世纪 100 年排放总量的 60%。

2.1.3 环境污染

每年与空气污染有关的死亡病例估计达到 650 万例，如果能源部门不采取更加有力的措施控制污染排放，这一数字将有增无减。目前由于室外空气污染导致的过早死亡人数为 300 万，预计到 2040 年将上升到 450 万，而且主要集中在亚洲发展中国家。据国际能源署预计，在清洁空气情况下，到 2040 年由于空气污染导致的过早死亡人数可减少 170 万，这一情况只需要增加 7%的能源总投资就能实现。

2.2 全球能源互联网的概念

2.2.1 为什么要进行大规模的互联？

要提供可负担的、安全的、可持续的能源供应，同时减缓气候变化风险，需要我们在新能源基础设施和技术研发上进行空前规模的投资，并大规模改造现有的能源输送系统。重要的是，未来能实现这些目标的能源系统将会大大减少对化石能源的依赖，提高供应效率，增加可再生能源和清洁能源使用比例。在这一挑战的重大决策关头，我们正在进行大规模的电力系统互联。

主要的可再生资源在很大程度上还受制于时间和空间。最优质的风能和太阳能资源往往远离能源需求中心；此类资源分布最密集的地区（如中国北部的风能或美国西南部的太阳能）往往远离主要的能源需求中心。虽然风能和太阳能的技术进步使得我们可以在资源分布不甚有利的地方进行开发利用，但扩展输电系统往往是利用最有吸引力资源的唯一可能途径。水电是目前世界上最大的清洁电源，但目前受到自然资源所处地理位置的限制，同样状况的还有地热、波浪和潮汐能等应用较少的可再生能源技术。

风能和太阳能的发电出力是有波动的，这种波动取决于给定时刻的风速和光照强度。电网互联已被证实在促进波动性可再生能源并网方面是非常有价值的灵活工具，能够平滑发电曲线。

同样，各国每小时的能源需求模式各不相同，这取决于时区、经济结构和行为。由于整体经济结构的差异以及空调和电加热在不同地区使用情况不同，各国对电量的需求模式也表现出相当大的差异。

电网互联能够在更大的范围内平衡电力需求，连接冬季用电高峰地区和夏季用电高峰地区，按时区划分用电地区能够平衡用电的峰/谷期和季节性负荷。同样，在可再生能源的生产模式和资源禀赋方面，各地区也存在差异。因此，强大的电网互联能够提高电力系统的灵活性，同时节约可观的装机容量以满足峰荷需求。

目前，许多国家呈现出广泛互联的趋势。虽然洲际互联与同频系统存在已有几十年了，但在大规模电力远程输送方面的应用仍然十分有限（通常关注的是远距离水电输送），而且互联通常是出于系统安全考虑。更大规模的区域和洲际互联可为可持续能源发展带来显著收益。在此背景下，实现全球能源互联有望成为解决多项能源挑战的可能方案。

2.2.2　GEI 是什么?

GEI 最终阶段将是自然发展形成的更大范围电网互联，即由智能电网基础设施支撑的全球互联的电力系统，优化利用特高压技术进行远距离电力传输。这种大规模的电网互联将为清洁能源的广泛使用提供骨干网架支撑，并可在资源最好的地方合理设置发电厂。

未来我们将受益于更高层次互联互通和全球能源互联网，在此情况下，电力需求同样远高于目前水平。依赖化石能源的传统工业生产过程，交通部门特别是私人交通的电气化水

平大大提高，住宅和商业部门的电力供热、制冷及设备用能需求不断上涨，所有这些情况导致电力需求不断增长。

GEI 的概念基于以下三大支柱:

（1）大规模的清洁能源利用，尤其是波动性可再生能源，以及较高的电气化水平;

（2）电力远距离传输，使特高压技术成为必需;

（3）可以在各级电压水平进行智能监视和控制的智能电网解决方案（见图 2-3）。

2.2.3　GEI 的潜在益处

实现地理广域范围内的高层次互联提供了电力交换的平台，可以进一步平衡电力供需，充分利用发电资源。这是全球范围内清洁能源利用和获得低碳电力的综合平台，通过平台可以获得潜在的经济效益、社会效益和环境效益:

（1）全球能源网络能够带来环境效益，因为这一网络为可再生能源资源的利用提供骨干网架支撑，而从电厂角度来讲，则可以获得最优的可再生能源资源;

（2）尽管从现在起至 2050 年的成本趋势还无法预测，但用于评估全球能源系统脱碳成本的各情景分析已经确认，可再生能源是脱碳的主要支柱;

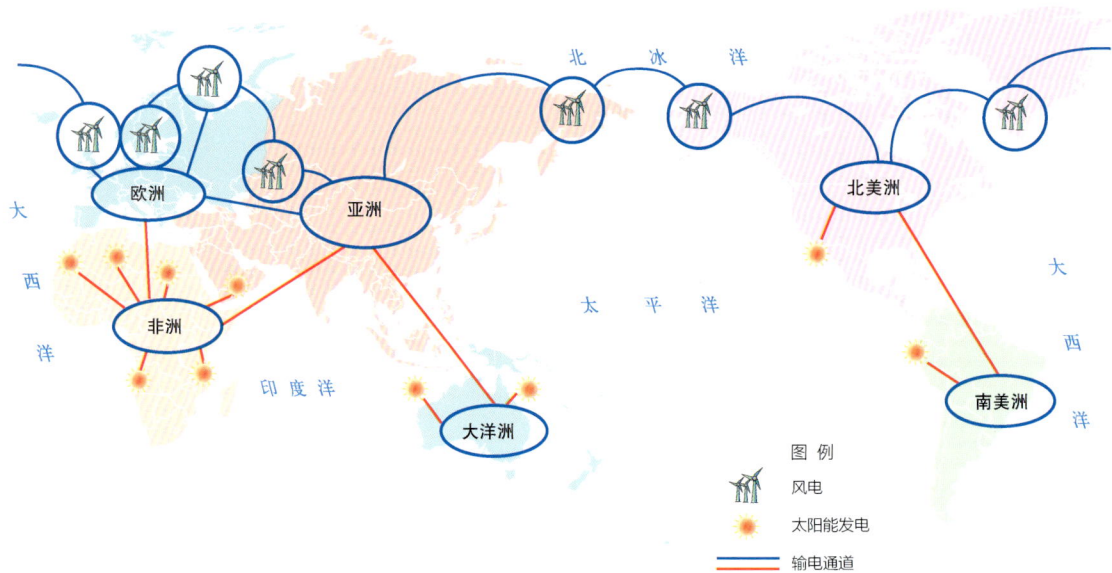

全球能源互联网（GEI）＝特高压电网＋智能电网＋清洁能源

图 2-3　全球能源互联网示意图

（3）大规模输电网络和低碳电力将为发展中国家带来社会效益，使其获得清洁能源，并有机会改善当地的能力建设和就业。

2.2.4　GEI 设想

GEI 将构成一个有机整体设想，使国家电网的发展与日益增长的跨国跨洲联网水平相协调。特高压输电技术、智能电力监控和电网控制技术构成了电网互联的支柱，互联电网的建成将有利于（环）北极风电、赤道太阳能以及各大洲的主要可再生能源基地和负荷中心互联。综合考虑目前的电气化水平、发电站分布情况、传输和配置能力，全球能源互联网的发展可以分为三个不同的阶段：

第一阶段，各国政府、电网系统所有者和运营商、公用事业单位和其他利益相关者深化共识，以提高互联水平为目标。这一阶段国内电网继续升级加强，国家电力系统逐步实现脱碳。

第二阶段，同一大洲的跨国互联水平大幅提升，大规模清洁能源基地得到开发（例如北欧的风能、中国西部的风能和太阳能、北非的太阳能）。

第三阶段，相距更为遥远的能源中心开始发展（环）北极地区的风能和赤道地区的太阳能，跨洲互联开始出现。

第 3 章

GEI 能源趋势与市场成熟度

3.1 全球能源资源与能源需求

世界一次能源总需求一直保持持续增长趋势，同时世界能源结构不断发生着变化（见图 3-1）。

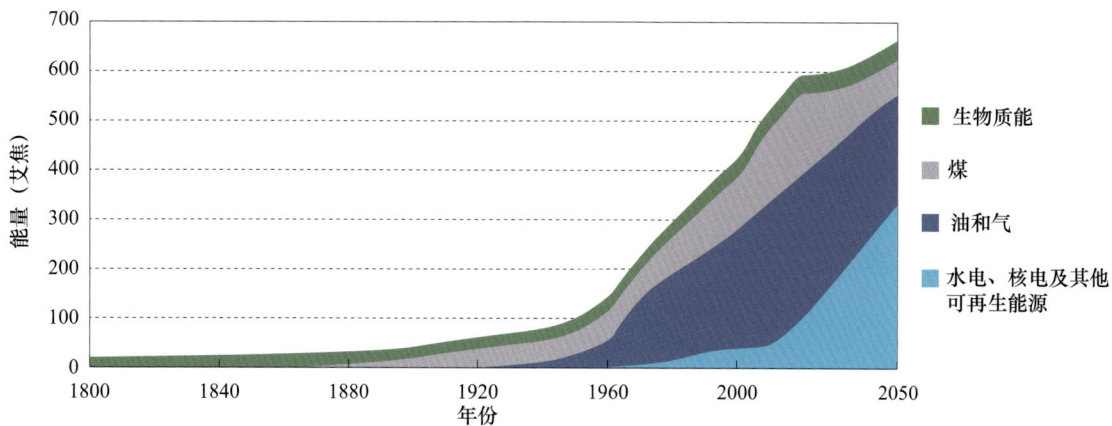

图 3-1 1800～2013 年全球一次能源供应结构及 2013～2050 年展望（IEA）

能源消耗由一种能源形式转变为另一种能源形式平均需要 20～40 年。19 世纪中期以前，传统的生物质能是全球能源消耗的主要来源。随着工业革命的开始，煤及其衍生物的消费量大幅增加，这是因为能源服务和燃料终端使用途径越来越多。20 世纪中期出现了第三次转变，能源形式转变为石油和天然气。在 20 世纪 70 年代末以前，世界一直处于另一个重大变革中，而在这之后，一次能源供应中石油的需求量达到了高峰，天然气的份额也在持续增长。中国的经济发展又一次促使煤炭的消费量回升，虽然增加幅度不大。更重要的是，低碳能源（水力，核能和其他可再生能源）的消费量大幅提升。

3.1.1 能源资源

地球上资源充足，但经济规模和

技术能力却因经济条件和地理位置的不同而存在差异。全球能源资源主要包括：化石能源（如煤炭、石油、天然气）、核裂变能（铀和潜在的钍）以及可再生能源（如水力、风能、太阳能、生物质能、地热能和海洋能）。

3.1.1.1 化石能源和核能

化石能源虽然资源丰富，但分布不均匀，且并非取之不尽用之不竭（见图 3-2）。全球剩余的可开采石油资源总量约为 6.1 万亿桶，其中已掌

握其开采技术（进行盈利性开采的可能性为 90%）的数量约为 1.7 万亿桶。以现在的生产速度计算，已掌握开采技术的石油储量将在 52 年后开采完，技术性可开采石油资源（一个更不确定的概念）将在 185 年后开采完。已掌握开采技术的煤炭储量可维持 122 年的生产，而天然气的储量将维持 61 年的生产，以 2012 年的消费量计算，铀储量可以持续开采 120 年。随着新科技的发展，不可再生能源资源的可开采量也在不断增加。

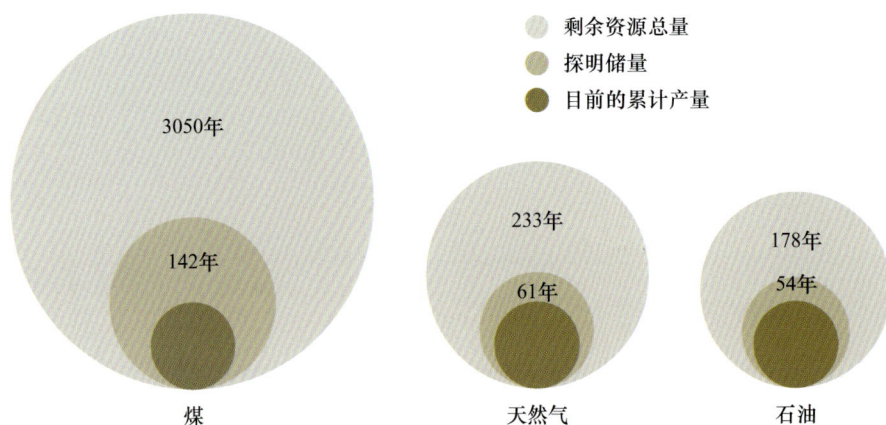

图 3-2　化石燃料储量时间线

化石能源在全球的分布极其不均匀，95%的煤炭分布在欧洲、亚欧大陆、亚太地区和北美，80%的石油分布在中东，美洲的北部、南部和中部，70%的天然气分布在欧洲、亚欧大陆和中东地区。

虽然资源基础十分雄厚，但化石能源的大部分，包括国内和国际石油

公司已有的资源都不可以进行进一步的开采，否则，二氧化碳的预计排放指标就无法实现。图 3-3 展示了在限制地球温升（50%的可能性）的情况下可以消费的最大能源量，重点指出了如果消费了全部列出的能源，地球温升将突破设定的上限，上升 3℃。

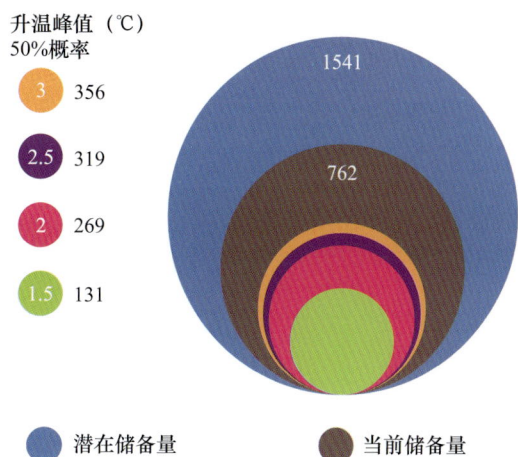

升温峰值（℃）
50%概率

3	356
2.5	319
2	269
1.5	131

● 潜在储备量　　● 当前储备量

图 3-3　50%的概率储备

3.1.1.2　可再生能源（RE）

总体来说，太阳提供了大量能量：每年大约有 8.85 亿 TWh 能量到达地球表面。根据《国际能源署当前政策情况》中的数据，这些能量相当

于 2008 年商业中一次能源消耗总量的 6200 倍或 2035 年人类能源消耗总量的 4200 倍（见图 3-4）。世界风能资源储量各不相同，但其总量也超过了全球电力需求量，而且世界大多数地区都有大力发展风能和水能的潜力。根据国际能源署（IEA）公布的转换方法，将电力供应量（TWh）换算为一次能源供应量（EJ），政府间气候变化专门委员会（IPCC）估计 2007 年陆上风能潜力为 180EJ/ 年（或 50 000TWh/年），相当于 2014 年全球电力需求的 2.5 倍。国际能源署估计全球水电潜力为 16 400TWh/年，足以满足全球 2/3 的电力需求。

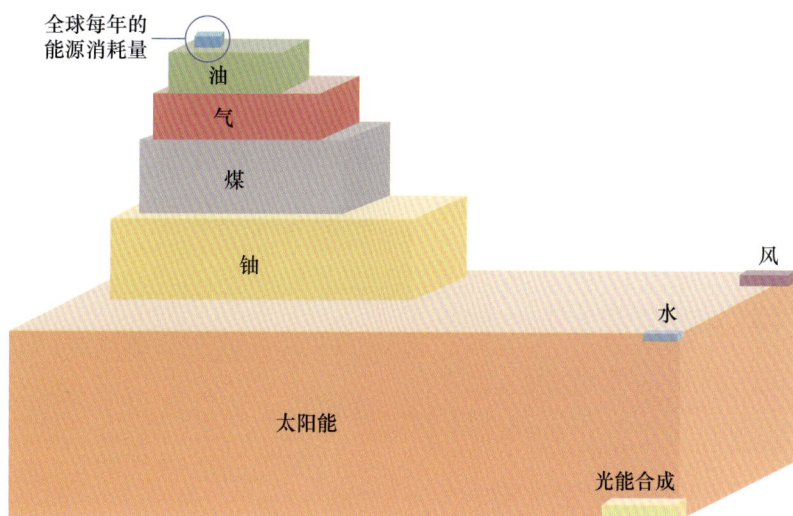

图 3-4　全球每年已知能源的消费量（IEA 2012 年）

全球的清洁能源分布也十分不均匀（见图 3-5）。水力资源主要分布在亚洲、南美、北美和中非的河流流域中。风能资源主要分布在北极地区、

中亚和南亚、北欧、北美中部以及东非，在每个大洲的近海区域也分布有少量的高质量风能资源。最佳的太阳能资源分布在北非、东非、中东、大

洋洲、中美、南美以及赤道附近的其他地区。此外，干旱地区，如戈壁、拉贾斯坦邦和其他沙漠也有优质太阳能资源。正如前面强调的，如果在距离负荷中心数百乃至数千千米的人烟

稀少地区大规模地开发可再生能源，且要求电力能够实现大规模远距离的输送，这样就可以利用偏远地区的优质发电资源。

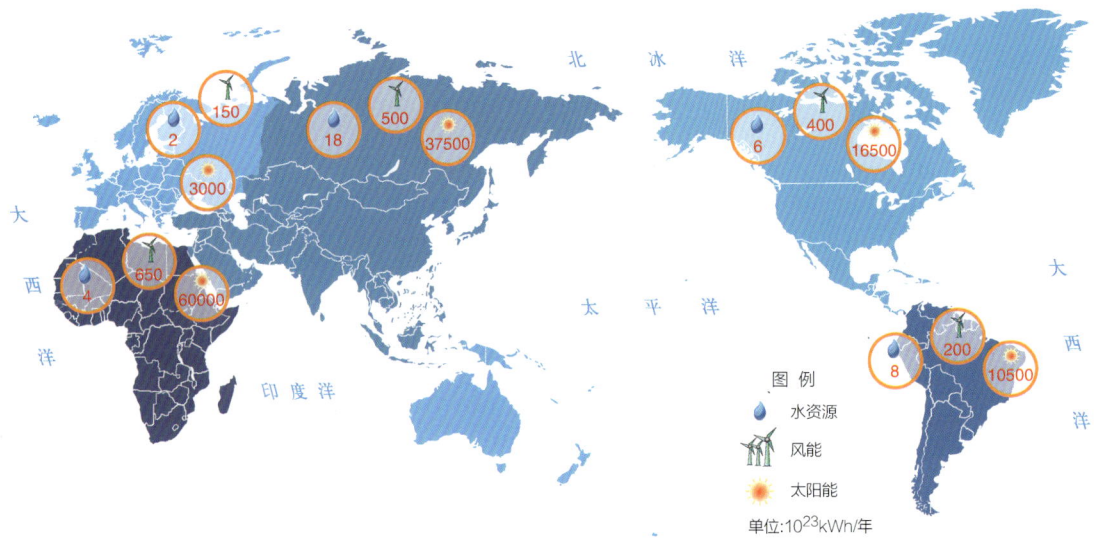

图 3-5　世界清洁能源分布

3.1.2　能源需求

在过去的几十年间，全球能源消费量的增长速度比 GDP 增速慢得多，这主要得益于经济结构的变化、能源效率的提高和燃料使用的转变。全球能源强度（每创造一个单位的国内生产总值所消耗的能源量）在 1971～2012 年间下降了 32%。尽管能源需求和经济增长之间出现了不同步变化（这一变化在经合组织中体现的尤其明显），这两者仍然是密切相关的（见图 3-6）。

然而，能源效率在 2000～2011 年

的提高平均速率远低于 1980～2000 年间的变化，且在 2009 年和 2010 年，能源强度实际上有所上升，这是由于全球经济活动将重心转向了亚洲发展中国家，这些国家具有相对较高的能源强度。而预测对于 GDP 增长率和增长模式是高度敏感的。

世界人口将由 69.2 亿持续增长到预计的 95.5 亿，而目前仍有 13 亿人无法享用清洁能源。对能源载体不断增加的能源需求，尤其是来自新发展区域的需求，如非洲、南亚和拉丁美洲，将成为未来能源系统的中流砥柱。

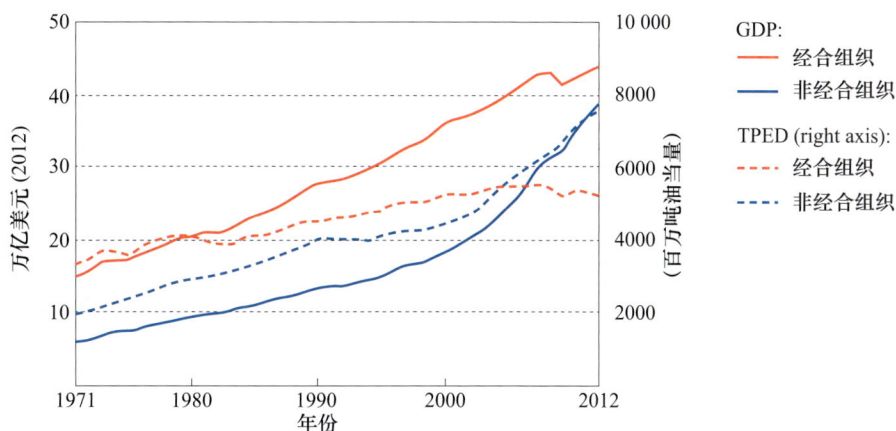

图 3-6　全球一次能源需求的总量和发展速度

3.1.2.1　全球能源需求

预计全球一次能源需求将继续增长，尽管增长速度不断降低。

电力已经成为全球能源体系的核心，而且还将发挥更加重要的作用。全球将近 40%的一次能源用于发电，但电力仅占全球终端能源需求的17%。在所有的终端能源载体中，人均电力增长速度最快，1974 年时仅为1263kWh/cap，2011 年翻番，达到了2933kWh/cap，按照这种趋势预计将持续增长到 2050 年。在过去 10 年内，风能和太阳能发电量每年以两位数的速度增长，但同期化石燃料在净新发电量中的占比超过 75%。

至关重要的是，新能源终端的应用和行业的电气化将有望补偿经合组织国家用电强度的下降。交通领域的电气化（特别是私人交通），供暖和制

冷，以及工业生产过程中电力使用的最大化，都将推动电力成为主流能源。

3.1.2.2　地区电力需求

电力需求的增长呈现出区域发展不平衡的现状，这在某种程度上反映了全球经济的衰退，或是经济由工业发展逐步转变为以服务业为导向。随着基础设施的老化，电力系统的可靠性受到了质疑，同时可再生能源的使用和相关天气变化也给电力系统带来了挑战。

欧洲和美洲发达经济体的电力需求在全球电力需求总量中的占比将会大幅下降，而亚洲、非洲和南美的占比将会上升。1990 年，非经合组织国家的用电量仅占世界总电量的 35%，而近期，由于新兴经济体电力消费量的不断增加，在 2010 年，非经合组织

国家电力消费量已经占到了世界总量的 51%，这一数字在 2013 年上升至 53%。

3.2 GEI 关键技术的成本降低趋势

虽然可再生能源技术在成本方面的竞争力不断提升，但在大多数国家中，公众支持对于促进可再生能源的应用仍很有必要。2014 年，可再生能源发电新增装机达到了 128GW，几乎占所有新增电源装机的一半。约 69% 的新增电源投资都流向了可再生能源发电。在电力投资中超过一半的投资

用于波动性可再生能源发电，即风电和光伏发电，另外 14% 的电力投资用于水力发电。在 2015 年投运的全部容量的预期年输出容量中，假定在当前负荷因子下，新增的风力和光伏发电站输出容量约占 20%。

在过去的二十年中，可再生能源尤其是风电和光伏发电的成本大幅下降。技术进步、新项目融资机制和条件的改善、向具有优良资源市场的扩展、市场的巩固及当地能力的建立，均促进了可再生能源发电度电成本的降低，且有望进一步降低（见图 3-7）。

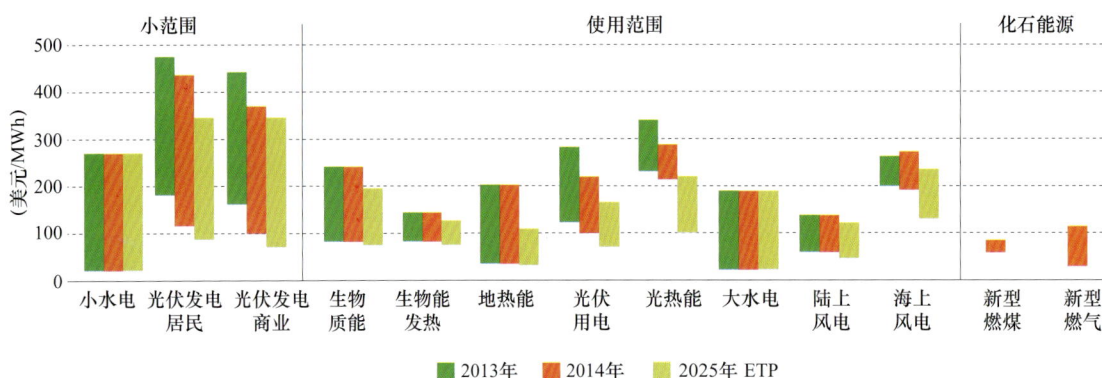

图 3-7 2013 年、2014 年和 2025 年目标发电平准化成本

3.2.1 风力发电市场趋势

风力发电的度电成本取决于多种因素，包括风能资源、投资成本、运行及维护成本、财务成本，以及将风力转换为电力的技术能力，一般用风能利用系数来衡量。同等条件下，轮

毂越高、扫掠面积越大，利用系数也越高，发电量也越大。

3.2.1.1 陆上风力发电

陆上风力发电是具有全球供应链的成熟技术。随着技术的发展，陆上风电已能够将单位装机的发电量最大

化。风电机组正在向更高轮毂、更大扫掠面积及更大容量发展。这些变化导致投资成本的增加，但利用率的提高也使度电成本降低（见图 3-8）。每

兆瓦具有更大扫掠面积的新型风机使之前无法利用的低风速和中风速地区的风电开发成为可能。

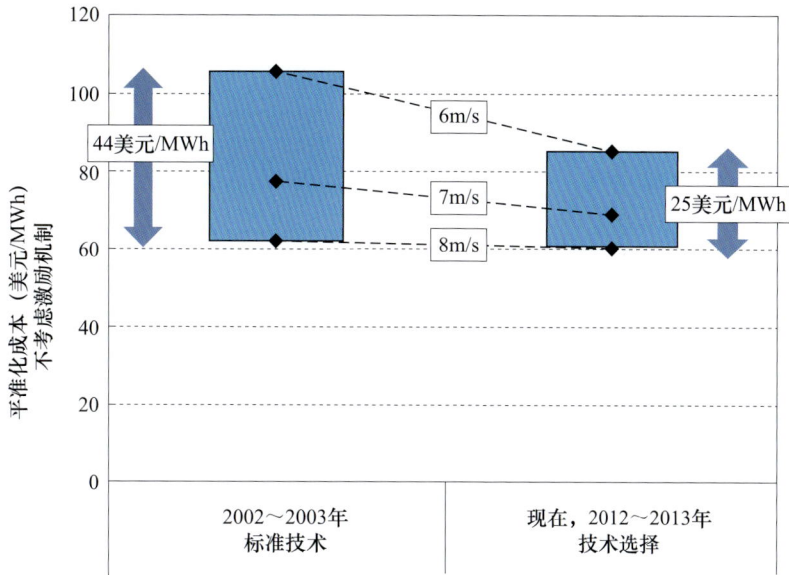

图 3-8　不同风速下的风电成本变化趋势

产生上述趋势有三个因素。首先，在诸如丹麦和德国的一些国家，随着风电穿透率的逐步提高，具有优质风能资源的场址正在逐渐减少；其次，一些国家可再生能源激励措施的减少挤压了风电场开发商的利润空间，增加了对单位装机发电量最大化的压力；最后，以拍卖和竞标取代非竞争性上网电价的趋势也增加了市场竞争。

据估计，风机的成本占到风力发电成本的比例约为 65%～80%。基建成本、并网成本及其他软成本也同样影响成本降低的趋势。虽然竞争机

制、本地生产和市场潜能是各国风机价格的主要指导因素，而其他系统成本的影响因素则更加复杂。图 3-9 显示了截至 2020 年所选部分地区预期的风电成本下降情况。

2015 年初，全球范围内的典型能源平准化成本（LCOE）范围从 60～140 美元/MWh。在大部分具有开发经验的国家中，陆上风电的平准化成本在 70～80 美元/MWh 的范围内。最低的平准化成本估计是在巴西和美国的各大型风电场，因其利用率接近于 50%，且开发商可获得较低的贷款利率。

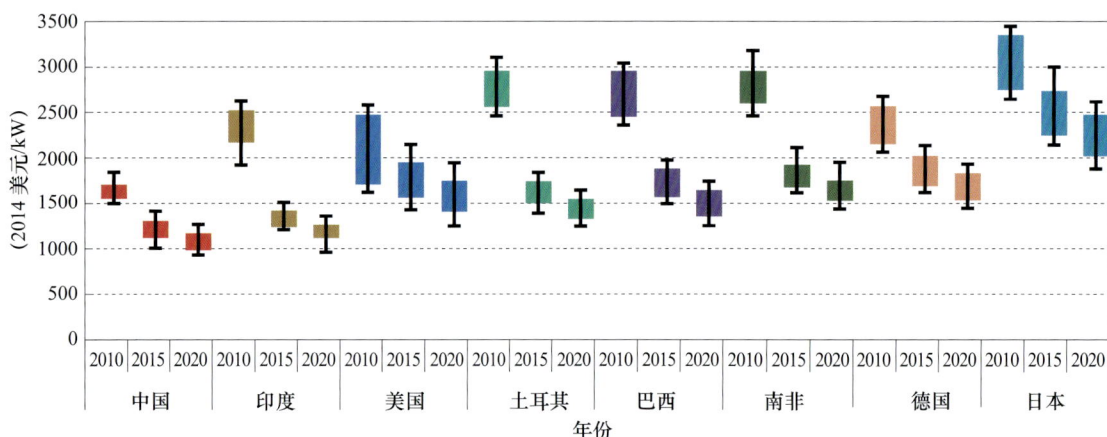

图 3-9　部分国家的陆上风电每千瓦投资成本（来源：IEA）

2014 年，中国的风电平准化成本约为 64～84 美元/MWh。在印度，国内的高融资成本和低利用率（17%～23%）导致其风电的平准化成本相对较高，尽管印度的系统成本只是稍高于中国。德国的风电项目典型平准化成本在 75～100 美元/MWh 范围内，在一些好的场区可低至 65 美元/MWh。

3.2.1.2　海上风力发电

欧洲大型海上风电工程的投运和大容量长叶片机组的商业化，是近几年海上风电的发展趋势。海上风电供应链继续向标准化方向发展。将于 2017～2020 年并网的丹麦和英国项目，以及德国的大型项目，均显示出成本在中期范围内大幅下降的可能性。但是，并网滞后、对长期稳定的市场及监管环境的需求，仍对海上风电的开发利用带来持续挑战。

现在的系统成本在 4000～5250 美元/kW 之间。这个成本范围包括风电项目投运所需的陆上和海上电气设施。不同项目的总投资成本会有很大的变化，但重要的是强调这些成本背后的各类动态因素。未来随着大型风电场的部署、风机制造商和其他供应链部件供应商间竞争的加剧、部分基础结构的标准化及运行管理效率的提升，海上风电投资成本有望下降（见图 3-10）。

作为风电投资成本的主要部分，风机成本仍具有最大降低的可能。海上风电机组制造商之间竞争的加剧将使投资成本在中期内下降。此外，风电机组发电容量的增加使得所需的风机基础和电缆量减少，能显著降低风电建造成本。漂浮式海上风电的安装方式可能成为未来几年的一种创新解决方案，包括垂直轴风机的使用。垂直轴风机虽然在陆上风电已被淘汰，但可能在漂浮式平台中存在优势。

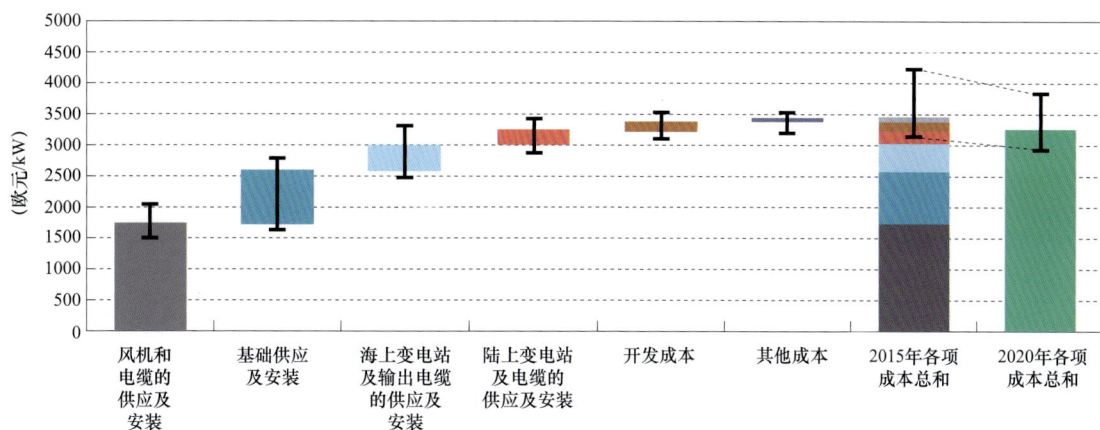

图 3-10　欧洲海上风电投资成本构成及趋势（来源：IEA）

3.2.2　太阳能发电市场趋势

3.2.2.1　光伏发电

截至 2014 年底，全球光伏发电装机容量达到 177GW，其中 2014 年新增容量为 40GW（见图 3-11）。从 2008～2012 年，光伏发电电池板模块的价格降至 1/5；在成熟市场（如意大利）中，由于持续的技术改进和大规模经济促进，光伏发电系统价格降至 1/3。2013 年和 2014 年，在包括日本和德国的市场中，光伏电池板模块价格每年降低 15%～18%；在中国市场，光伏电池板模块价格虽在个别月份较高，但总体是持续稳定的。2015 年初，光伏电池板模块平均价格为 0.60～0.70 美元/W，虽然中国市场仍占据较低价格的位置，实际上不同市场间的价格差异已经缩小。对于中国市场，持续增加的国内市场需求是光伏电池板模块价格稳定的一大驱动因素。2014 年，中国市场占据了全球约一半的光伏电池板模块供货量。

图 3-11　不同范围的全球光伏发电容量及趋势（来源：IEA）

技术改进是光伏发电系统投资成本持续下降的重要驱动因素（如图 3-12 所示）。技术改进主要有如下三大趋势：

（1）向更高转换效率的持续改进，可使组件的尺寸更小；

（2）降低材料的使用；

（3）更合理和更具创新性的制造过程。

但是，由于技术趋势预测的不确定性和工业竞争的影响，针对光伏电池板模块学习曲线轨迹出现了一些争议。

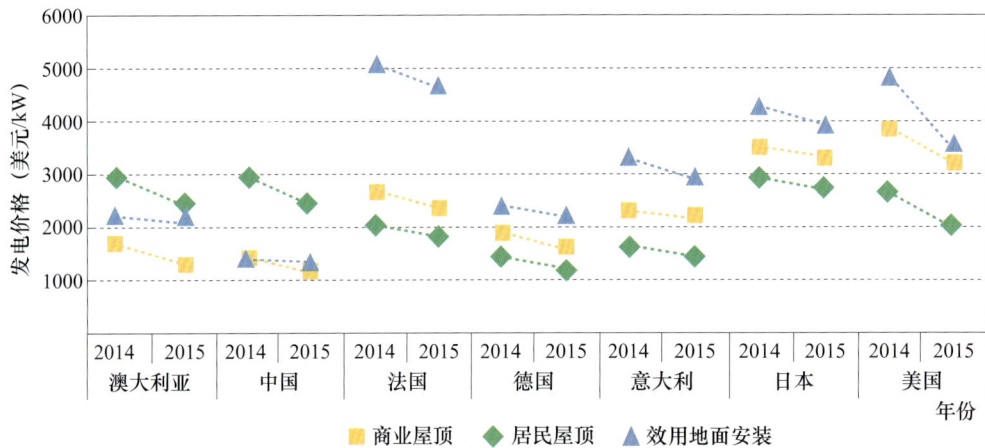

图 3-12　光伏发电技术的系统成本趋势（来源：IEA）

虽然电池板模块的价格下降开始变缓，平衡系统成本却开始加速降低。2015 年，中国和德国的典型公共事业单位规模的太阳能光伏发电价格低至 1300 美元/kW；中国商业规模的光伏发电价格为 1150 美元/kW，澳大利亚的商业规模的光伏发电价格为 1300 美元/kW；同时，居民使用的光伏发电系统价格仍保持在 2000 美元/kW 或略高的水平。总体来说，世界上大多数新的公共事业单位规模项目的投资成本在 1000～2000 美元/kW 之间，具体数值取决于市场情况。

由于全球范围内发电模块生产经验的积累以及软成本的局部改进，太阳能光伏发电的投资成本有可能将继续下降。晶体模块的平均价格预期在 2020 年达到 0.50 美元/W（如图 3-13 所示）。

除了安装成本，光伏发电系统的平准化成本主要取决于光照资源。全球范围内，不考虑补贴的情况，2015 年早期建设的典型公共事业单位规模项目的平准化成本在 100 美元/MWh 和 200 多美元/MWh 之间。中国和印度靠近该成本区间的下部，而日本则靠近上部。然而，全球统计数据表明，加权平均开发成本在 125 美元/kWh 左右。

分布式光伏发电（如小规模和屋顶光伏）的成本虽然在 2015 年约为 220 美元/MWh，但预计在 2020 年将达到 160 美元/MWh。

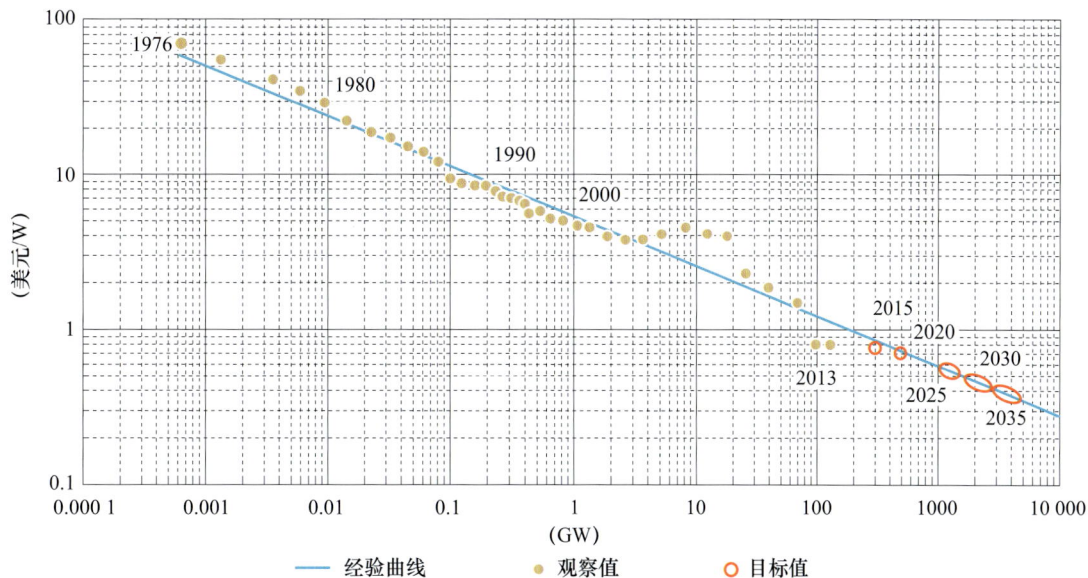

图 3-13　晶体模块的价格下降趋势（来源：IEA）

一般来说，对于不可调度电源，比如光伏发电，其成本价格趋势通常并不能完全反映其竞争性。为了对光伏发电与其他电源的竞争性进行更全面的评估，应考虑光伏发电的系统价值，比如光伏发电的部署地点、发电时间，以及如何与需求侧和输电侧的系统需求和容量进行协调。

3.2.2.2　太阳能热发电

基于聚光太阳能发电（CSP）的太阳热能（STE）是已证实可行的一种可再生能源能源利用技术。由于储热系统与/或混合系统的存在，如图 3-14 所示，太阳能热发电可以提供稳定

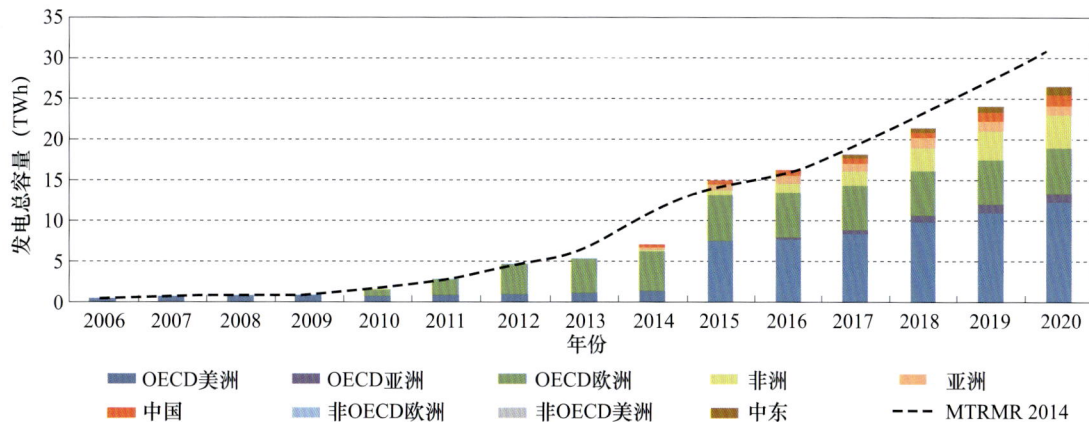

图 3-14　全球光热发电总容量及趋势（来源：IEA）

的峰值容量、中间容量或基荷容量。截至 2015 年，全球太阳能热发电装机容量达到 4.94GW，其中约 3.2GW 未配储能系统，而 1.8GW 配有储热系统。到 2020 年，80% 的新装容量将配有储能。然而，目前仍有一定的风险存在，需要技术的更加进步以降低成本，从而获得更快发展。

太阳能热发电的储能特性和混合性使其比光伏发电对系统而言具有更高的价值。光热投资成本较高，大型光热电站（大于 50MW）的投资成本在 4000～9000 美元/kW。在未来一段时间，光热电站的投资成本有望进一步下降。例如，太阳能场站的大小与其发电容量直接相关，其厂址的投资占整个电站投资的一半。开发商期望通过提高电力转换效率而减小场站规模，其成本可通过使用熔盐增加储热容量的方式得到进一步下降。IEA 预测，到 2020 年，美国配 6h 储热容量的光热发电投资成本将下降到 3000～4000 美元/kW，配 12h 储热容量的光热发电投资成本将下降到 4500～5500 美元/kW。图 3-15 显示了当前及 2020 年预期的太阳能热发电的平准化成本趋势。不同电站的平准化成本变化很大，且不完全反映太阳能热发电的经济优势，因为该优势也取决于所发电力的价值。

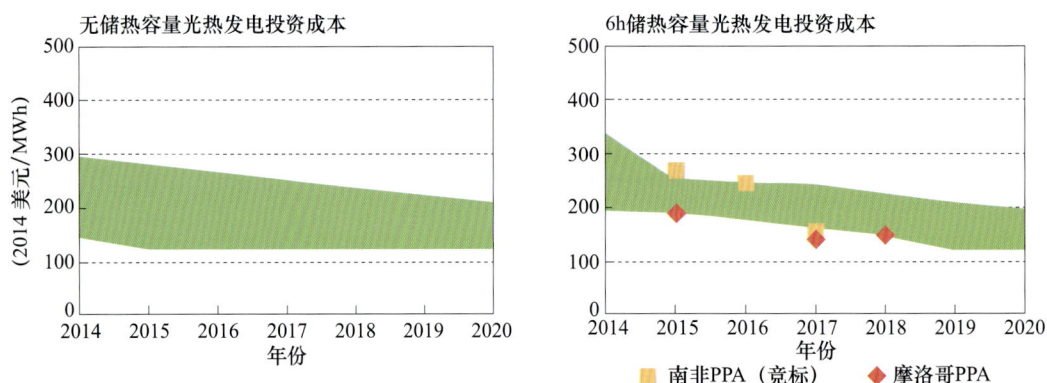

图 3-15　当前及 2020 年预期的光热能源平准化成本趋势（来源：IEA）

3.2.3　受地域限制的其他可再生能源技术市场趋势

3.2.3.1　海洋能

目前，海洋能在全球能源构成中的比例依然较小。但巨大的资源储量和正在开展的示范项目表明，海洋能在中期有商业化扩张的可能。2014 年，海洋能发电总容量约为 0.53GW，约等于一个大型天然气电站容量，其中包括位于法国和韩国的两个大型潮汐发电项目。

IEA 的海洋能系统（IEA-OES）技术合作项目预估一个 3MW 波浪能电站的投资成本约为 18 100 美元/kW，但一个 75MW 电站的投资成本可降低一半至约 9100 美元/kW；10MW 潮汐能项目的投资成本约为 14 600 美元/kW，而较大型的 90MW 潮汐能项目的投资成本可降至约 5600 美元/kW。

3.2.3.2　地热能

全球的地热能资源储量非常丰富，由于其具有可调度性，因此地热能是一种很有吸引力的可再生能源发电技术。地热能开发的工作量较大，包括钻井和土木工程开发，从而具有很长的开发周期（即 5～7 年）。

由于地热能的这些特性，其投资成本因地而异，典型的高温电站投资成本约为 2000～5000 美元/kW。双循环电站的投资成本略高，约为 2400～5600 美元/kW。地热电站的容量系数较高，其平准化成本为 35～200 美元/MWh。

3.3　全球范围内电力系统互联实践经验

结合 2.2.4 中提到的全球能源互联

三部曲策略，本节着重就上述三个阶段相关的实践经验进行论述。

3.3.1　国家大型输电网互联经验

3.3.1.1　中国

在过去的几十年间，中国的电力网络在互联规模及电压等级上都取得了长足的发展。在 1950 年后，中国的国家电网从数百个相互孤立的网络系统发展成 30 个省级电网，并最终形成了大型地区性电网。目前中国大陆有 6 个同步电力网络，分别为：华北与华中同步电网，并且在 2009 年随着第一条 1000kV 特高压交流输电线（UHVAC）的建成，合并为一个同步电网；华东电网、东北电网、西北电网、西藏电网及南方电网。这些电网之间通过高压直流（HVDC）线路连接，如图 3-16 所示。

随着一些正在建设中及规划中的特高压骨干输电线路的陆续投入使用，这些区域性电网在未来的相互联系将会加强。在一份新的五年电网发展规划中，中国国家电网公司（SGCC）计划在 2020 年形成两个同步电网，分别为东部和西部电网，如图 3-17 所示。鉴于中国西部地区丰富的资源状况，西部电网将致力于整合中国几大电力基地。东

部电网将致力于整合中国大的负荷中心。上述两个电网的建设将大幅提高电力的外送及馈入能力，支撑

88GW 风电、20GW 太阳能发电及 60GW 水电的跨区域输送，从而帮助政府实现低碳目标。

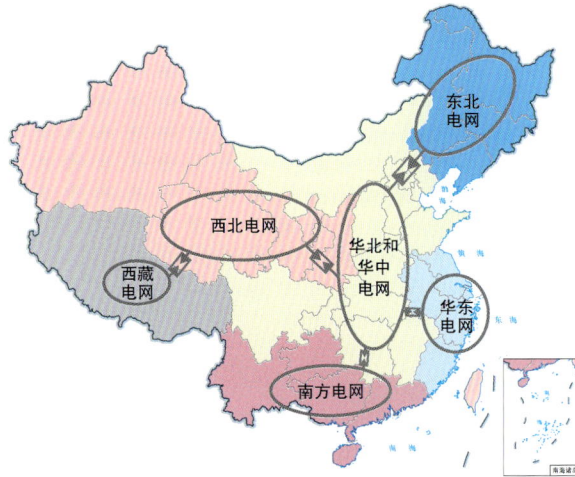

图 3-16　中国电网互联现状

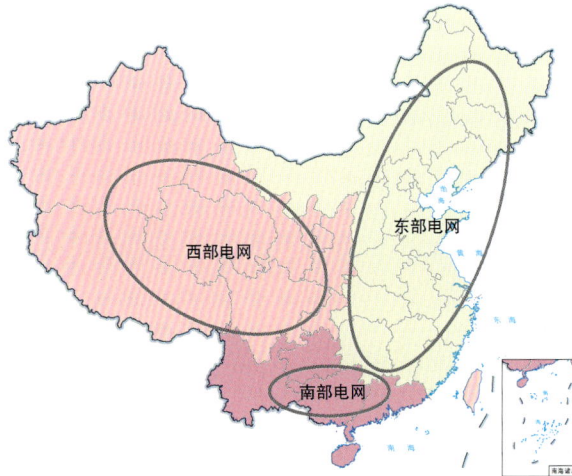

图 3-17　2020 年中国电网互联规划（国家电网有限公司）

3.3.1.2　韩国

　　韩国电力工业由韩国电力公司（KEPCO）主导，该公司持有全国范围内的输电网和配电网（如图 3-18 所示）。KEPCO 通过推进特高压电网（UHV）建设解决首尔地区高需求负

荷中心与发电区域之间严重的供需不平衡问题。东亚首个商业化运行的特高压工程（765kV 输电线路及变电站项目）于 2002 年在韩国投运。该工程采用了诸多环境足迹少的先进电网技术，如对环境影响较小空气隔离开关及铁塔。韩国的经验表明，相较于

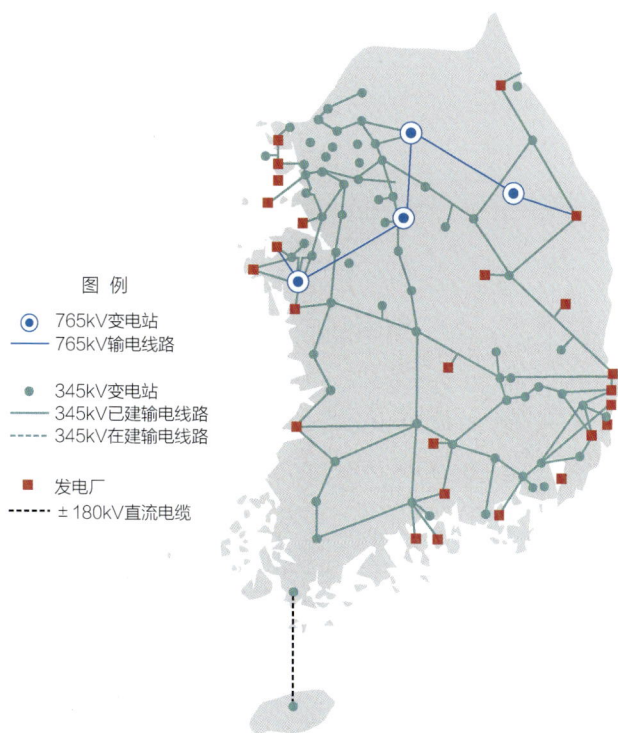

图 3-18　韩国国家电网

345kV 电压等级主网，采用特高压技术对已建电网进行升级和互联可使其输电能力提升 3.4 倍，土地占用率减少 22%，输电损耗及建设成本均可下降 1/5（见图 3-19）。

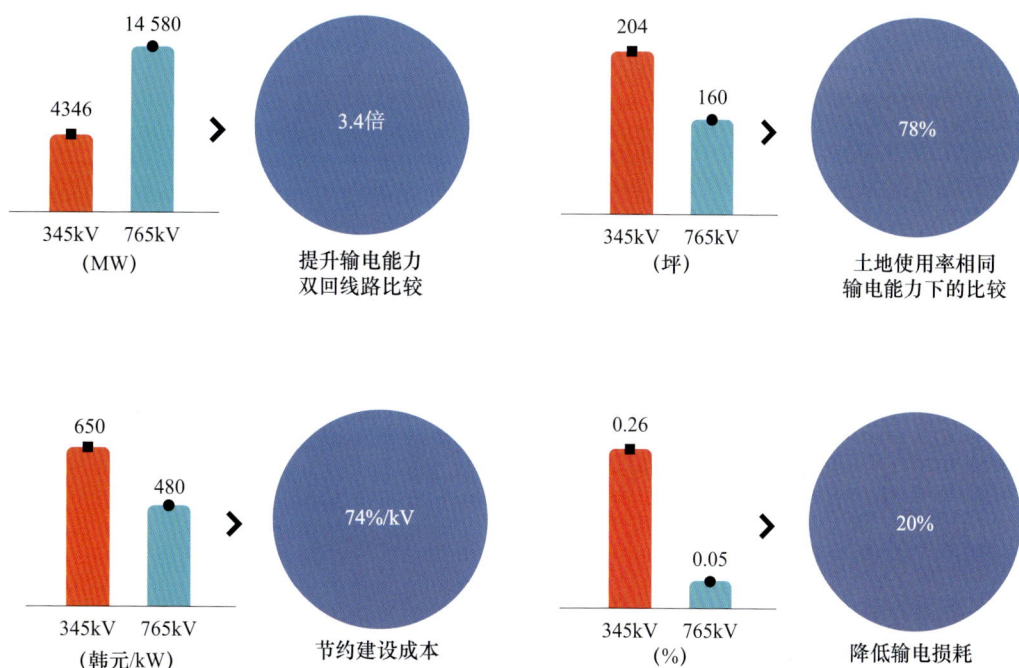

图 3-19　韩国特高压输电系统的主要优势

3.3.1.3 日本

日本国内的互联输电网如图 3-20 所示。日本的 9 个区域电网（除冲绳外）均通过高压直流海底电缆、高压交流架空线、背靠背系统及频率变流器相连接。通过分析世界范围内电网互联的实际经验，日本电力系统主要有两个特点。

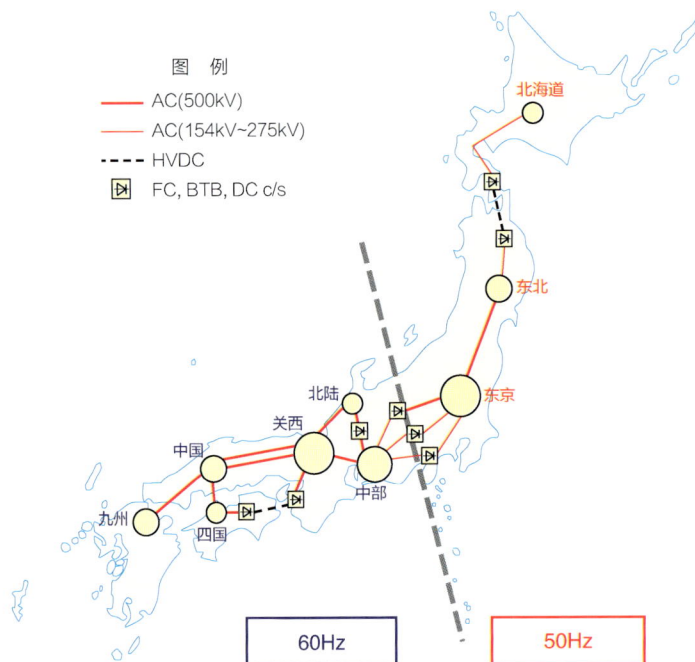

图 3-20 日本国内电力网络互联（TEPCO）

首先，日本东部及西部地区的电网频率不同，东部为 50Hz，西部为 60Hz，这是历史原因造成的。在日本电力工业发展的早期，位于东部的东京采用了德国制发电机，而位于西部的大阪采用的则是美国制发电机。这种差异导致日本国家电网需要使用变频设备（FCFs）来连接西部与东部电网，以实现东西部之间的电力交换。目前三台 FCFs 设施正在运行中，容量为 1.2GW。东西电网间的联络线是电网间电力交换的瓶颈所在。

其次，日本九个独立运行的电力公司负责建设充足的电源以满足各自的电力需求，并监管各自电力系统的发展与运行。各个区域内的电力供需关系很大程度上由当地的电力生产与消费情况决定，电网互联通常只用于远距离电源的电力传输及应急情况下的电力系统干预等。因此，日本目前几乎所有的电网互联仅根据以上用途提供最低限度必需的输送容量。

近几年日本不得不重新思考电网规划的传统观念。主要是由于 2011 年东日本大地震后东北部与东京地区的电力供应不足及供需不平衡所致。此外，日本在 2016 年 4 月电力零售业务的全面自由化增加了跨区电力交换需求，这也是原因之一。

东京与中部之间电网互联升级方案如图 3-21 所示，该方案通过 900MW 高压直流输电线路实现互联，计划于 2020 年投运。

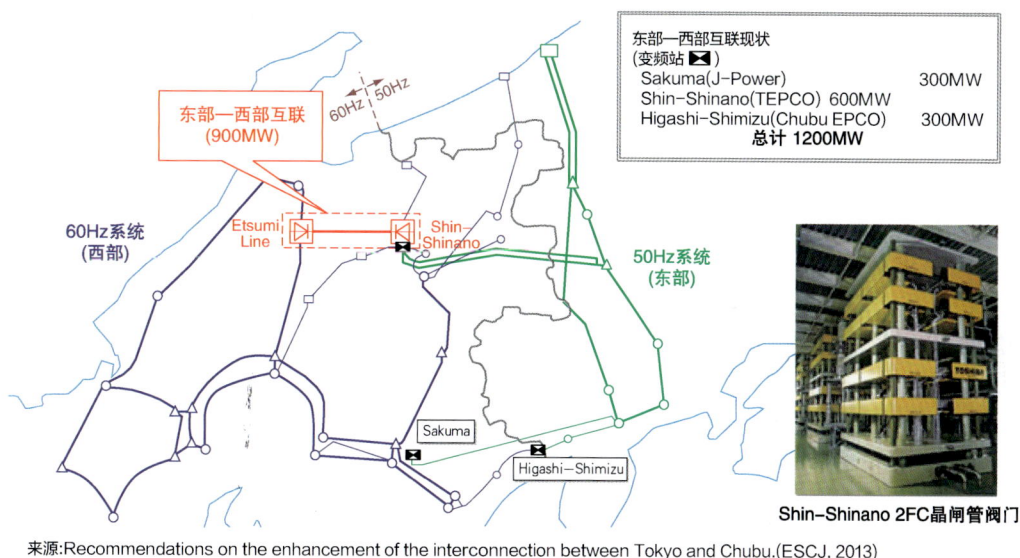

东部—西部互联现状
（变频站 ⊠）
Sakuma(J-Power)　　　　　　　300MW
Shin-Shinano(TEPCO) 600MW
Higashi-Shimizu(Chubu EPCO)　300MW
总计 1200MW

东部—西部互联
(900MW)

60Hz 系统
（西部）

Etsumi Line

Shin-Shinano

50Hz 系统
（东部）

Sakuma

Higashi-Shimizu

Shin-Shinano 2FC晶闸管阀门

来源:Recommendations on the enhancement of the interconnection between Tokyo and Chubu.(ESCJ, 2013)

图 3-21　东—西部电网 900MW 高压直流互联升级计划

3.3.1.4　印度

印度的电网发展可分为三个阶段：

（1）1947～1960 年，连接诸多孤立的小型电网，逐渐形成邦级电网。

（2）1960～1980 年末，连接邦级电网，形成 5 个区域电网。

（3）1990 年至今，连接区域电网，形成国家级同步电网。2012 年印度的 5 个区域电网见图 3-22。

与中国类似，印度电网的布局及互联很大程度上是其能源资源与负荷中心在地理分布上的不平衡所导致的。印度的能源资源主要分布在北部、东北部及东部地区，但印度的主要负荷中心在北部、南部与西部。因此大量的电力需要从印度东部传输到西部、从印度北部传输到南部。未来，印度将规划更高电压等级的输电线以加强区域间电网互联。印度的第十二个五年电网规划明确提出，2017 年建设至少两条 400kV 交流或 765kV 交流或背靠背高压直流线路，以连接区域电网。规划还提出，在印度北部及东北部建设 ±800kV 特高压直流线路及

1200kV 特高压交流线路。印度第一条从阿萨姆邦（Assam），穿过西孟加拉邦（West Bengal）至北方邦

（Uttar Pradesh）的±800kV/6000MW特高压直流线路已经于 2015 年 8 月31 日投运。

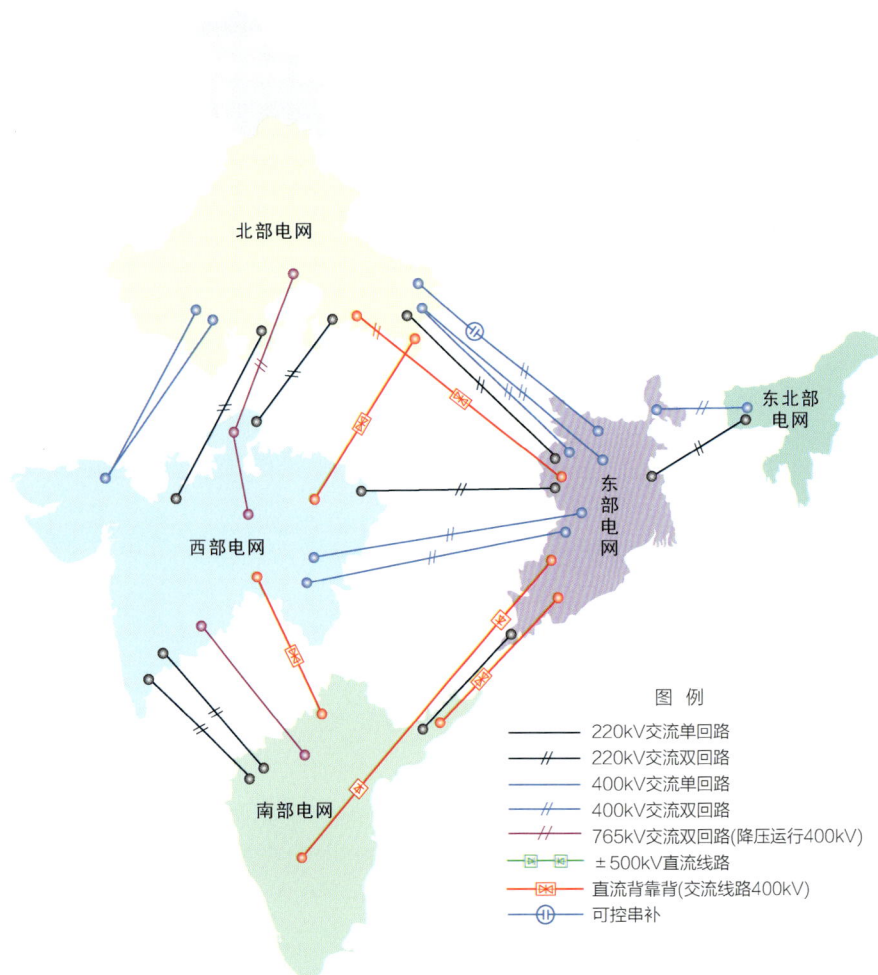

图 3-22　2012 印度电网互联（印度电力部[3]）

3.3.1.5　巴西

巴西水力资源丰富，水电在巴西电源中占据主导地位。在水电站大规模建设的同时，巴西跨区电网互联也在加速。20 世纪 80 年代已经形成了 4 个 500kV 线路为主干网架的区域性电网，分别为北部、东北、

东南及南部电网。20 世纪 90 年代末，上述 4 个电网分别通过 765、500kV 及 345kV 线路连接，形成了全国统一的同步电网。此外还有两条在运的±600kV 高压直流线路用于输送伊泰普（Itaipu）水电站的电力。巴西计划继续发展水电，尤其是在西北部及北部地区。计划进一

步增强巴西的跨区电网互联。巴西当前及未来规划的电网互联情况如图 3-23 所示。一条 ±800kV 特高压直流线路正在建设中，用于输送巴西贝罗蒙特（Belo Monte）水电站（装机容量 11GW）的电力。

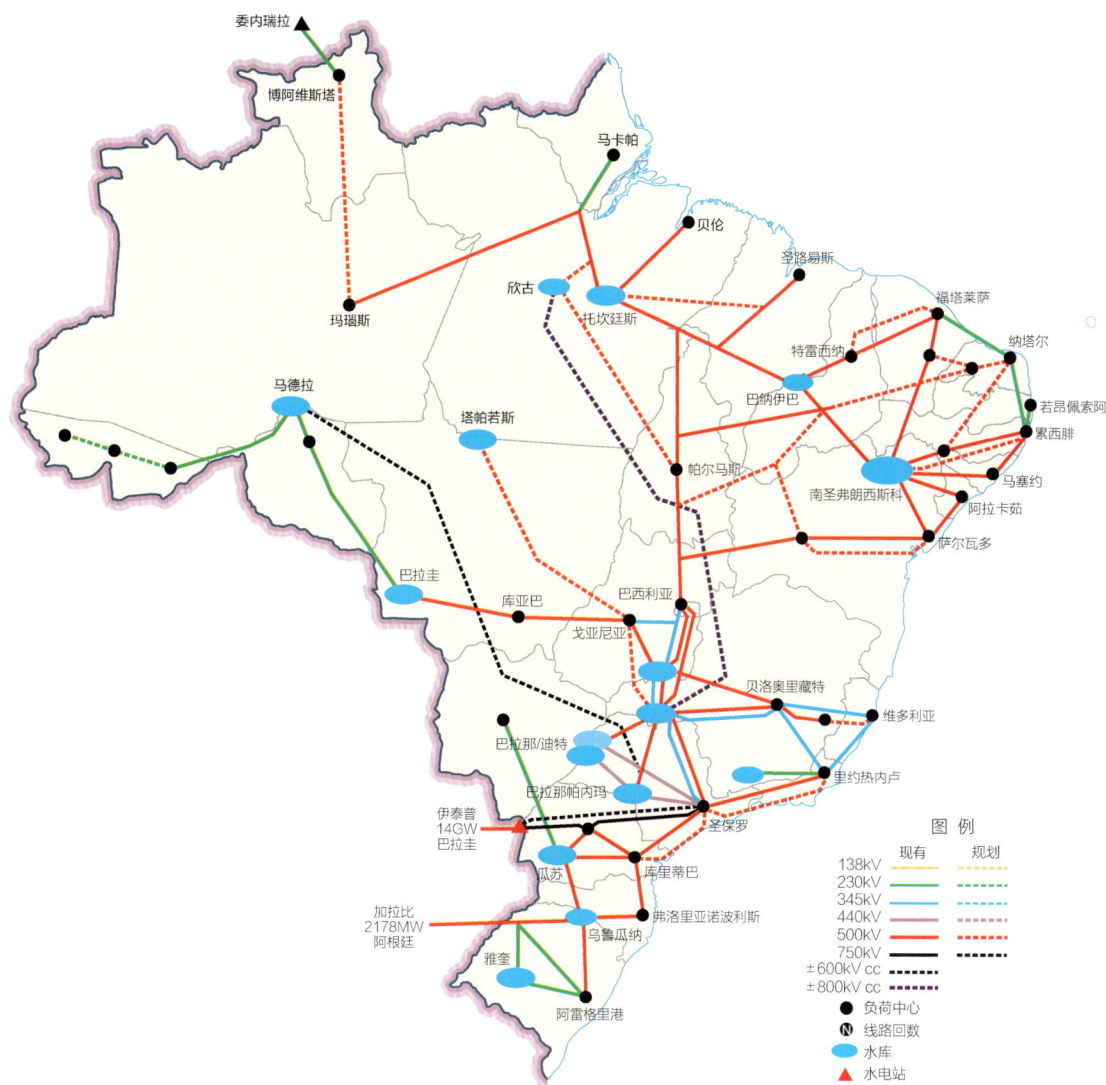

图 3-23　巴西当前及规划电网互联情况（ONS[4]）

3.3.2　区域互联的实践经验

3.3.2.1　亚洲

亚洲范围内多条互联线路的建设运行预示了更大区域电网互联的可能性。

在东北亚地区，中国电网已经通过一条 110kV 交流线路、两条 220kV 交流线路及一条 ±500kV 背靠背直流线路与俄罗斯电网互联。此外，还有两条 220kV 交流线路将中国内蒙古自治区的电力送往蒙古国。2020 年前，另有两条互联线路正在规划中，分别是±800kV/8000MW、长度为 1830km 的直流输电线路用于中俄两国之间的电力传输，以及 ±660kV/4000MW、长度为 1220km 的直流工程，用于将蒙古国的电力送往中国。

在亚洲中部，哈萨克斯坦与俄罗斯之间有三条 500kV 交流互联线路，其中一条为 1150kV 特高压线路。此外哈萨克斯坦与吉尔吉斯斯坦、塔吉克斯坦及乌兹别克斯坦之间已经形成了 500kV 电力环网。土库曼斯坦同样与伊朗及乌兹别克斯坦进行了电力连接。目前在中亚五国，以及伊朗和阿富汗，正在建设多条 500kV 线路，用于增强电网互联。中亚现有及规划中的电网互联情况如图 3-24 所示。

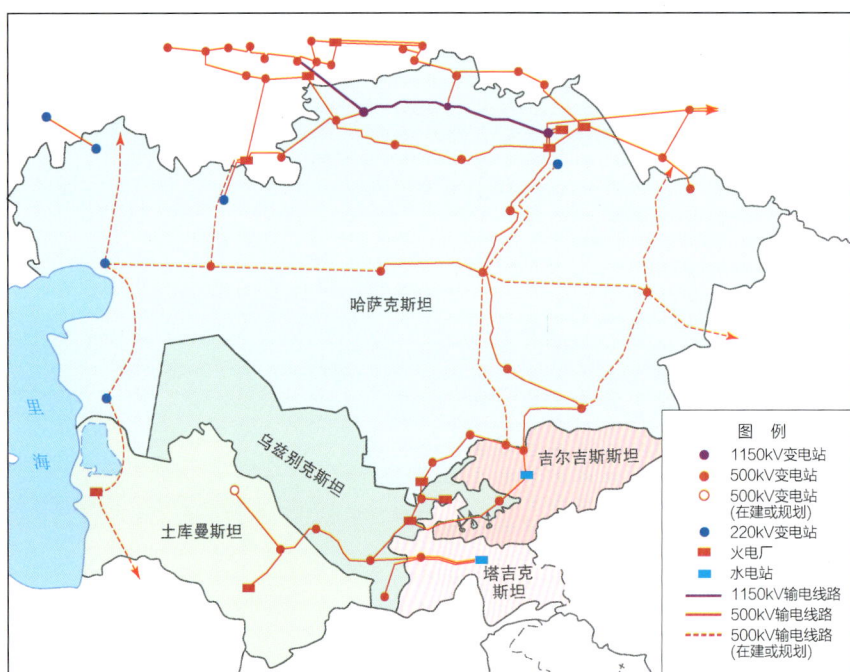

图 3-24　中亚地区电网互联情况（GENI[5]）

西亚已通过跨国输电线路形成两个同步电网。第一个为中东半岛北部与伊朗同步电网，包括伊拉克、叙利亚、约旦、黎巴嫩及伊朗电网，由电压等级为 400kV 及/或 220kV 交流线路连接而成。该电网同时还向北连接土耳其、亚美尼亚和阿塞拜疆电网，并向西与埃及电网相连。第二个同步电网为海湾电网，连接沙特阿拉伯、科威特、巴林、卡塔尔、阿联酋及阿曼（见图 3-25）。2015 年，海湾合作委员会建议通过与中东及北非电网连接来扩大海湾电网。

在南亚地区，印度电网通过±400kV背靠背直流线路与孟加拉国电网相连，通过一条 132kV 交流线路与尼泊尔相连，通过三条线路与不丹国相连。亚洲发展银行计划以印度为中心改善南亚地区电力网络互联水平，增强印度与不丹、尼泊尔、斯里兰卡、孟加拉国及巴基斯坦之间的电网互联，同时加强印度与中亚电网的连接，如图 3-26 所示。

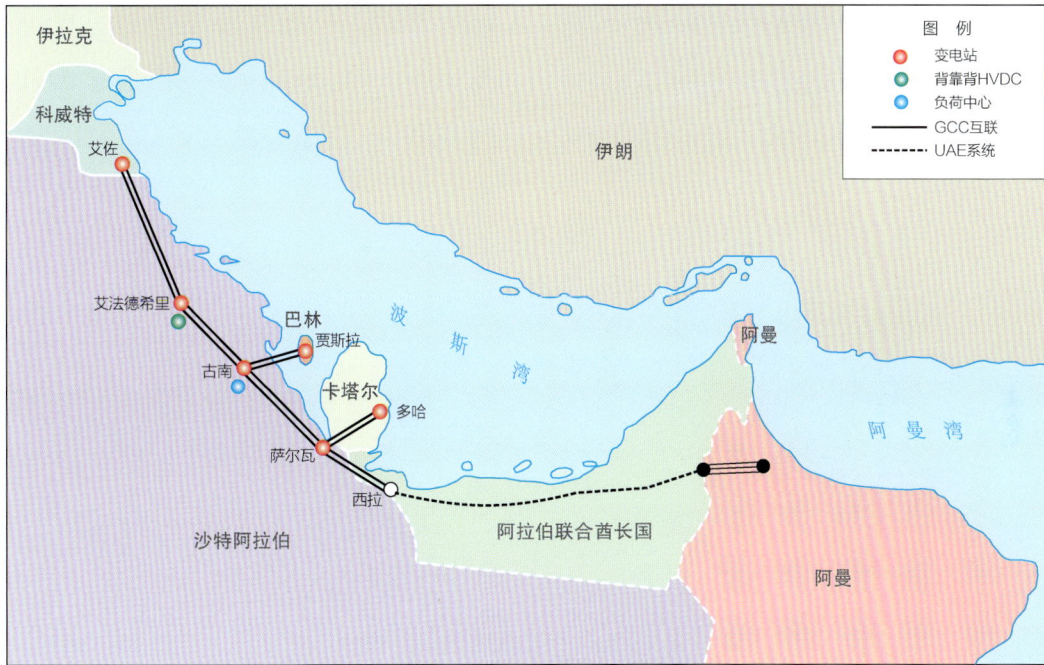

图 3-25　海湾电网（海湾合作委员会互联局）

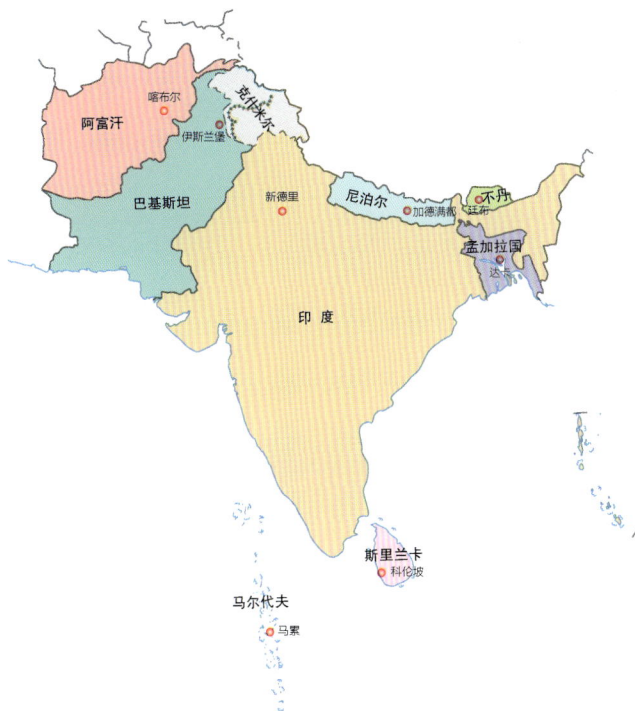

图 3-26　南亚地区电网互联规划（尼泊尔能源论坛[6]）

目前在东南亚，中国电网与越南电网通过三条 220kV 及两条 110kV 交流线路相连接。中缅两国电网通过一条 500kV 和一条 220kV、从中国到缅甸的点对网交流线路连接。印度支那半岛上部分国家的电网也已经通过多条 500、220、110kV 交流线路及一条±330kV 直流线路相连。根据亚洲电力公司/电力局负责人（HAPUA）提出的东南亚国家联盟（ASEAN）电网发展规划建议，2025 年底前将建设 16 个交直流工程，从而加强东南亚诸国的电网互联（见图 3-27）。

图 3-27　东南亚国家联盟电网规划（EPRI）

3.3.2.2　欧洲、俄罗斯及其他国家

欧洲国家间的电网互联已经打造了一个延伸至欧洲大陆东部地区的大型同步区域，系统频率 50Hz（见图 3-28）。欧洲诸国的电网互联始于 20 世纪 50 年代。西欧首先开始电网互联，并于 1996 年与欧洲中部实现同步连接[7]。

目前欧洲电网互联容量是欧洲各国装机容量的 11%。如图 3-28 所示，目前欧洲电力系统主要由位于欧洲大陆、北欧、波罗的海诸国、英国及爱尔兰五个跨国互联同步电网组成，此外还包括冰岛和塞浦路斯两个独立电力系统。电网互联及电力市场一体化使成员国之间的电力交换空前频繁。2013

年全欧洲约进行了 387.3TWh 的电能　交换，约占总用电量的 12%。

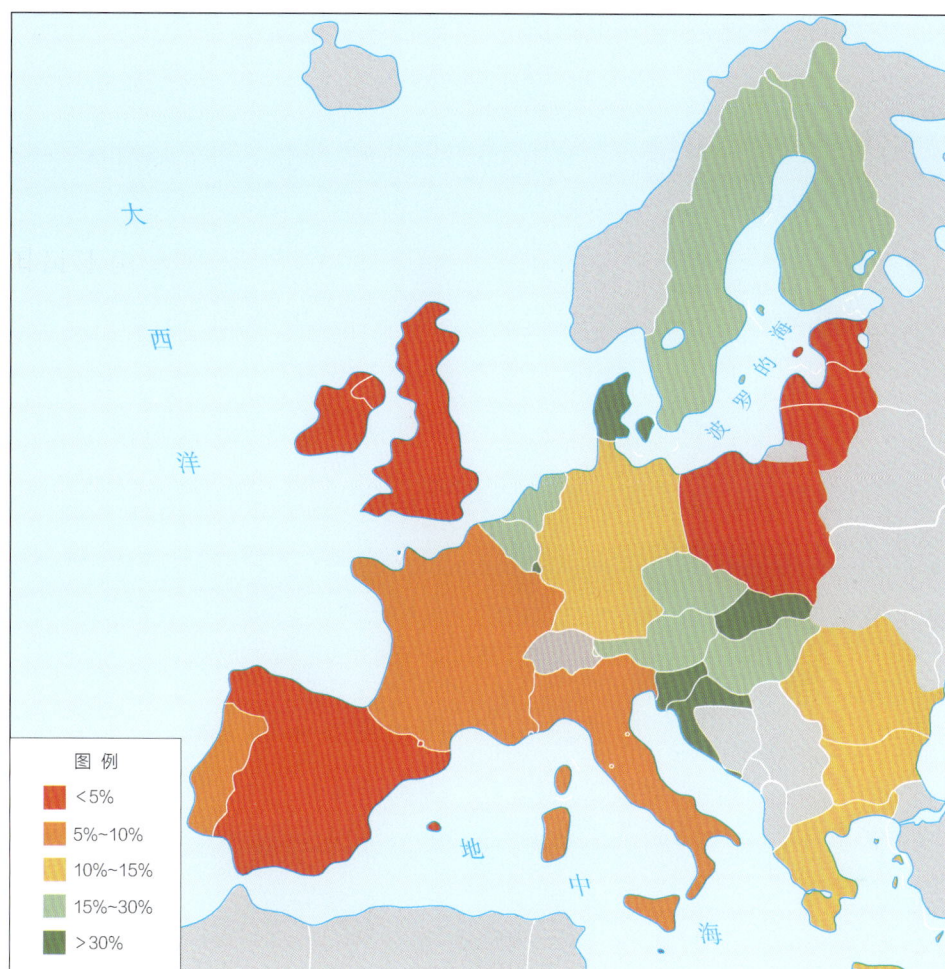

图 3-28　2020 年欧洲电力交换（IEA）

　　然而区域性差异仍然存在。以波罗的海诸国为例，为了提升电力供应的安全性、降低发电机的市场功率，该区域对电网互联有较大需求。为了促进输电网运营商（TSO）间更加紧密的合作，前欧洲输电系统运营联盟（ETSO）与五家 TSO 组织（分别为 ATSOI、BALTSO、Nordel、UCTE 及 UKTSOA）在 2008 年进行了整合，成立了欧洲输电系统运营商联盟（ENTSO-E），覆盖了来自 34 个欧洲国家的 41 个 TSO[8]。

　　一个连接更为紧密的欧洲能源网络，能为欧洲居民带来显著的市场经济效益。预计到 2030 年，该网络的实施每年将为欧洲广大能源消费者节约 120 亿～400 亿欧元。对于欧盟脱碳政策要求的高比例可再生能源消纳，该网络也被证明是至关重要的。2014 年，欧盟理事会讨论了欧盟成员国间电网互联率达到 15%的目标。尽管这个实施目标使电网互联问题变得更直观，但还需要从投资、公众的可接受性与理解程度等角度，对能源互联的优势及相关费用进行全面评估，这些都是输电线路能够最终建成所必需的前提条件。只有当全面的成本效益分析结果显示出一个项目的正面价值，才能促进公众接受该项目。

俄罗斯与欧盟正尝试对综合电力系统/统一电力系统（IPS/UPS）和 ENTSO-E 电网进行整合，创造一个跨越 13 个时区的同步超级网络。以地理覆盖范围计，IPS/UPS 互联形成的电网是目前世界上最大的同步电网，横跨八个时区，连接俄罗斯、阿塞拜疆、白俄罗斯、格鲁吉亚、哈萨克斯坦、吉尔吉斯斯坦、摩尔多瓦、蒙古国和乌克兰及其他国家。它通过背靠背直流线路与芬兰电网异步连接，通过交流线路与波罗的海电网同步连接。

3.3.2.3 美洲地区

早在 20 世纪 30 年代，随着大规模水力发电的开发，北美地区电网的互联水平得到最大程度的提升，在 20 世纪 50～80 年代期间得到进一步发展，通过不断提高电压等级来满足快速增长的电力需求。北美电网已经发展成四个主要的同步系统，即西部互联电网、东部互联电网、德克萨斯（ERCOT）互联电网和魁北克互联电网，四个系统形成的网络横跨加拿大、美国和墨西哥北部，如图 3-29[7]

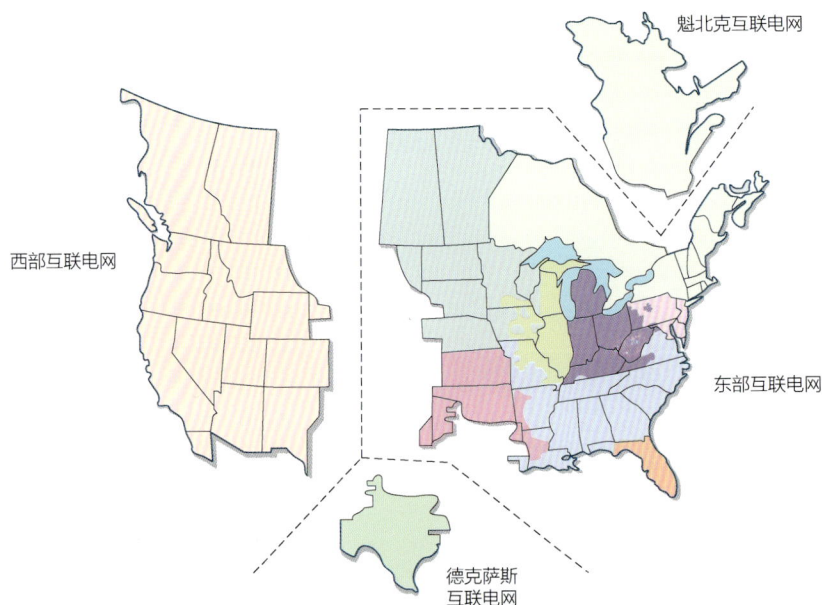

图 3-29　现阶段北美电网互联图

所示。这些电网互联线路通常是背靠背直流线路，主要以紧急备用为目的。它们的功率交换容量有限，在正常工作条件下交换的功率可忽略不计[9]。这些互联电网间均不同步，不使用交流互联器并限制与直流线路联接的物理互联器的容量大小。目前，在西部和东部互联网络之间仅有几条约 2GW 容量的直流互联线路，在东部和德克萨斯互联网络之间有一条 2.6GW 容量的互联通道。

这些传输区域间相互孤立、且传输能力不足，已经被确认为影响美国实现其较为激进的可再生能源目标以及提高整个美国电力系统的可靠性和效率的潜在障碍。美国中西部区域、大平原区域及德克萨斯州拥有丰富的风能资源，可进行大规模开发并传输到位于东部和西部海岸的各负荷中心。美国于 2008 年提出了 Tres Amigas Super Station 方案，计划通过一个单一的电网联接方式实现美国西部、东部和德克萨斯州电网互联，从而起到可再生能源枢纽作用。该方案实施的前期工作已经于 2016 年启动（见图 3-30）[10]。

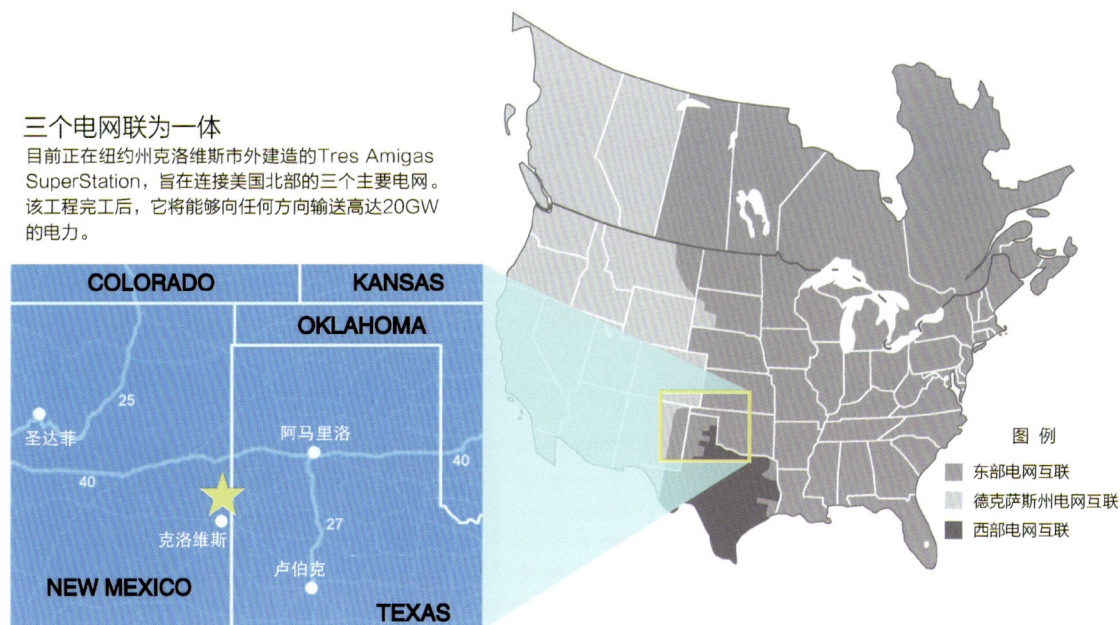

图 3-30　Tres Amigas Super Station 的位置布局图（NERC[10]）

在南美洲，已建、建设中或计划建设的电网互联主要集中在两个地理区域，如图 3-31 所示。北部区域包括哥伦比亚、厄瓜多尔和委内瑞拉，南部为阿根廷、巴西、巴拉圭和乌拉圭。哥伦比亚、厄瓜多尔和秘鲁之间的电网互联预计将于 2017 年完成。完成后将继续向南延伸到玻利维亚和智利，要求在 2020 年底完成，并作为一个更大的计划的一部分对五个安第斯共同体国家的电力系统进行全面整合[7]。在中美洲区域，哥斯达黎加、危地马拉、洪都拉斯、尼加拉瓜、巴拿马和

萨尔瓦多通过一条串型输电线路相互连接，如图 3-32 所示。该系统由 15 个变电站和 1800km 长的 230kV 跨国线路组成[7]。

图 3-31　南美电网互联图[7]

图 3-32　中美地区电网互联图[7]

3.3.2.4　非洲

自 1995 年南部非洲电力联盟（SAPP）成立以来，该机构一直积极促进跨国电网互连。该联盟共有 12 个成员，分别是安哥拉、博茨瓦纳、刚果民主共和国、莱索托、马拉维、莫桑比克、纳米比亚、南非、斯威士兰、坦桑尼亚、赞比亚和津巴布韦。这些国家中有 9 个，其中不包括安哥拉、马拉维和坦桑尼亚，已经通过 400、275、220kV 和 132kV 交流电线路进行电网互联。南非计划中的电网互联项目分为两大类：一类涉及安哥拉、马拉维、坦桑尼亚和其他成员国之间的互联；另一类涉及建设中央输电线路通道，通道将津巴布韦—赞比亚—博茨瓦纳—纳米比亚互联，还包括津巴布韦中部的输电走廊和赞比亚的输电项目[7]。

非洲国家还计划通过电网互联，在 2020 年前形成包括非洲南部、西部、中部和北部在内的泛非电力网络。

3.3.3　电网跨国互联计划

该计划以长期性的视角，对电网跨国互联在更广阔地理区域内的影响进行了研究，制定了若干倡议，开展了初步的可行性研究，提出了具体计划。计划中含有的项目包括欧洲超级电网、Desertec 项目、Medgrid 项目以及 Gobitec 项目和亚洲超级电网项目。这些项目将在以全球能源互联网（GEI）概念为依托的电网互联后期阶段逐步予以实施。

3.3.3.1　欧洲超级电网计划

该计划对多个欧洲超级电网进

行了评估，比如，通过特高压直流技术联接欧洲国家与邻近的北非、中东国家的电网，并最终与里海国家电网进行互联[11]。成本效益分析结果显示，这种电网相较于其替代方案的优势仍然有待进一步论证，但它将有利于高水平地大规模利用北欧沿海地区的海上风电资源和南部地区丰富的太阳能资源［该地区较高的直接辐照度（DNI）将有利于 CSP 的开发］，以及将电力从这些基地输送至欧洲的负荷中心，并使用丰富的水电资源实现系统平衡（见图 3-33）。

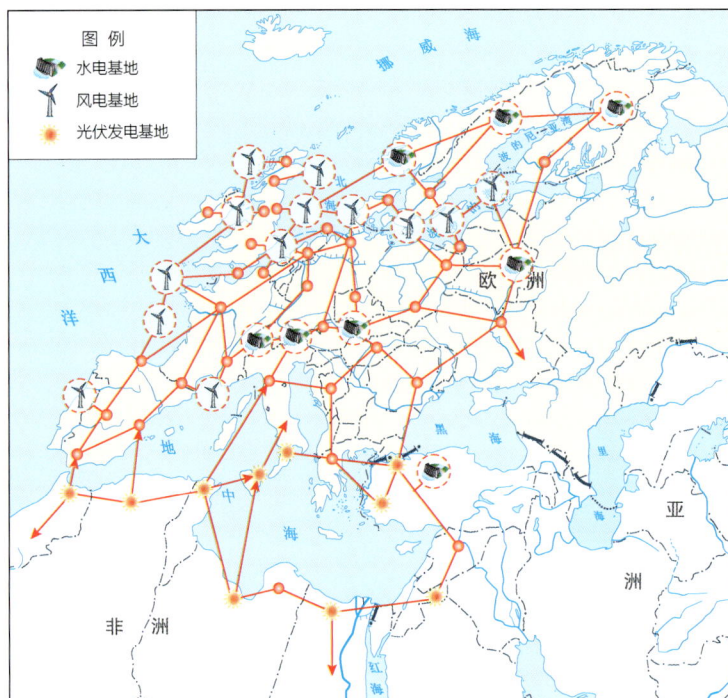

图 3-33　欧洲超级电网概念图（超级电网之友）

起步阶段。

3.3.3.2　Desertec 项目

Desertec 项目的重点是利用北非和中东沙漠的太阳能为这些地区提供清洁电力，通过淡化海水为这些地区提供淡水，并向欧洲输送大量电力（见图 3-34）。尽管该项目最近重新获得了关注度，但沙漠电力的开发利用仍然处于

3.3.3.3　Medgrid 项目

2010 年，Medgrid 项目由 20 多家公共事业机构、制造商和投资者组成的联盟发起，联盟大部分来自地环中海的欧洲和北非国家。Medgrid 项目的目标是开发 20GW 的可再生能源，大部分来自太阳能发电，其中 5GW 专门向欧

洲输送电力。虽然 Medgrid 项目组成的联盟于 2016 年 1 月停止运作，但在这之前已进行了一些电网互联规划研究，其中包括设计连接北非和欧洲的三条输电走廊（见图 3-35），并完成西部和中央输电走廊的预可行性研究。

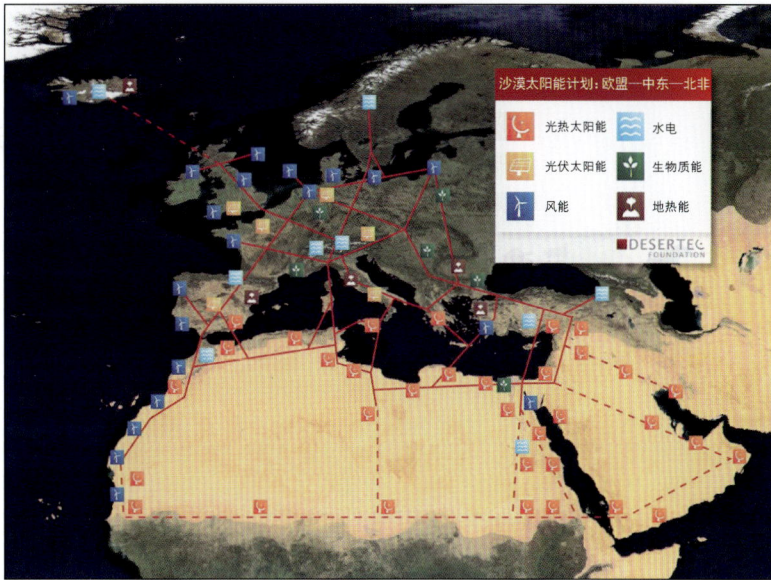

图 3-34　Desertec 项目概念图（Desertec 基金）

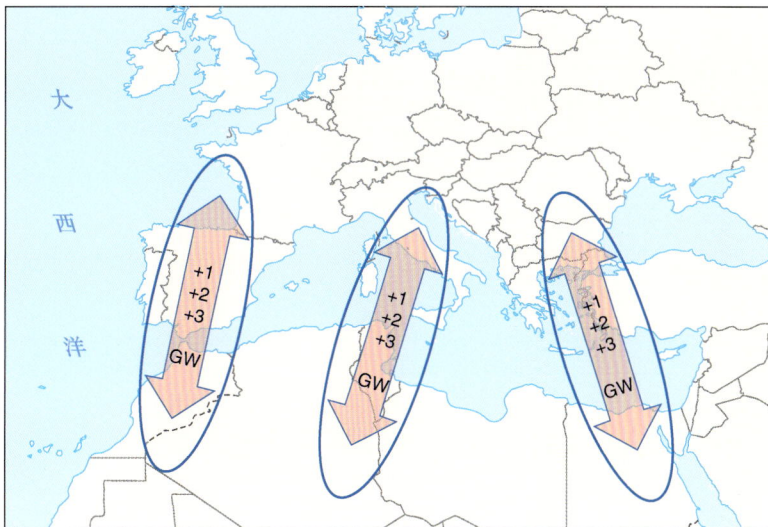

图 3-35　北非与欧洲之间潜在的输电走廊（Medgrid）

3.3.3.4　Gobitec 项目和亚洲超级电网项目

在 1998 年首次提出的 Gobitec 项目和亚洲超级电网（ASG）项目，旨在开发利用戈壁和塔克拉玛干沙漠以及俄罗斯远东的大量可再生能源资源，将大量的电力传输到中国、韩国和日本的负荷中心。这些项目自 1998 年以来一直在讨论与研究。由蒙古、日本、俄罗斯和韩国的研究和政府机构撰写的 2014 年报告[12]提出了 ASG 的愿景（见图 3-36）[12]。利用 UHVDC 输电线路作为骨干网架，ASG 将戈壁沙漠

的风电和太阳能发电基地以及俄罗斯伊尔库茨克的水电站与北京、上海、首尔和东京的负荷中心连接。尽管涉及政治、法律、体制和财政等方面的重大挑战，亚洲开发银行和国家电网有限公司正在支持该项目的进一步研究。

图 3-36　ASG 愿景

3.4　GEI 的经济可行性

如前所述，总体而言，国家间电力系统互联是一个十分具有吸引力的议题。借助系统互联，可提升系统的安全性和可靠性，为电力平衡、

确保资源充足提供支持，提高资产利用率、降低成本，并推动电力系统脱碳。实现互联不可避免的需要营建新的输电线路，这方面的成本和收益，需要应用严谨的成本效益分析方法（CBA）进行谨慎评估。随着大范围电网互联概念的提出，监管、政治

和经济方面需考虑的问题也变得更加复杂。

互联提案所针对的主要经济效益包括：共享资源、更高的可靠性和供给安全性、促进竞争、节省生产和运营成本、在容量需求方面的节省、回收（部分）闲置投资、通过降低碳排放、降低阻塞成本等减轻环境影响。

需要与上述收益进行权衡考虑的是提案带来的成本支出包括：直接成本如资产注入的投资成本，间接成本如输电投资引发的社会和环境成本。互联带来的一大变化在于，两个区域之间的价格差异，由此可能会出现不同的收益和成本分摊问题。对电力价格较低的地区而言，由于扩大的互联区域会指定一个更高的电价，实现互联可能给该地发电企业带来效益。反过来，这也可能引起发电企业在具有更高电价的地区聚集。在输电能力充裕的条件下，这种供给侧的变化将推动区域间电价趋同，这给不同地区消费者的带来的影响将是截然不同的。最终，只有当实现互联的增益高于成本时，才可认为项目的实施从经济角度而言是合理的。

对于新的电网投资而言，需要考虑以下两条基本性原则：

（1）净收益评估：综合比较收益和成本，通常应当认识到新投资对市场的全面影响。

（2）与已确认的受益人间事前按比例分摊投资成本，有助于降低融资不确定性，并提高项目的接受程度。

在规划阶段引入 CBA 有助于提高项目的透明度，并帮助在所有市场参与者之间开展协商。这样，对那些未来可能会影响成本和效益的重要因素所做的假设才可能为各方所接受。协调投资人对上述未来发展条件的假设至关重要，因为任何投资计划只能基于预期发展。同时，这些假设应与风险评估相结合，因为假设中的不确定性可能会改变收益。如需求、燃料源或供给能力等所有这些相关假设，在风险评估中通常被认定为价格和/或数量风险。远期收益规划的不确定性随时间跨度而上升，对于 GEI 而言尤其如此。如此巨大的地理覆盖范围和时间跨度，不可避免地增加了规划的不确定性，以及对效益的低估或高估的风险。因此依据经济规划原则，采取适当措施进行长期收益和风险评估是必要的。

第 4 章

构建全球能源互联网所需技术

对于全球能源互联网概念中所设想的电网互联水平，需要一系列技术支持其实现。本章对这些技术进行了分析，对这些技术的描述为第 5 章标准需求的探讨奠定基础。

4.1 输电技术

4.1.1 特高压输电技术

4.1.1.1 特高压交流输电

特高压交流指额定电压 1000kV 及以上的交流输电技术，是实现远距离输电的两项关键技术之一。特高压交流技术自 20 世纪 60 年代在前苏联、美国、日本和意大利开始平行发展，至今已成为成熟技术[7]。埃基巴斯图兹—科克切塔夫输电线路是世界上第一个特高压交流输电工程，长 495km，1985 年开始试运行。中国自 1986 年开始特高压交流技术研究。2006 年，中国国家电网公司开始 1000kV 特高压交流试点工程建设，单

回线路总长 640km，联结华北电网和华中电网，于 2009 年投运。2011 年，经扩建输送容量达到 5GW[13]。在试点项目获得经验的基础上，中国在华东地区相继建成另外 2 条 1000kV 特高压交流线路，还有 4 个在建工程。

相对于较低电压等级交流输电技术，特高压交流输电技术具有更远距离、更大容量、更低损耗、节省线路走廊和成本的特征。图 4-1 提供了 1000kV 和 500kV 交流输电技术和经济指标的比对[14]。

4.1.1.2 特高压直流输电

特高压直流指额定电压 ±800kV 及以上的直流输电技术，是实现大容量远距离输电的另一关键技术。目前，只有一个技术，即基于线换相换流器的高压直流（LCC-HVDC），也称作基于电流源换流器的高压直流（CSC-HVDC），能够达到特高压电压等级。LCC-HVDC 是一种成熟的技术，于 1954 年首次投入商业运行。当

500kV交流（双回线）		1000kV交流（双回线）
2—2.4	输电容量（GW）	8—9
250—800	经济输电距离（km）	500—2000
0.46—0.69	线损率（%/100km）	0.17—0.21
0.029—0.035	架空线足迹（m/MW）	0.008—0.009
39	变电站足迹（m²/MW）	29
1938	成本［RMB/（MW·km）］	1346

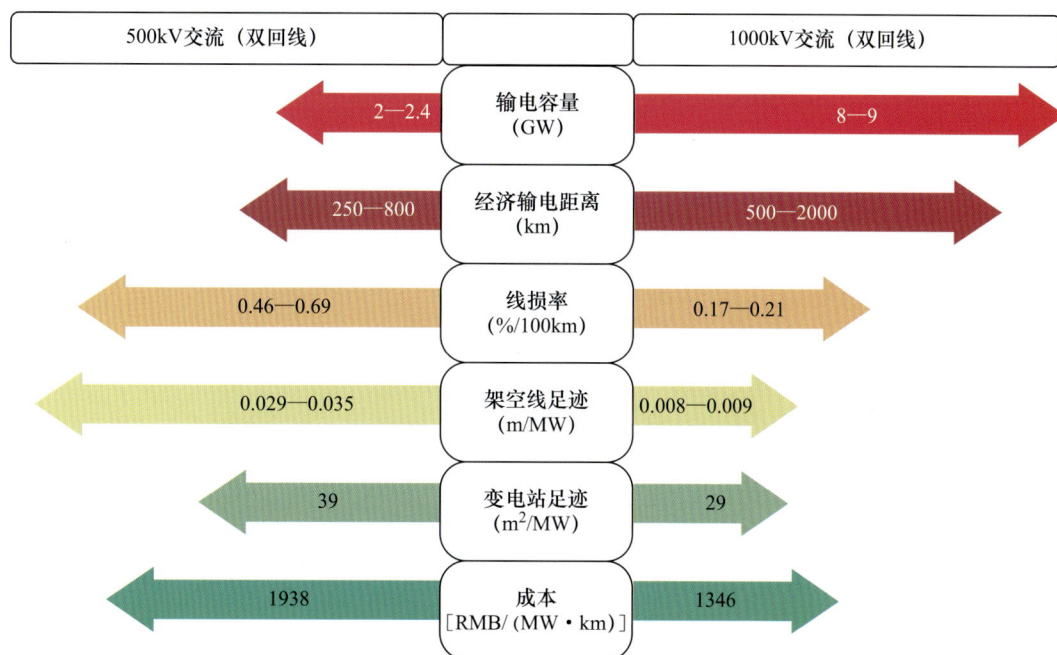

图 4-1　1000kV 和 500kV 交流输电特性比对（SGCC）

前这是一种实现远距离、大容量、点对点输电，以及实现不同频率交流电网互联的选择。相比于传统交流输电，这种特高压直流输电具有更低损耗、更低成本、更小的输电走廊、更高可控性的特点。在几大新兴国家，如巴西、中国、印度、南非，大量电力基础设施仍有待建设，对大容量远距离输电有很大的需求，特高压直流输电工程在近几年正在大量的规划和建设。

目前世界上大部分在运和在建特高压直流工程都在中国，主要作用是将西部和北部能源中心发出的电输送到中部和沿海负荷中心。中国国家电网公司目前在运 4 条±800kV 特高压直流工程，另有 5 条在建线路。中国南方电网公司运营 2 条特高压直流线路，另有 1 条在建线路。这些±800kV 特高压直流工程的输电距离从 1100～2400km 不等。2016 年 1 月，中国国家电网公司开始建设世界上首条±1100kV 特高压直流工程，输电线路长度 3324km，额定功率 12GW。

图 4-2[14]对特高压直流和±500kV 高压直流输电的技术和经济性能进行了对比。与普通高压直流输电相比，特高压直流技术具有远距离、大容量、低损耗、低成本、节省线路走廊的特点。±800kV 和±1100kV 特高压直流输电线路在输电距离分别达到 2500km 和 5000km 时可实现经济输送。

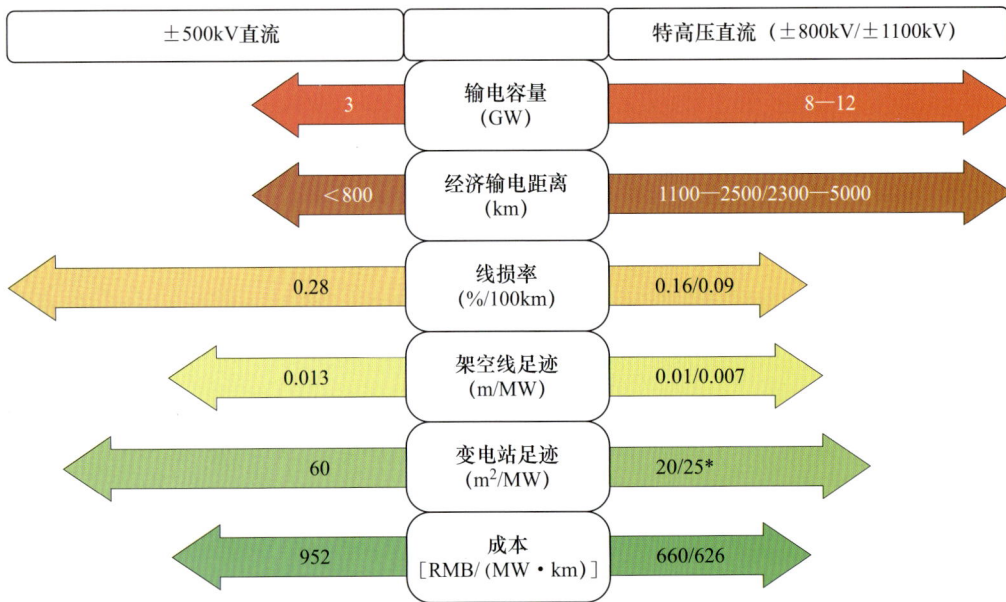

* 换流站连接两个不同电压等级的交流系统。

图 4-2　±500kV 直流和特高压直流（±800/±1100kV）输电特性比较（SGCC）

4.1.1.3　全球能源互联网背景下的特高压输电技术

当前的特高压输电技术已经可以满足修建大规模区域互联，跨国互联，甚至最终全球能源互联的主干网络。如表 4-1[7]所示，全球主要能源基地和负荷中心之间的距离都在 2000～5000km 之间，在特高压输电的经济输电距离之内。不同电压等级的特高压交流和特高压直流资产设施可以根据不同的目的和输电距离进行配置。如特高压交流电网主要用于在供电侧汇集功率或在需求侧分配电能，而特高压直流可以用于点对点输电。若输电距离超过 5000km，可以考虑采用 ±1500kV 特高压直流输电技术，目前正在示范论证阶段。

表 4-1　所选的主要新能源基地和负荷中心的距离[7]

起始	末端	长度（km）
北极喀拉海（风电）	华北	4400
白令海峡（风电）	中国北部、日本、韩国	5000
白令海峡（风电）	英国西部	4000
北极格陵兰岛（风电）	英国北部	2100
北极格陵兰岛（风电）	加拿大魁北克	2000
北非（太阳能发电）	欧洲	<2000
中东（太阳能发电）	印度西部	4000

4.1.2　柔性交/直流输电技术

4.1.2.1　柔性交流输电技术（FACTS）

基于先进的大容量电力电子设备和创新控制技术，20 世纪 90 年代以来各种柔性交流输电系统得到快速发展，极大地提升了交流输电系统的可控性、灵活性、稳定性和输电容量。FACTS 还可用于易变的可再生能源并网的电压和潮流控制。

4.1.2.2　VSC 高压直流输电和高压直流电网

基于电压源型换流器的高压直流输电（VSC-HVDC）和高压直流电网是现代电网互联的基本组成部分，也将成为未来区域和跨国电网的重要支柱。不同于采用半控阀的传统的 LCC-HVDC，CSC-HVDC 输电采用全控阀，是一种更新的选择，于 1997 年首次投入商业运行。与传统高压直流输电相比，这种直流输电的优势包括：

（1）可以进行有功功率和无功功率的快速独立控制，甚至可以黑启动。因此，它不依赖于所连接的交流系统的强度，也不需消耗大量的无功功率，可以给交流系统提供动态的无功和电压支撑。这些特点也使其适用于远距离可再生能源发电并网，尤其是海上风电并网。

（2）简化了换流变两侧设备的设计，从而减小换流站规模，简化换流站配置。LCC 和 VSC 高压直流换流站配置如图 4-3 和图 4-4 所示。

（3）潮流反转更加容易，不易受换相失败的影响，从而使得该技术更适用于多端直流（MTDC）和高压直流组网，传统的 LCC 直流输电技术很难实现这一点。

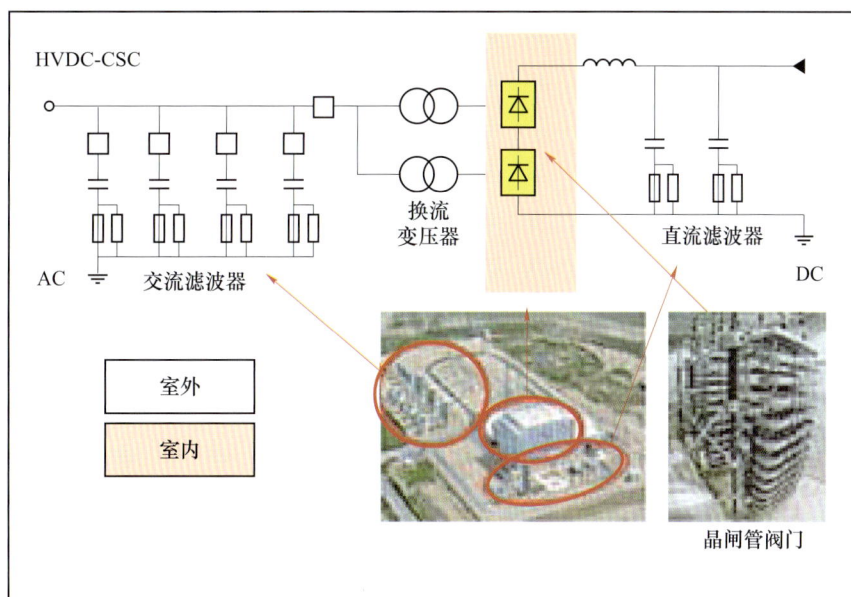

图 4-3　传统 LCC 高压直流换流站配置[20]

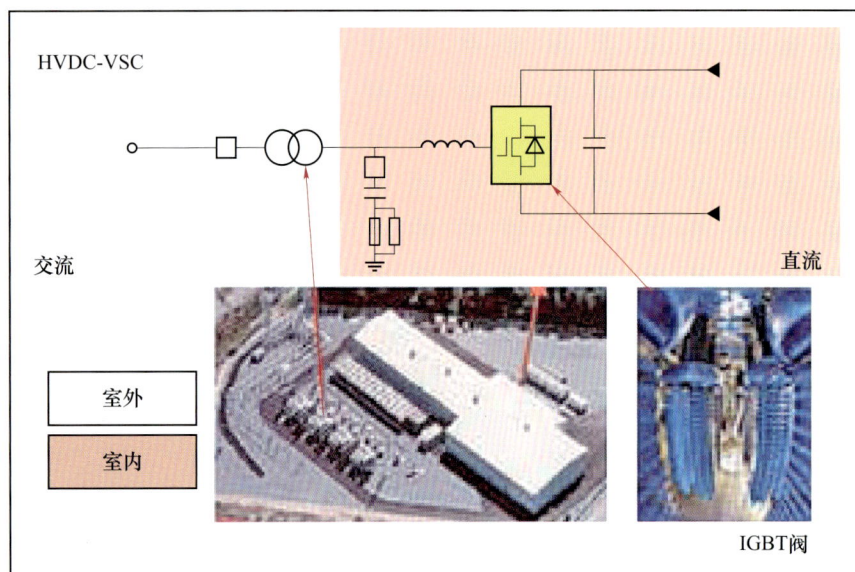

图 4-4　VSC 高压直流换流站配置[20]

在欧洲、中国、美国，多项 VSC 高压直流工程已经投运、或在建和规划中。这些工程主要用于电网互联，海上风电并网，以及向海上石油或天然气平台和大城市供电。典型例子包括法国和西班牙间 ±320kV/2×1000MW 工程，意大利和法国间 ±500kV/2×600MW 工程，北海海上风电向欧洲北部多项输电工程，美国 ±200kV/400MW Transbay 工程，以及 2015 年竣工的中国厦门 ±320kV/1000MW 真正的双极工程[8],[16],[17],[18]。

与 LCC 高压直流相比，受换流阀和电缆高成本和可用性限制，VSC 高压直流系统的电压和功率等级相对较低。目前，VSC 高压直流系统的最高电压和额定功率分别为 500kV 和 2GW[19]，但未来会不断提升。

高压直流电网是大范围、跨区域，最终实现全球电网互联的一个关键组成部分。在 VSC 高压直流输电技术不断改进的基础上，对高压直流电网的展望和详细研究已经展开[21]。一个高压直流电网由至少 3 个换流站和由若干输电线路组成的至少一个网架构成。根据电网重新配置需要，也可以包括一个高压开关站。高压直流电网已经具备了技术可行性，但仍然面临包括适当的保护、控制，以及电网仿真等方面的挑战。许多情况下，在分散、易变的可再生能源并网时，直流组网可能比点对点高压直流系统具有更高的成本效益。实践中，高压直流电网可以通过逐渐扩展多端直流电网实现，如将具有两个以上换流站的高压直流系统连接起来[17]。

在欧洲，旨在实现北海海上风电、北非和地中海太阳能并入欧洲电网的超级电网（Super Grid）、Desertec 电网、Medgrid 电网等概念和计划的提出都是基于高压直流电网技术。在美国，从新泽西州到马里兰州和特拉华州的将多个海上风电场经海底电缆并网工程也已提出计划[17]。最后，中国已建成投运世界上首个和第二个 VSC 多端直流项目，分别是 2013 年竣工的广东省南部沿海的南奥三端海上风电并网工程[22]和 2014 年竣工的浙江省东部沿海的舟山五端并网工程（见图 4-5）[23]。高压直流电网在中国西部和北部地区用于可再生能源并网项目也正在研究之中[24]。

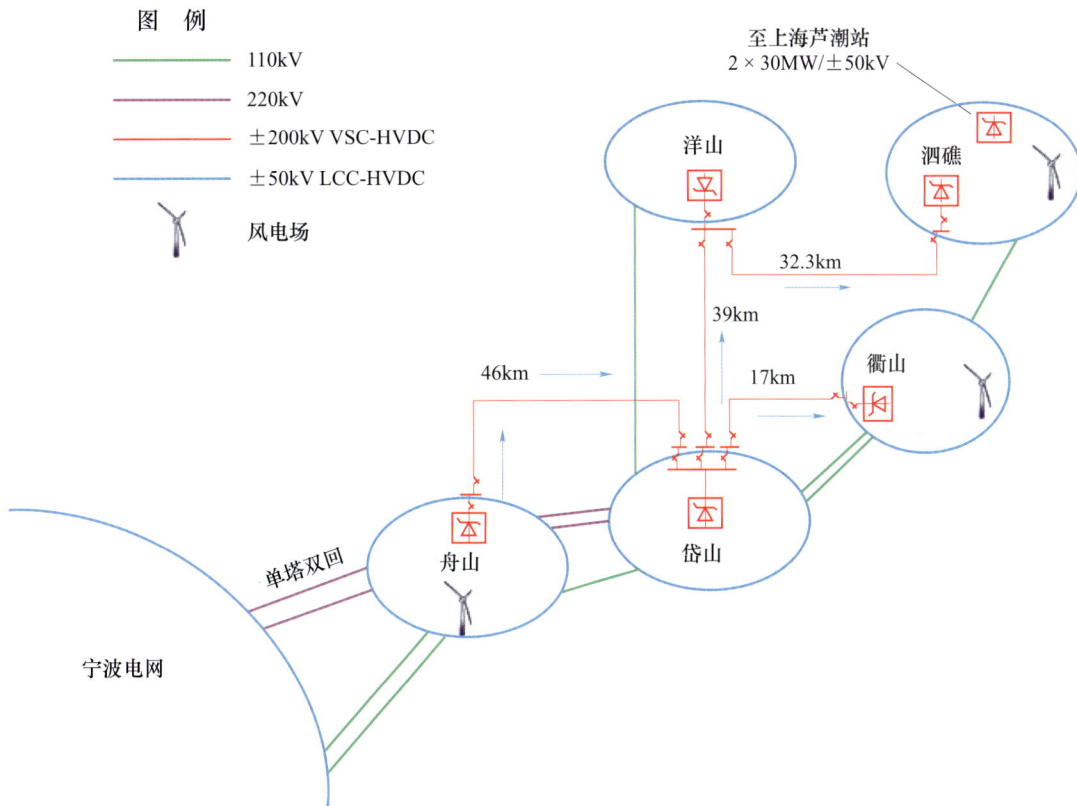

图 4-5　舟山多端直流工程配置图[23]

VSC 高压直流和高压直流组网技术的不断发展将使得跨越大地理区域的可再生能源基地并网和大范围电网互联以及跨区和洲际乃至全球电网互联更加具有可行性和更有效。

4.1.3　其他新兴技术

4.1.3.1　半波长交流输电

半波长交流输电（HWACT）是一项正在开发的能够实现远距离、大容量输电的有前景的输电技术。顾名思义，这是指输电的电气距离接近 1 个工频半波长，即 3000km（50Hz）或 2500km（60Hz）的超远距离三相交流输电[25]。半波长交流输电概念首次于 20 世纪 40 年代由前苏联学者提出，用于将哈萨克斯坦火电和西伯利亚水电输送到西部负荷中心。在 21 世纪的第一个十年，半波长输电技术又重新引起人们的关注，CIGRE 已成立新工作组 A3.13 并开展可行性研究。

特高压半波长交流输电是在距离超过 3000km 或为 3000km 倍数（工频 50Hz）的大容量输电时，替代特高压直流输电的又一经济可行选择，该技术的示范项目正在进行中。该技术可以在跨国、跨洲电网互联，及最终实现全球电网互联中发挥重要作用[25]。

4.1.3.2 高温超导输电

高温超导输电（HTS）是指采用高温超导电缆（–180℃及以上）的输电方式。理论上，高温超导输电较传统输电方式有下述优势，而这些都是大范围及全球电网互联极为需要的[26]：

（1）输送容量极大：一条±800kV 的高温超导特高压直流线路的输送容量可达 16～80GW，是目前传统特高压直流输电的 2～10 倍。

（2）损耗极低：是常规电缆损耗的 25%～50%。

（3）很小的空间足迹，重量轻，可以通过改变温度灵活调整输送容量，通过相变限制故障电流。

尽管具有技术上的优势，在高温超导输电用于实际输电工程项目之前还需要在物理学和材料学方面取得相应的进展，从而使该技术在远期可以在电力系统互联和全球电网互联中发挥作用。20 世纪 90 年代以来，主要在美国、欧洲、日本、韩国和中国，针对高温超导电缆（最初聚焦于交流电缆研究，后转向直流电缆研究）的深入研究、开发和示范工作都有所开展[26]。

目前，这些电缆的长度、电压和额定功率水平都比较低。对于交流电缆来说，长度从 30～1000m 不等，额定电压从 10～138kV。对于直流电缆，长度从 200～2500m 不等，额定电压范围从±1.3～±80kV。

4.2 智能电网技术

4.2.1 大电网运行和控制技术

除电力系统物理资产和技术外，实现 GEI 理念中跨区域、跨洲电力传输，需要着力提升大电网运行、监测和控制能力。

4.2.1.1　大规模电网的控制和保护

传统上，电力系统的监测和控制是基于监测控制和数据采集/能源管理系统（SCADA/EMS）实现的，保护则依赖于局域量测探知故障和异常情况。SCADA/EMS 系统可通过现场监测单元（FTUs）测量电压、频率、功率数据，以及断路器和开关状态，并发送到控制中心，在控制中心通过状态估计对必要技术性能进行计算。SCADA/EMS 系统的一大缺陷在于采集的数据在时间上不同步，意味着状态估计在测量中可能有所不同。

得力于卫星导航系统，相量测量装置（PMU）可直接记录各条母线的同步电压幅值和相位角度，并传送至控制中心，从而实现由"状态估计"到"状态测量"的跨越[27]。基于 PMU 网络开发的大量应用组成了广域监测系统（WAMSs）[28]，包括：广域可视化、振荡检测和阻尼控制、发电机模型和参数校验，孤岛监测、电压失稳监测、事后分析、广域保护等，这些应用显著提升了大电网的控制和保护水平。未来 PMU/WAMS 应用的发展趋势包括：开发高精度 PMU，离线系统到在线系统的转换，单纯监测向控制的转换，以及 PMU/WAMS 技术与大数据技术的结合[29]。在 GEI 背景下，PMU/WAMS 技术将发挥基础性作用（见图 4-6）。

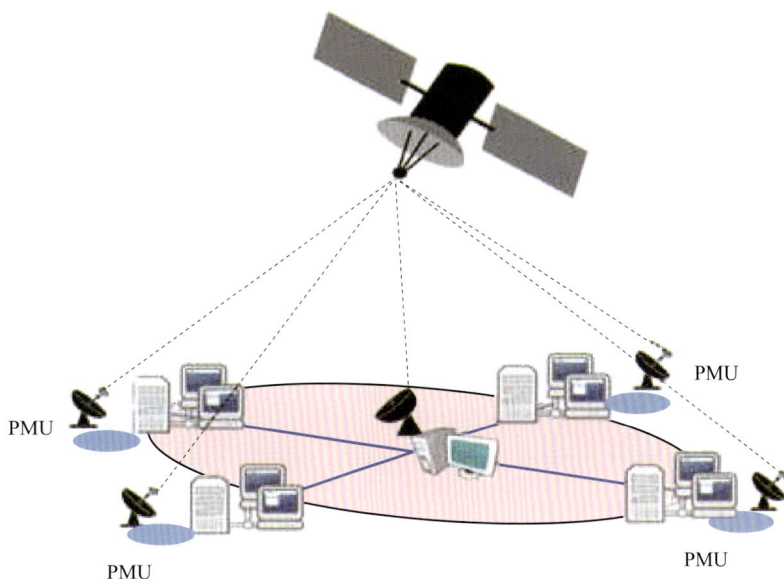

图 4-6　PMU/WAMS 系统图解

随着在线故障监测和诊断、新型继电保护、广域后备保护、故障恢复策略优化和智能配置等技术的进步，未来电网在面对不同运行环境和各类故障时将具有更强的安全性、稳定性和自愈能力。上述技术可显著提高大电网抵御连锁故障、极端天气状况、外部有害因素的能力。随着 ICT 技术和控制理论的发展，电网运行和控制正逐步向预测、预警和自动故障恢复的方向演进。预计高度自动化运行控制将在 GEI 建设中期实现，支持高精度可再生能源发电日前预测（偏差率将低于 5%），并有助于可再生能源、常规能源和负荷的低成本接入[7]。

4.2.1.2　大电网仿真和分析

鉴于无法在实际运营电网进行故障和扰动试验，仿真和仿真结果分析就成为探索特定电网特性的不可替代的工具。随着算法、模型和计算软硬件的不断升级，仿真在保障电网安全和稳定运行方面发挥了关键作用，电网的技术也随着时间的推移而不断发展。

大规模互联推动电网规模不断增长，对电网运行分析和决策支持的时间性要求达到了前所未有的高度。过去，受限于计算机技术发展水平，电力系统分析只能基于离线仿真开展。然而，随着 ICT 技术的进步，越来越多的仿真可在线进行，从而实现了在线动态安全评估和预警。通过在线暂态稳定分析，不仅可以评估电网的现有安全水平，还可以辅助电力系统调度员制定预防控制策略，以进一步提高电网安全性。目前，已经实现了对一定规模电网的实时❶和超实时仿真，这将进一步提高大型电网的运行和控制水平。

在大规模互联和 GEI 背景下，电力系统运行的复杂性将急剧增加，对仿真和分析的准确性、速度和效率也提出了更高要求。因此，需要应用超级计算和机电—电磁混合暂态仿真技术提升仿真能力，以支持对拥有数百万母线的电力系统的分析，还需要建立高渗透率可再生能源电厂、直流输电和新型电网控制和保护装置的准确模型。在准确建模困难的情况下，可以通过数模混合仿真，以硬件在环的形式，实现控制和保护物理设备与数字化系统模型的连接（见图 4-7）。此外，在全球范围实现设备和网络数据的管理和共享，对于实现集中式和分布式仿真及分析也是不可或缺的。

---

❶ "实时"仿真是指仿真一个系统事件所用的时间与实际系统中物理系统中事件所持续的时间相等。

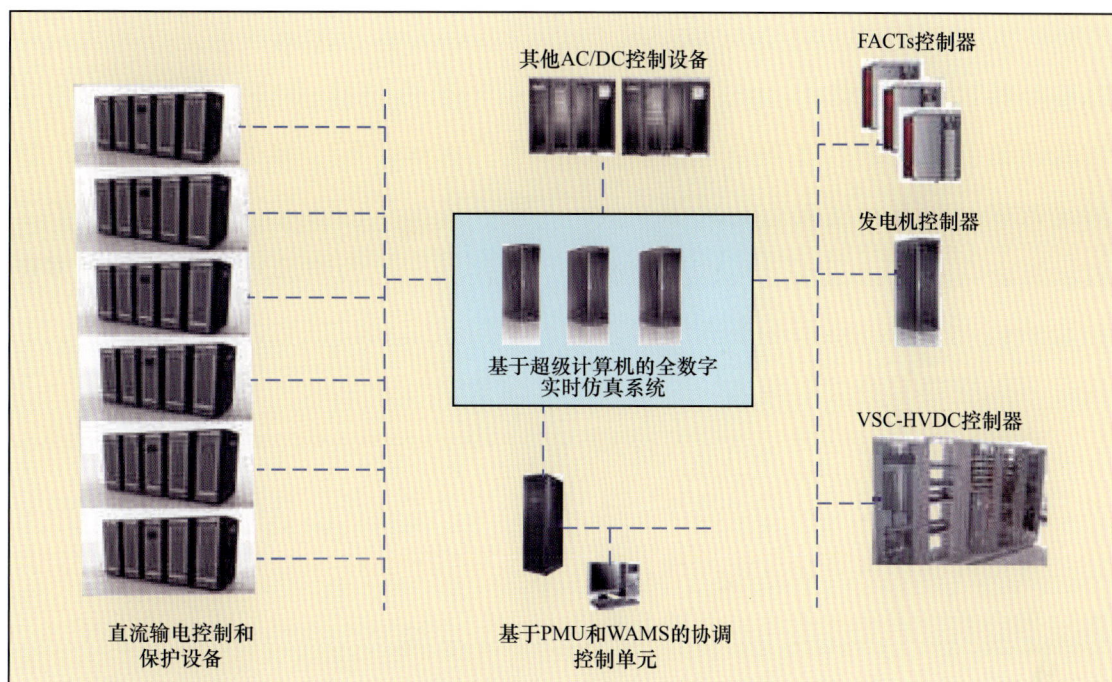

图 4-7　中国国家电网公司数模混合仿真平台架构

4.2.2　信息和通信技术（ICT）

构建 GEI 网络相当于在全球建立一个超级、智能、高压电网，这一宏伟蓝图的实现需要基于最现代化的标准部署复杂的新一代 ICT 技术。

运营如此智能、复杂的技术网络，有赖于运营和商业数据/流程的有效集成，以便实时地实现关键决策和商业交易。而这需要建立新型技术平台，打破传统 OT 和 IT 系统的信息隔离，从而实现超大范围跨区交易。

上述 IT/OT 集成平台也将成为综合信息系统应用的技术基础，以实现对电网规划、运行和维护等核心过程

能量流的计量、计费、结算和相关服务的管理，并通过实时连续过程分析，即刻发现诸如技术损失、欺诈、停电风险等技术和商业问题。

该平台还将基于通用市场标准和流程，并协调扩展性资产信息和业务网络，在相关合作公司之间实现自动数据交换，以优化与供应商和市场合作伙伴的协作。

4.2.3　IT/OT 集成平台的必要性

当前的 IT 环境由数十乃至上百个系统组成，虽然个别系统进行了集成，但在绝大部分情况下，各个系统完全分离，例如业务和业务智能化系统（BI）、能源投资组合管理和交易系

统、SCADA、地理信息系统（GIS），以及网络信息系统等运行系统和历史数据系统等。随着 GEI 智能电网的发展，数据量和颗粒度都将快速增长，对于受影响的 TSO 来说，一个越来越重要的问题就是如何减少数据复制的次数，以提高自身分析能力。长期将如此庞大的数据从一个孤立系统复制到另一个，并保持数据的一致性，从经济角度而言不具有可行性。此外，对于大多数分析和业务流程，数据集的时效性、综合性和一致性决定了其能否提供更好的结果和更深入的见解。除数据量的增长外，数据采集和提交业务流程的时间间隔将不断缩短，在很多情况下甚至需要提供（近）实时数据。

在 GEI 背景下，上述变化要求 TSO 平台实现三个重要的高级别功能：

（1）处理急速攀升的数据量和许多不同的数据类型。

（2）整合不同来源的数据，以实现业务和运行系统的集成（IT/OT 系统集成）。

（3）实现数据（近）实时可用。

下列业务过程列举了 GEI 背景下 TSO 平台需要具备的功能。这些功能示例旨在重点强调一些关键性要求，并非业务流程支持功能的详尽清单。

（1）电网分析支持电网的近实时分析，以提高电网的稳定性和效能，并防止停电。这需要采用相关性分析，例如需要了解在哪些情况下，特定设备如变压器等将过载，还需具备峰值负荷的预测能力。分析结果将触发人工交互或主动管理电网资产的其他系统的干预。

该过程很大程度上依赖于电网中的传感器和事件数据，但表计数据也不可或缺。如果数据和分析近实时可用，即在收到数据后的几分钟或甚至几秒钟内便可用，那么电网分析解决方案将达到非常好的效果，可快速采取措施。

（2）预见性维护即基于电表、传感器数据和历史数据估计资产何时将发生故障或效率下降，并根据结果触发维护动作。总体而言，预见性维护符合电网和电厂的利益，特别是对于处于边远地区的资产，如离岸风电场、偏远地区的输电设备等。

预见性维护的数据要求与电网基础设施分析过程相似，但通常不需要实时数据，每日数据即可。非结构性数据，例如来自工作指令或客户信息的文本也将支持这一分析过程。

（3）泄漏管理支持如欺诈管理、技术损失的早期探测等流程，可辅助判断损失发生的位置，以及是否由欺诈造成，并作为后续流程的起始点，在安全方面也有积极作用。

除电表、资产和 GIS 数据外，还需要来自用户关系管理及计费系统产生的用电预测数据、事件数据和用户数据的支持。非结构性数据，如社交媒体平台数据，也可用于检测可能的欺诈行为。虽然每日上传数据即足以支持欺诈管理，但采用实时数据对于发现技术损失是非常有益的。

（4）能量结算对特定时间间隔内一组传输点的计量数据进行聚集，作为输电服务商业结算的基础。该信息随后可通过市场消息系统发送给运营区域内所有参与方进行进一步处理。

采用统一平台提供统一数据存储库、通用工具及功能，将为上述业务流程及相对应的各个应用带来更好的实施效果。其背后的原因在于，业务流程可基于综合性、一致性的实际数据进行操作，从而减少数据复制需求。应用层面获得好处在于，通过采用通用功能，可避免各个独立应用中的重复开发问题。此外，由于数据交互和交互接口需求的降低，不同应用间的集成也将更为简化。

上述统一平台总成本预期远低于由多个不同产品组成的一种系统环境的总成本，前者可通过在顶层应用中复用大量通用功能，有效降低数据复制、清理和保持一致性的投入，而后者中每个产品都采用独立数据表、工具和技术，成本更高。

为满足以上所有要求，TSO 平台需要支持上述业务流程，并具备异构应用支持功能，并满足以下要求：

（1）快速上传大量不同类型数据；

（2）处理不同来源的各类数据，包括电表、传感器、事件、地理、价格、天气等数据；

（3）支持从月度到日以下（直到实时）的不同频率数据上传；

（4）具备月度到分钟甚至秒级不同颗粒度数据处理能力；

（5）具备等时间间隔和非等间隔（离散）值处理能力；

（6）具备非结构性数据处理能力。

除上传和存储数据外，该平台还需要具备以下功能：

（1）数据验证、估算和编辑；

（2）在发生变化的情况下，存储数据的不同版本；

（3）支持审计功能，例如在监管要求下提交报告；

（4）支持超过一年期数据存储和数据老化；

（5）此外，该平台还需支持可供所有运行于其上的应用使用的通用功能，包括：

1）计算工具，例如利用原始数据计算消费情况、替代值，或能量消耗、发电成本等；

2）具备聚集引擎以实现电网多点数据聚集，例如属于一家控股公司的所有传输点，或接入同一变压器的所有电表数据的聚集；这些数据将用于业务过程中的分析和模式识别，例如网络基础结构分析或欺诈管理；

3）维护的预测算法和资产的替换策略；

4）支持如预见性维护等数据分析的数据挖掘工具；

5）具备大量业务流程所需的复杂事件处理能力，例如停电管理等，平台不需要支持完整的业务流程，只需为相应的系统提供分析结果；

6）具备与外部系统、外部数据供应商及 GEI 其他参与方数据的接口。

为应对上述要求，大规模能源互联网和 GEI 运营商需要建立 IT/OT 集成平台，实现不同产品的优化和协同运行，以妥善应对当前的数据管理挑战。主要数据管理要素包括：海量跨存储数据处理、高速流数据处理、数据可视化及进一步处理等。应对这些挑战需要具备主数据处理能力、信息治理和信息建模能力。支持多样化数据类型也是当前面临的需求之一，包括结构性数据、半结构性（或基于文本的）数据，以及图片、音频、视频等非结构性大数据。结合 Hadoop®分

布式文件系统和 Hadoop®分布式计算（MapReduce）框架进行海量非结构性数据预处理和处理，正成为一种标准化做法。

未来的 IT/OT 平台需要彻底解决这些数据管理挑战，且解决方案需具备可扩展性。平台需为各类组织提供稳健而又灵活的环境以实现其管理数据需求，包括在线交易处理、数据处理和分析、数据建模和传送，信息治理，以及统一管理和监测工具。除其他要素外，IT/OT 平台需覆盖以下产品或组合。

（1）具备以下功能的内存计算平台：可实现内存在线交易处理（OLTP）、支持代码库嵌入、应用先进统计算法进行数据分析。

（2）通过传统数据库技术增强和补充内存需求，以满足更好的经济和价格/性能要求，这一点在越来越多的客户数据规模向千兆字节量级发展的趋势下尤为关键。该技术以本地 MapReduce 并行计算框架为特征，并为大数据分析提供 Hadoop 集成技术。

（3）用于高速流数据分析的事件流处理能力，以及对于超低时延应用的过滤能力，从而实现不间断智能化处理。

（4）具备非常先进的安全通信协议和数据加密能力的数据安全扩展组

件，以有效抵御入侵、保障关键任务技术数据安全。

此外，IT/OT 集成平台应为合作方和用户提供数据建模和数据迁移工具，使其能够在同一平台构建自己的应用。

IT/OT 集成平台的所有元件都必须向第三方工具开放集成，例如支持商业智能、信息管理或基础设施管理。

实现上述平台，需要将商业企业资源规划（ERP）系统与电表数据管理（MDM）、SCADA 等技术应用，

以及文件管理系统（DMS）进行有机融合。图 4-8 介绍了由 SAP 设想的 IT/OT 平台的概念架构。该架构中的数据融合是将 SAP 的商业 MDM 应用与来自某一合作伙伴的技术头端系统（HES）数据在一个通用、云端就绪、支持内存数据库的通用平台（SAP HANA 云平台）上进行数据集成，以实现商业交易流程与海量实时技术数据的对接，并支持引入如输电负荷实时预测等全新流程。

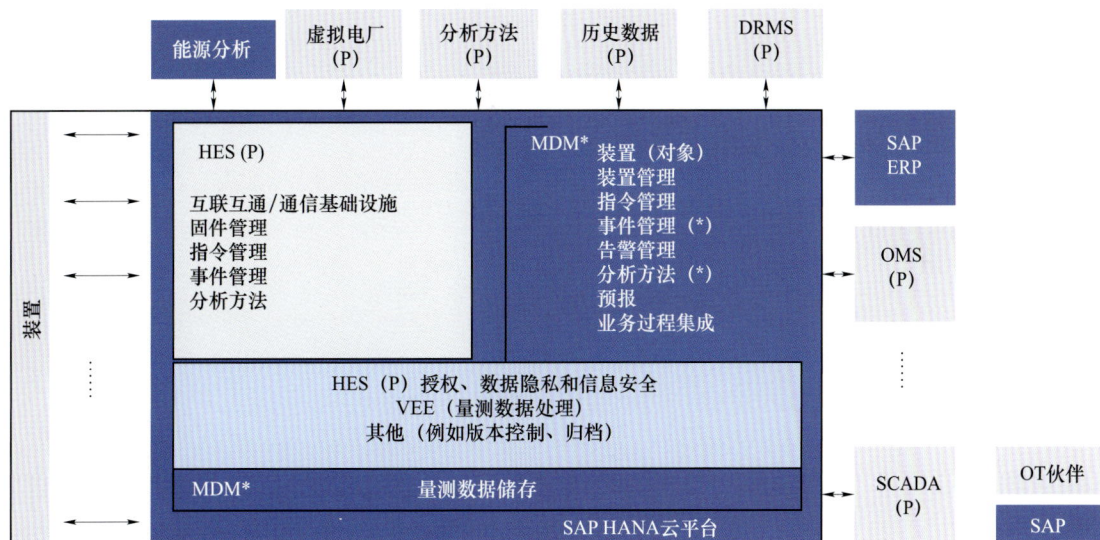

图 4-8　IT/OT 集成平台（SAP）概念

4.2.4　应用资产智能管理网络提升电网规划、运行和维护水平

技术资产的有效和安全管理从一开始就是能源产业面临的核心需求之一。因此，市场上涌现了多种经验证的 IT 解决方案，在支撑电网规划、运行和维护方面效果显著。

但在复杂的 GEI 框架下，TSO 可能面临一些特殊需求，需要提升资产管理流程的智能化和互联互通水平。要实现 GEI 的可持续发展，一项关键需求在于全球资产管理流程的标准化，利用最佳实践推动 TSO 间的国际合作，保障能源跨国传输的可靠性。

《IEC 电网资产战略性管理报告》对相关标准的重要性进行了全面而详尽的阐述。

当前，业界尚未实现对资产管理链的全面集成。在模型信息定义方面缺乏一致性，另外，原始设备制造商（OEM）和运营商通常都会采用手动方式上传数据，由此可能引入误差和延迟，造成数据不正确。缺乏完整、一致、消耗性设备的数据阻碍了后续对设备购入和维护的决策。资产管理的业务流程很少跨企业集成，造成信息的不透明、不完全。但 GEI 的成功

实现，需要基于公共标准，对技术资产和流程进行有效的协调管理，这就需要引入集成化资产智能管理网络（AIN）。

向数字化经济的转化，以及物联网、云端网络等新技术应用的快速增长，为自动数据交换提供了发展机遇，并通过资产管理网络为利益相关方提供了更为简单的协作模型。AIN 被视为应对上述挑战的有效解决方案，它为 GEI 资产管理的所有利益相关方提供了一个安全的云平台，作为中央结算所和通信枢纽，其概念如图 4-9 所示。

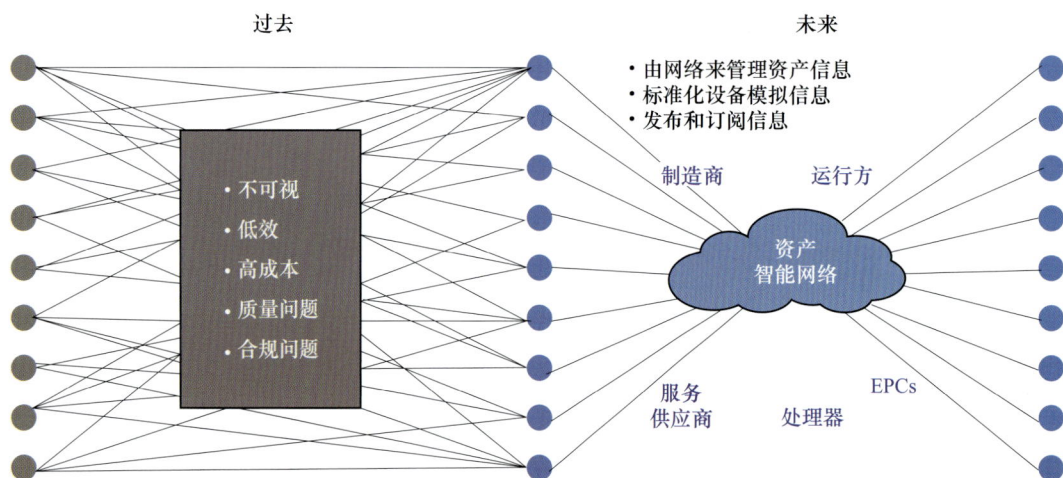

图 4-9 AIN 概念图：以一个无缝连接的网络中实现不同地区资产和企业的互联

AIN 为资产管理生态系统中不同参与方构建了统一平台，将推动运营商、原始设备制造商（OEM）、EPC 公司、服务商等不同组织合作迈向新高峰。AIN 是一个单一的云物联网，将所有设备接入同一生态系统。运行

在这个协作平台上的一系列应用简化了设备维护，并加强了复杂任务之间的协同效率。其内嵌的分析技术将激发资产管理服务创新，或基于性能进行重新设计（见表 4-2）。

表 4-2 AIN 的 巨 大 潜 力

种类	价值	性能	应用领域
高效资产管理流程	提高项目验收速度、增加收入	运营商和承包商可通过网络查找资产信息来源并验证丢失资产信息	标准化设备管理
	降低资本支出	工程团队可调整替代方案并降低生产支出	协作网络服务
	提高资产的可用率	通过与 OEM 合作，利用更新信息和预见性维护，利益相关方可降低资产停工时间	维护流程执行协作网络服务
	降低备用件库存	每次网络更新后，仓库可减少老旧及积压的 B-和 C-级库存	维护流程执行标准化设备管理
	降低维护成本	通过与 OEM 和服务供应商密切合作，运营商可对维护活动进行优化	维护流程执行协作网络服务
用户生产效率	减少查找和更新资产信息的工作量	所有成员都可访问与企业系统集成的最新信息	标准化设备管理维护流程执行
	缩短维护工作时间	现场工人可随时获得最新的任务时间指导和备件详细信息	维护流程执行协作网络服务

AIN 内设备信息应采用由 OEM 或第三方内容供应商提供的标准化性模型（如基于 API 610 数据表的泵）。模型中的数据表将提供设备的技术属性和内容，如推荐的维护策略、标准工作指令、物料清单、备件清单、图示等。制造商只需提供数据表一次，即可供所有认可的业务伙伴使用。此外，运营商可在此唯一网站检索来自不同制造商的一致性数据表，即可将其应用于自己的环境评估和管理（EAM）环境。

AIN 将为 GEI 利益相关方提供诸多效益（见图 4-10）。

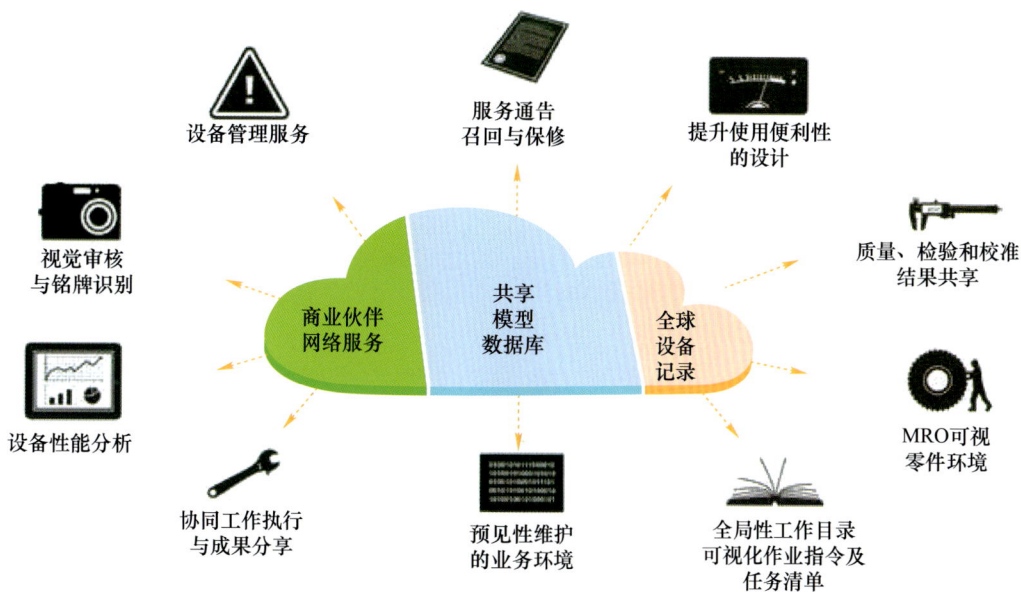

图 4-10　AIN（SAP）效益

4.2.4.1 全局性工作目录、可视化作业指令及任务清单

AIN 能够帮助运营商建立一个全局性工作库，包括推荐性维护策略、维护计划、标准作业和安全须知，供运营商在其工作管理系统中采用。原始设备制造商（OEM）将会发布这些推荐性维护策略、维护计划和标准作业作为其模型信息的部分内容。

4.2.4.2 预见性维护的业务背景

AIN 为预见性维护和服务提供了业务环境，无论运营商、制造商或服务提供商均可对设备进行监控和维护。通过向运营商和制造商预警即将发生的故障，可显著改善 TSO 和制造商间的协作。

4.2.4.3 性能提升

AIN 为 OEM、服务提供商和运营商提供了平台，帮助其改善机械设计以减少故障、降低运营成本、改善可维护性，并最终提高利润。这需要建立包括以下信息的设备信息流：设备是如何使用的，在何处安装，发生了哪些故障，应用了哪些服务公告等，以及来自于运营商的故障类型和影响分析信息。

4.2.4.4 一体化工作计划和实施

AIN 可协助运营商和服务提供商

协作开展设备维护工作，一些复杂活动可能需要分解为多个顺序步骤，部分由资产运营商完成，而一些更专业的部分则由服务提供商完成。

4.2.4.5 设备管理服务

运营商希望最大限度降低其资本支出和风险，而 OEM 则希望将产品与增值服务捆绑在一起。这些需求的融合，以及 IoT、合作网络等新技术的涌现，催生了设备管理服务这一新型商业模式。

4.2.4.6 设备性能分析

AIN 可协助运营商推行资产改善计划，利用不同运营场所信息建立可靠性基准指标，在全球范围内发现最佳运营和维护案例。根据各方供应和消费信息的需求，还可对信息进行匿名处理。

4.2.4.7 智能化市场

公司收集的设备信息日趋增长，用于数据分析、预测和预后判断的算法也越来越先进和多样化，由运营商自行完成所有数据处理的方式是否依然可行或理想？是否可以由制造商、服务提供商甚至个人在竞争市场环境下提供此类"智能化"服务，且择优采用？AIN 可为此提供市场环境，商

业伙伴可与其他第三方合作参与竞争，提供更加优质的智能化服务。网络化的资产信息为智能化市场提供了坚实基础，有望催生新的企业级解决方案及相应的新型服务。

4.2.4.8　质量、检验和校准结果共享

质量、检验认证和校准结果可通过 AIN 共享。法定管理当局和独立保险公司如 Lloyds Register、DNV GL、TüV 等（假定此类公司已取得有效授权）都将有权访问最新相关信息，包括是否按时进行了法定检验并具有相关检验结果。另一类案例是获取基于状态检修任务的结果和报告，例如引擎油料分析等，通常这类检测是送交外部实验室完成。

4.2.5　能量流的计量、计费和结算及相关服务

正如其他输电网一样，GEI 将在商业框架下运营，向电力接收方和/或送出方按输送的能量收取输电服务费用。这就需要配置专门的客户信息系统，能够对典型行业流程进行管理，包括编制抄表流程、按时间序列获取和管理海量抄表数据（负荷曲线），根据性能和可靠性计量输电服务费等。

市场上已有多种解决方案可满足上述商业需求，但是随着基于高颗粒

度数据（如基于分钟级价格）结算规则的重要性日趋提高，以及相关数据量的增长，理想的解决方案是对信息实现实时处理。这就需要采用基于内存的现代应用程序，以显著缩短海量数据复杂计算的处理时间。此类系统将在同一数据库下集成交易和分析数据的处理，去除批处理这一典型的耗时流程。此外，基于最新数据，该解决方案还可实现复杂操作的实时报告。

4.2.6　GEI 市场通信平台

GEI 将以由众多国家级 TSO 共同组成的网络形式运营，为了确保跨国甚至跨洲际输电的可靠性和可持续性，则有必要强制性的规定一种基于国际认可的通信格式、高度自动化的数据交互流程。典型的数据交互流程包括指定输电容量、输电预测和安排、支持跨境辅助服务的技术数据交换、优化资产管理协作所需的资产和运行数据交换，以及为输电服务结算或输电服务计费提供计量数据。

目前，已有多种可供 TSO 使用的市场通信标准，可考虑作为未来扩展延伸的 GEI 市场通信的基础。

例如，欧洲输电系统运营商联盟（ENTSOE-E）一直在维护其电子数据交换（EDI）库，保存了 ENTSO-E 核

准的所有文件和定义，以保证标准化电子数据交换的协调性和有效实施。

在未来 GEI 市场模型背景下，应研究探讨对 GEI 市场通信枢纽采用集中式操作是否有利于提高 GEI 流程效率。可考虑采用一种类似 IEC 的组织提供的云服务，集中协调所有 GEI 参与方间的通信流和跨公司数据交换。此类平台所必需的 IT 技术已经可得，且已在各类数据交换项目中的取得良好效果。

第 5 章

GEI 标准化

标准化对于 GEI 的成功是至关重要的，同时也是最大挑战之一。它要求在跨越主权边界、技术领域边界、分层边界和设备生命周期阶段等各个方面实现史无前例的系统集成。为了取得这一成功，基于共识的标准和规范是 GEI 不可或缺的基础。

现有及未来基于共识的标准将为下列各项技术采购创造坚实基础：通过标准化术语和概念来支持通信，确保互操作性，验证技术适用性及确定市场相关性。通过基于共识的标准化流程，以及研究人员、行业、监管和标准化机构之间的密切合作，在早期阶段描绘 GEI 概念，是多阶段成功实施 GEI 的核心要求之一。

为了获得成功，这些原则应该与支持 GEI 核心技术（即特高压、清洁能源和智能电网）的现有标准相一致。这不仅有利于今后设备、接口和技术的推广和应用，而且还将为在能源网和相关设备之间建立国际层面上的互联创造条件。

5.1 当前情况

目前存在的标准已覆盖 GEI 的一些基本技术领域，如特高压、清洁能源和智能电网。将多种技术纳入一个非常复杂庞大的电力能源系统的各个部分，这些标准都是非常需要的，这不仅将连接大范围的基础设施，还将支持信息通信系统。其涉及的标准与 IEC 中的许多技术委员会以及 IEC 以外的其他协调组织相关。以下列出了目前与 GEI 相关的 IEC 技术委员会（TC）和分委员会（SC）。

5.1.1 电力传输

TC7：架空电力导线

TC14：电力变压器

SC17A：开关设备

TC20：电缆

TC28：绝缘配合

TC36：绝缘子

TC115：100kV 及以上的高压直流输电系统

TC122：特高压交流输电系统

ACTAD：输配电咨询委员会

5.1.2 清洁能源——可再生能源发电和储能

TC4：水轮机

SC8A：可再生能源接入电网

TC21：蓄电池和蓄电池组

TC82：太阳能光伏能源系统

TC88：风能发电系统

TC114：海洋能—波浪能、潮汐能和其他水流能转换设备

TC117：太阳能光热电厂

TC120：电力储能系统

5.1.3 智能电网

TC8：电能供应系统方面

TC13：电能测量与负荷控制设备

TC22：电力电子系统和设备

TC57：电力系统管理和信息交换

TC64：电气装置和电击防护

TC77：电磁兼容

PC118：智能电网用户接口智慧能源系统委员会

ISO/IECJTC1：信息技术

CISPR：国际无线电干扰特别委员会

5.2 未来标准化需求

为构建全球能源互联网建立全球能源系统，这将提供一个全球性平台，让新技术得以最好的应用，并实现最好的性能和可靠性。如根据国际能源署预测，到2040年，陆上和海上风电装机容量将超过 1300GW，陆上风电容量占总数的 85%，而这个数字在 2011 年为 98%，风电的发展前景非常好。这种扩张将需要增加一些国际标准覆盖这些新的领域。新能源技术的自身特性要求其标准化紧跟各个领域的发展。

此外，智能电网和储能比以往任何时候都要与发配电系统、区域能源中心和远距离特高压线路统一在一起。

特高压交流最广阔的市场发展趋势是长距离大规模输电及与现有电力系统的互联。还有一种趋势是建立强大的消纳电网以接收更大规模的电力馈入。电网变化的驱动因素为：新兴国家负荷中心用电的快速增长，发电结构从煤、天然气和核能发电转变到处于远方发电场所的风电、太阳能发电、大型水力发电和其他能源的全部为可再生能源发电。随着主要来自风能、大型水电和太阳能的可再生能源

发电的增加，电能将与石油、天然气和煤炭能源竞争，但电能需要新的传输系统来满足预期的需求。

随着负荷增长和能源需求与供应之间的不平衡，就需要有些发电厂远离负荷中心（如大型水电和火电站），清洁的可再生能源分布式发电（如风力发电和太阳能发电）也将大量出现。前者的特点是容量大、距离远，采用高压直流传输技术具有明显的优势。

在极端环境条件下建造高压直流输电系统，比如在非常高的海拔高度（3000～5300m）建设换流站和直流输电线路，对高压直流输电技术提出了更高的要求。

智能电网建设工作已经开启，并且将在未来几十年里随着接连不断的项目呈进阶式推进。

现在有必要对使用期限低于传统网络资产（电子和通信产品的使用期限为 3～5 年，而电线、电缆及变压器则为 40 年以上）的新设备集成进行管理。

智能电网是一项技术挑战，远非简单地将信息技术基础设施叠加在电工技术基础设施上。连接到智能电网的每个设备既是电工设备，也是智能节点。现在的"连接"标准需要同时兼顾这两方面。

采用先进的监测和控制技术是未来智能电网的关键目标。

为了支持 GEI 未来标准化工作的需求，下文提供了一些重要的一般性考量。

5.2.1　系统标准

智慧能源活动在全球能源互联方面将面临新的问题和疑问，必须开发新工具（如创建使用案例库和系统级别标准）以弥合标准制定组织（SDO）和利益相关方等完全不同领域组织间的差距。在起草一份系统级标准前，需要了解其他组件间在物理上和电气上的相互关系，以及电网和系统性能变化的信息流。

就合格评定而言，还需要了解标准使用期限如何随着组件周围环境的变化而发生变化。最重要的是，GEI 的系统标准化还需了解系统中各子系统与 GEI 系统不断壮大的设备资产之间相互关系。

IEC 已经成立了一个智慧能源系统委员会（SyC），旨在开展智能电网和智慧能源领域（包括热与气相互作用）系统级的标准化、协调和指导工作。为确保变电站的设备和通信兼容，已经出台了一些重要的国际标准，如 IEC 61850；而编制 IEC 61970 是为了定义能源管理系统的应用程序接口。智慧能源系统委员会已开始接触各种内部和外部利益相关方，但仍有许多工作有待协调。

5.2.2　管理标准

数据公开和共享有利于数据分析和模拟，这为规划、调度、运行和控制提供了基础。然而，只有当所有利益相关方能够有效地合作并同意共享数据或信息时，才能实现集成和互操作性带来的巨大效益。数据将成为 GEI 的一个关键问题，包括数据分析、数据利用、数据隐私和网络安全。利益相关方强调，缺少客户、基础设施和运行方面的基础数据交流是最重要的障碍之一。数据共享规范和数据格式标准都是必需的。另外，还需要一系列的管理规范或指导方针，以确保对所有参与者之间的规划、交易和运营进行协调。

尽管许多地区性和国家组织都有自己的可靠性标准，诸如 NERC、Nordel、UCTE、ENTSO-E 和 NGET，但是在进行全球能源互联时仍需要对这些标准进行协调。如需要规范协调互连链路和电网连接代码的控制和保护策略。

5.2.3　信息交换标准

基于适当 ICT 架构的有效信息交换是 GEI 控制、保护和调度的基础。因此，智能电网核心国际标准 IEC 61850、IEC 61968 和 IEC 61970 也是非常重要的，但是必须进一步研究其是否适用于 GEI，或者是否有必要制定新标准或修改现有标准。网络安全是 GEI 的另一个重大挑战，这也需要相应的标准。许多联盟以及 ISO/IEC JTC 1 都将需要对此方面进行重新评估。

5.2.4　新材料和设备标准

正如本报告中所述，为了实现 GEI，智能电网将以 UHV 网络为核心、清洁能源作为主要能源，在全球范围内实现能源互联。因此，新领域的标准化工作应考虑可能促成建设 GEI 网络的新材料发现或环境挑战。

例如，北极地区和赤道地区的庞大能源基地将向全球客户提供风能、太阳能和海洋能源等可再生能源。更高电压等级的 UHV 技术是将这种大容量电力远距离输送到偏远地区的先决条件。UHV 输电系统必须适应这种极端的环境运行条件，因此可能需要设计新能源导电材料并为其制定新的可靠性导则。

此外，随着智能电网和微电网的推出，这意味着客户端需要安装电储存器，预计额外的 RE 将被转化成气

体中或以氢气形式储存，因此需要制
定能源转换和存储技术标准。预计小
型和分布式 EES 的市场将会大幅增
长。EES 不仅可用于单一应用，还可
以通过集成 GEI 所需的多个分散的存

储站点，同时应用于多个目标。

在大多数情况下，标准化会起到
稳定的作用，通过研究活动来建立真
正的市场机会。

第 6 章

结论与建议

GEI 是一项宏伟的计划，将由波动性可再生能源为主的清洁能源的大规模开发应用整合起来。即整合具有不同级别的互操作性及目前尚未以适当规模部署的 IT 和 OT 集成能力的智能电网，大规模部署用于远距离输电并形成大容量和高压电网的先进技术，以及涉及新设备的众多能源服务的电气化。

大型能源网络和最终 GEI 中的许多构建模块现在已经存在。大规模可再生能源已经实现，特高压输电领域的成果为正在重新划定将多大功率、传输多少距离是成本效益合算的边界。第 4 章中描述的技术水平只会进一步提高。同时，电力系统中信息通信技术和智能技术的巨大潜力才刚刚开始利用。

虽然 GEI 所需的技术大部分可用或正在发展中，但大规模洲际或全球能源互联的挑战之一是实施过程，在实施时需要克服众多障碍和挑战。因此，本报告中的分析为评估和实施大型互联和 GEI 提供了一些关键建议。

6.1 向决策者和监管者提出的建议

政策制定者和监管机构应考虑用于评估大规模、区域、洲际以及最终全球能源互联成本效益的开发工具和方法的需求。互联通常由相关国家根据具体情况进行评估。即使在相对较长的输电系统运营商（TSO）规划时间框架内，像大规模区域和洲际互联这样宏伟的项目可能还达不到规划的程度，这样做的目的是需要鼓励对效益作出全面的评估。第 3 章介绍了区域能源互联的实践经验，这些经验为能够获得联网效益提供了信心，而这种效益是可以由大量参与者之间采用长期系统性的视角看问题积累起来的。

虽然应继续鼓励大规模开发可再生能源，但重点还是应转移到发输电资产的联合规划。监管机构和政府应该认识到联合规划所有电力系统要素的需求。这方面的评估可以揭示不少优势，例如建立与遥远资源的连接，加强电网为在指定地区加速发电能源开发铺平道路，或为开发新的资源而制定更好的激励措施。

政策制定者和监管机构应该为大规模电网互联倡议建立论坛讨论。虽然行业利益相关者、政府或监管机构已经设有大量召集小组，但是用于讨论大规模电网规划组织一般都是高度区域性的。各地的 TSO 组织已逐步合并了跨越较大区域的论坛。下一个自然而然的步骤则是建立国际论坛，分享世界各地的互联经验，并就新的机会开展对话。

6.2　针对满足工业需求的建议

应进行关于建立遥远可再生能源基地的市场准备程度和经济可行性的研究，即在高北纬地区、北极或赤道。虽然适用于极端条件的技术已经具备，但在这些极端的气候条件下大规模部署发电和输电资产所涉及的人力和实施挑战仍需确定。

设备的规模将对工业构成挑战，因此需要事先协调并共同参与示范工作（如技术开发），以避免在智能电网上使用时第一次就失误。很明显，智能电网技术是一个很好的投资，但部署新技术相当昂贵。这里所学到的教训是要避免"大爆炸"式的方法，而采用基于试点示范的方法。这就建议全面部署 GEI 将分阶段进行，并使工业界有更多的投资机会。

应促进和鼓励相关机构、区域机构和 TSO 的联合规划。充分利用每个国家在能源技术、战略规划、市场建立、政策创新和合作研究方面的成就，以及利用全球最佳实践，可以显著提高所有利益相关者对此的认知。

需要用协调和协作的方式来编写和执行导则，以确保系统运营商的活动符合电网导则。在 GEI 市场模型的背景下，应探讨一个中央操控的 GEI 市场通信中心是否有助于提高 GEI 各个流程的效率。这可能涉及由其他类似 IEC 组织所提供的云服务，其集中协调所有 GEI 参与者之间的通信流和公司间数据交换。

6.3　向 IEC 及其委员会提出的建议

IEC 市场战略局（MSB）应考虑新的内部途径，让 IEC 能够更快地响应行业。鉴于大量的利益相关者对 GEI 有兴趣，MSB 应通过其项目团队的活动来加强与行业的联系。后者应该调查对革命性 GEI 相关技术的需求。

建议 IEC 标准管理局（SMB）组成 GEI 咨询委员会，帮助确定这一领域的优先需求，并根据这些需求协调开展标准化工作。具体来说，咨询委员会应考虑开发架构框架的内部协调，澄清 GEI 概念以及互操作性和系统集成的规则。这将涉及确定相关技术委员会制定的现有互操作性标准与 GEI 需求之间的空缺。

IEC 应考虑扩大赤道地区附属国家充分参与 GEI 国际标准制定的机会。由于全球赤道地区将为 GEI 贡献大量的太阳能和风能，IEC 应鼓励具有 IEC 附属国家高级成员地位的国家电工委员会（NEC）积极参与太阳能和风能的标准制定。众所周知，IEC 附属国家计划是将参与 IEC 的益处和优势带给全世界许多国家的先驱，许多国家不仅通过该计划直接获益，而且还可以通过针对发展中国家的开放参与合格评定系统等措施。这样的附属国家将受益于大规模可再生能源并网的直接投资，从而享受清洁能源带来的社会效益和为当地的能力建设和就业带来的机会。

参考文献

[1]   WISER, R., LANTZ, E., HAND, M., et al., *IEA Wind Task 26: The Past and Future Cost of Wind Energy*, IEA Wind, May, 2012.

[2]   International Energy Agency, *Medium-Term Renewable Energy Market Report 2015*, [Online]. Available: www.iea.org/bookshop/708-Medium-Term_Renewable_Energy_Market_Report_2015. [Accessed 19 September 2016].

[3]   *Report of the enquiry committee on grid disturbance in Northern Region on 30th July 2012 and in Northern, Eastern and North-Eastern Region on 31th July 2012*, [Online]. Available: powermin.nic.in/ sites/default/files/uploads/GRID_ENQ_REP_16_8_12.pdf. [Accessed 19 September 2016].

[4]   Operador nacional do Sistema Eléctrico (ONS), *Mapas do SIN*, [Online]. Available: www.ons.org.br/ conheca_sistema/mapas_sin.aspx. [Accessed 19 September 2016].

[5]   Global Energy Network Institute (GENI), *The Water-Energy Nexus in the Amu Darya River Basin: The Need for Sustainable Solutions to a Regional Problem*, [Online]. Available: www.geni.org/ globalenergy/research/water-energy-nexus-amudarya-river/Water-Energy   Nexus-AmuDarya-River-RD.pdf. [Accessed 19 September 2016].

[6]   Nepal Energy Forum, *Pros and cons of regional electricity grid*, [Online]. Available: www. nepalenergyforum.com/pros-and-cons-of-regional-electricity-grid. [Accessed 19 September 2016].

[7]   LIU, Z., *Global Energy Interconnection*, Elsevier, 2015.

[8]   BONPARD, E., FULLI, G., ARDELEAN, M., MASERA, M., *Evolution, Opportunities, and Critical Issues for Pan-European Transmission*, IEEE Power and Energy Magazine, Vol. 12, no. 2, pp. 40-50, 2014.

[9]   ZHANG, Yi, ZHANG, Yang, *Overview of the Practice of Renewable Generation Integration and Transmission Planning in North America*, Energy Technology and Economics, Vol. 23, no. 8, pp. 1-7, 23, 2011.

[10]   KUMAGAI, J., *The U.S. may finally get a unified power grid*, IEEE Spectrum, Vol. 53, Issue 1, pp. 35-36, January 2016.

[11]   ANDREWS, D., *Why Do We Need The Supergrid, What Is Its Scope And What Will It Achieve?*, A Claverton Energy Reseach Institute Presentation, 19 June 2009.

[12]   MANO, S., OVGOR, B., SAMADOV, Z., et al., *Gobitec and Asian Super Grid for Renewable Energies in Northeast Asia*, Spotinov print Ltd., 2014.

[13]   IEC, *Grid integration of large-capacity Renewable Energy sources and use of large-capacity Electrical Energy Storage*, White Paper, 2012.

[14]   HUI, L., *Research on the Economics of Ultra-High Voltage and Global Energy Interconnection*, Presentation, Sino-Europe Workshop on Technology and Equipment of Global Energy Interconnection, Berlin, 10-11 December 2015.

[15]   ADAPA, R., *HVDC Technology: The State of the Art*, IEEE Power and Energy Magazine, Vol. 10, no. 6, pp. 18-29, 2012.

[16]   MAJUMDER R., BARTZSCH, C., KOHNSTAM, P., et al., *High-voltage DC on the New Power Transmission Highway*, IEEE Power and Energy Magazine, Vol. 10, no. 6, pp. 39-49, 2012.

[17]   ANDERSEN, B. R., *HVDC Grids – Overview of CIGRE Activities and Personal Views*, CIGRE, 2014, [Online]. Available: www.e-cigre.org/.../ELT_275_2(2).pdf. [Accessed 19 September 2016].

[18]   YUE, B., MEI, N., LIU, S.-Y., et al., *Overview of HVDC Flexible*, China Electric Power (Technology Edition), no. 5, pp. 43-47, 2014 [in Chinese].

[19]   CHEN, G., HAO, M., XU Z., et al., *Review of High Voltage Direct Current Cables*, CSEE Journal of Power and Energy Systems, Vol. 1, no. 2, pp. 9-21, 2015.

[20]   BAHRMAN, M. P., JOHNSON, B. K., *The ABCs of HVDC Transmission Technologies*, IEEE Power and Energy Magazine, Vol. 5, no. 2, pp. 32-44, 2007.

[21]   LUNDBERG, P., CALLAVIK, M., BAHRMAN, M., SANDEBERG, P., *High-Voltage DC Converters and Cable Technologies for Offshore Renewable Integration and DC Grid Expansion*, IEEE Power and Energy Magazine, Vol. 10, no. 6, pp. 31-38, 2012.

[22]   RAO, H., *Architecture of Nan'ao Multi-terminal VSC-HVDC System and Its Multifunctional Control*, CSEE Journal of Power and Energy Systems, Vol. 1, no. 1, pp. 9-18, 2015.

[23]   TANG, G., HE, Z., HUI, P., et al., *Basic Topology and Key Devices of the Five-Terminal DC Grid*, CSEE Journal of Power and Energy Systems, Vol. 1, no. 2, pp. 22-35, 2015.

[24]   YAO L., WU., J., WANG, Z., et al., *Pattern Analysis of Future HVDC Grid Development*, Proceedings of the CSEE, Vol. 34, no. 34, pp. 6007-6012, 2014.

[25]   XUMING, L., *Technology Research and Application Prospect of Half-wavelength Alternating Current Transmission*, Smart Grid, Vol. 3, no. 12, pp. 1091-1096, 2015 [in Chinese].

[26]   LIYE, X., LIANGZHEN, L., *Status Quo and Trends of Superconducting Power Transmission Technology*, Transactions Of China Electrotechnical Society, Vol. 30, no.7, pp. 1-9, 2015 [in Chinese].

[27]   SOONEE, S. K., AGRAWAL, V. K., AGARWAL, P. K., et al., *The view from the wide side: wide-area monitoring systems in India*, IEEE Power and Energy Magazine, Vol. 13, no. 5, pp. 49-59, 2015.

[28]   NUTHALAPATI, S., PHADKE, A. G., *Managing the grid using synchrophasor technology*, IEEE Power and Energy Magazine, Vol. 13, no. 5, pp. 10-12, 2015.

[29]   LU, C., SHI, B., WU, X., SUN, H., *Advancing China's smart: phasor measurement units in wide-area management system*, IEEE Power and Energy Magazine, Vol. 13, no. 5, pp. 60-71, 2015.

White Paper

Global energy interconnection

Executive summary

Global energy interconnection (GEI) represents the ultimate evolution of the trend towards greater interconnection of power systems. It embodies high-level integration of the flow of energy, flow of information and flow of business as an intelligent, automated and networked-based system for ensuring energy security on a universal scale.

Fueled by global economic growth, world energy consumption rose from 5,4 billion tons of coal equivalent in 1965 to 18,5 billion tons in 2014. Fossil energy accounted for more than 85% of the total. The world's energy consumption will maintain a growing trend in the future, as it is difficult to reverse the long-established patterns of intensive energy consumption.

Seeking a solution to these trends, the implementation of GEI would integrate a large-scale deployment of clean energy led by variable renewables with a Smart Grid incorporating high levels of interoperability and supported by a ultra-high voltage (UHV) grid backbone including extensive interconnections across countries, continents, technical domains, hierarchies and equipment life cycle phases.

Though such levels of deployment are highly ambitious, the technologies themselves are largely available or are currently in the pipeline.

The technical difficulties for large-scale, transcontinental or global energy interconnection, on the other hand, will come from the unprecedented degree of system integration that will be required. To help surmount this challenge, consensus-based International Standards and Specifications will form an indispensable basis on which to build concrete solutions. Standards, specifically those at the systems level, will facilitate procurement and national and international acceptance and will play a stabilizing role by pursuing research activities on which real market opportunities are built.

This White Paper examines the readiness of potential markets for GEI, identifies the technical and economic trends in related technologies and evaluates at a high level the impact on energy, environment, technologies and policies.

Taking the large-scale concepts connected with GEI to actual realization will require significant efforts in standardization – e.g. development of initiatives to enable multi-system interoperability. Thus this White Paper aims to highlight the concept of GEI and begin laying the foundations for identifying and addressing the standardization needs for large-scale, transcontinental and global energy interconnection.

Acknowledgments

This White Paper has been prepared by the Global Energy Interconnection project team, in the IEC Market Strategy Board (MSB), with major contributions from the project partner, the International Energy Agency (IEA) and the project leader, State Grid Corporation of China (SGCC). The project team met three times – in January 2016 (Beijing, China), March 2016 (Beijing, China) and June 2016 (Paris, France). The project team is listed below:

Dr. Yinbiao Shu, SGCC, IEC Vice President, MSB Convenor, Project Director

Dr. Luis Munuera, IEA, Project Partner

Dr. Jun Yu, SGCC, Project Manager

Dr. Jianbin Fan, SGCC

Dr. Caihao Liang, CEPRI

Dr. Geng Dan, Climate Parliament of China

Dr. Wei Wang, SGCC

Dr. Xing Lu (Ms.), State Grid Energy Research Institute (of China)

Mr. Richard Schomberg, EDF

Dr. Dongil Lee, KEPCO

Dr. Jae Young Yoon, KERI

Dr. Chan-Ki Kim, KEPCO

Dr. Ho-Keun Kim, KEPCO

Dr. Stefan Engelhardt, SAP SE

Dr. Alexander Rentschler, Siemens AG

Mr. Shinichi Suganuma, TEPCO

Mr. Chengwei Dai, China Datang Corporation

Mr. Yan Qin, China Datang Corporation

Dr. Hao Hu, SGCC

Mr. Peter Lanctot, IEC, MSB Secretary

Table of contents

Table of contents

List of abbreviations

Technical and scientific terms

AC	alternating current
AC	advisory committee (of the IEC)
AIN	asset intelligence network
BI	business intelligence
BOS	balance of system
CBA	cost-benefit analysis
COP	conference of the parties
CRM	customer relationship management
CSC	current source converter
CSP	concentrated solar power
DC	direct current
DMS	document management system
DNI	direct normal irradiance
EAM	environmental assessment and management
EDI	electronic data interchange
EES	electrical energy storage
EPC	engineering, procurement and construction (company)
ERP	enterprise resource planning
FACTS	flexible AC transmission system
FCF	frequency converter facility
FMEA	failure mode and effects analysis
FTU	field terminal unit
GDP	gross domestic product
GEI	global energy interconnection
GHG	greenhouse gas
GIS	geographical information system
HES	head-end system
HTS	high-temperature superconducting

HVAC	high-voltage alternating current
HVDC	high-voltage direct current
HWACT	half-wavelength AC transmission
ICT	information and communication technology
IEA-OES	Ocean Energy Systems Technology Collaboration Programme of the IEA
IoT	Internet of Things
IT	information technology
LCC	line-commutated converter
LCOE	levelized cost of energy
MDM	meter data management
MTDC	multi-terminal direct current
OEM	original equipment manufacturer
OLTP	online transaction processing
OT	operational technology
PMU	phaser measurement unit
PV	photovoltaic
RE	renewable energy
SC	subcommittee (of the IEC)
SCADA/EMS	supervisory control and data acquisition/energy management system
SDO	standards developing organization
STE	solar thermal energy
SyC	systems committee (of the IEC)
TC	technical committee (of the IEC)
TSO	transmission system operator
UHV	ultra-high voltage
UHVAC	ultra-high-voltag alternating current
UHVDC	ultra-high-voltage direct current
VSC	voltage source converter
WAMS	wide area monitoring system

Organizations, institutions and companies

ASEAN	Association of Southeast Asian Nations	
ASG	Asian Super Grid	
ATSOI	Association of the Transmission System Operators of Ireland	
BALTSO	Baltic Transmission System Operators	
CEPRI	China Electric Power Research Institute	
CIGRE	International council on large electric systems	
COP21	21st Conference of the Parties, 2015 United Nations Climate Change Conference	
CSPG	China Southern Power Grid	
EDF	Electricité de France	
ENTSO-E	European Network of Transmission System Operators for Electricity	
EPRI	Electric Power Research Institute	
ERCOT	Electric Reliability Council of Texas	
ETSO	European Transmission System Operators	
EU	European Union	
HAPUA	Heads of ASEAN Power Utilities/Authorities	
IEA	International Energy Agency	
IEC	International Electrotechnical Commission	
IPCC	Intergovernmental Panel on Climate Change	
IPS/UPS	Integrated Power System/Unified Power System	
ISO	International Organization for Standardization	
KEPCO	Korea Electric Power Corporation	
KERI	Korea Electrotechnology Research Institute	
MSB	Market Strategy Board	
NEC	National Electrotechnical Committee	
NERC	Northern American Electric Reliability Corporation	
NGET	National Grid Electricity Transmission	
OECD	Organisation for Economic Co-operation and Development	
SAPP	Southern African Power Pool	
SE4ALL	United Nations Sustainable Energy for All initiative	
SGCC	State Grid Corporation of China	

SMB	Standardization Management Board (of the IEC)
TEPCO	Tokyo Electric Power Company
TüV	technischer Überwachungsverein (technical inspection association)
UCTE	Union for the Coordination of the Transmission of Electricity
UKTSOA	United Kingdom Transmission System Operators Association
UN	United Nations
UNFCCC	United Nations Framework Convention on Climate Change

Glossary

asset intelligence network
AIN

cloud-based hub that facilitates collaborative asset management and allows companies take full advantage of the Internet of Things (IoT)

back-to-back system

two independent neighbouring systems with different and incompatible electrical parameters (frequency/voltage level/short-circuit power level) that are connected via a DC link

NOTE   High-voltage direct current (HVDC) transmission systems connect two separate high voltage AC systems via a DC link. The basic principle of operation of an HVDC system is based on the conversion of AC to DC and vice-versa by means of converter valves, which are the heart of a converter station.

balance of system
BOS

quantity encompassing all components of a photovoltaic system other than the photovoltaic panels

NOTE   This includes wiring, switches, a mounting system, one or many solar inverters, a battery bank and battery charger.

conference of the parties
COP

governing body of an international convention

NOTE The most well-known United Nations conference of the parties involves countries that have ratified the UN Framework Convention on Climate Change (UNFCCC) adopted in 1992 at the Earth Summit in Rio de Janeiro, Brazil. The 2015 United Nations Climate Change Conference, or COP21, was held in Paris, France, from 30 November to 12 December 2015. The conference was the 21st such event to take place since the signing of the UNFCCC, hence COP21.

exajoule
EJ

unit of energy equal to one quintillion (10^{18}) joules

NOTE   In describing national or global energy budgets, it is common practice to use large-scale units based upon the joule: 1 EJ = 10^{18} J. A joule is the SI unit of work or energy equal to the work done by a force of one newton when its point of application moves one metre in the direction of action of the force, equivalent to one 3 600th of a watt-hour.

frequency converter facility
FCF

facility where an electronic or electromechanical device converts alternating current of one frequency to alternating current of another frequency

global energy intensity

amount of energy used to produce a unit of gross domestic product (GDP) at market exchange rates

levelized cost of energy
LCOE

measure of a power source which attempts to compare different methods of electricity generation on a comparable basis

solar thermal energy
STE

form of energy and technology for harnessing solar energy to generate thermal energy or electrical energy

terawatt
TW

unit of power equal to one trillion (10^{12}) watts

TüV
technischer Überwachungsverein (technical inspection association)

German organization that works to validate the safety of products of all kinds to protect humans and the environment against hazards

UHV
ultra-high voltage

voltage above 800 kV

Section 1

Introduction

Achieving a sustainable, secure and affordable supply of energy has traditionally been the goal of both national and international energy policies. At the centre of achieving sustainability in the energy system lies the challenge of climate change, a factor recently brought to the fore by the Paris accords. The rise of electricity as the key energy carrier due to its high quality and versatility has determined its current role as a central vehicle for decarbonizing the supply of energy. Dramatic cost reductions in renewable energy (RE), particularly wind and solar, have made extensive deployment of such energies attractive on a global scale, with emphasis being placed on how to integrate these resources widely. Reducing reliance on fossil fuels by substituting low carbon electricity for the input of energy end-uses that rely on them (e.g. through electric vehicles in transport or electrification of industrial processes), will only increase overall demand for electricity. At the same time, large portions of the global population remain without access to electricity. Following a logical progression in power systems, as generation and demand continue to evolve in response to these trends, power grids will become more and more interconnected at the transnational and regional levels. This is reflected in the recent introduction of the concept of global energy interconnection (GEI).

GEI would represent the ultimate stage in the evolution of power grids towards greater levels of interconnectivity: a global energy network of intercontinental and cross-border backbone networks of high and ultra-high voltage (UHV), as well as smart power grids (transmission and distribution networks) in all interconnected countries at various voltage levels. A GEI could connect the power grids of all continents and take advantage of the diversity of different time zones and seasons, thus supporting a balanced coordination of power supply for all interconnected countries.

As one of the international organizations participating in the United Nations Sustainable Energy for All initiative (SE4ALL), the IEC and its International Standards play a major role in meeting fundamental energy challenges. IEC's purpose in issuing this White Paper is to highlight the concept of GEI and begin laying the foundations for identifying and addressing the standardization needs of large-scale, transcontinental and global energy interconnection.

The main objectives of this White Paper are as follows:

- To provide a high-level assessment of the potential worldwide needs, benefits and conditions of GEI

- To examine the readiness of potential markets for the technologies that would underpin GEI

- To identify technical and economic trends in related technologies

- To evaluate at a high level the impact on energy, environment, technologies, policies and relevant Standards

- To provide an outline of how standardization could be conducted from a high level and recommendations for different stakeholders to participate in the standardization work

1.1 Scope

This White Paper begins by assessing worldwide industrial, commercial application needs and energy resource allocation, development and utilization, as well as the potential benefits in light of the GEI concept, by collecting relevant data from international organizations. Several global transmission schemes are discussed and analyzed by scenario comparison.

The White Paper then examines the readiness of potential markets for GEI. Based on the current status of equipment and technologies from transmission system operators (TSOs) and suppliers, it identifies the technical and business trends (i.e. economic aspects) and challenges in related areas, including clean energy, UHV, Smart Grid, energy storage and grid control. The White Paper also addresses the environmental impact aspects of the concept, including carbon emission reduction, footprint of transmission lines, etc.

Finally the White Paper discusses how GEI will influence present energy system standards and highlights the need for new standardization.

Section 2

A vision for GEI

2.1 Global energy challenges

Global primary energy supply has grown ten-fold in the last 100 years, and more than doubled in the last 40 years. But for the first time in 2006, developing countries [i.e. those not members of the Organisation for Economic Co-operation and Development (OECD)] accounted for a larger share of energy use than developed economies; in 2013 the ratio was 61:39. The shifting of the traditional centres of energy demand to China, India and South Asia are reflected in global trends: China has accounted for the largest increase in primary energy demand and CO_2 emission over the last decade, and yet the added pace of RE deployment and drastic improvements in energy intensity have reduced its annual growth in CO_2 emissions to levels not seen before 2004, with recent signs of decoupling. India alone has been responsible for almost 10% of the increase in global energy demand since 2000, while Indonesia has seen the largest growth in coal use globally. A combination of emissions caps, a reduction in economic activity, and rapid growth in renewables has drastically altered the energy landscape in Europe. Developments in unconventional oil and gas technology and exploitation are dramatically changing energy prospects in the US and its status as an energy importer. Moreover clean energy added more capacity for the first time in 2014 than all other power generation sources combined.

In spite of these developments, anthropogenic energy-related global CO_2 emissions reached a record 31,6 gigatons CO_2 ($GtCO_2$) in 2012, warming reached a $1°C$ increase above pre-industrial levels, and 1,3 billion people remain without access to clean energy around the world.

The challenges facing the world in terms of providing secure, affordable and clean energy are greater than they have ever been, framed against an array of pressures at an unprecedented scale and a landscape of rapid technological change.

2.1.1 Energy security

Fueled by global economic growth, world energy consumption rose from 5,4 billion tons of standard coal in 1965 to 18,5 billion tons in 2014. Fossil energy accounted for more than 85% of the total. The world's energy consumption will maintain a growing trend in the future, as it is difficult to reverse the long-established pattern of intensive energy consumption.

Energy security can be understood as "the uninterrupted availability of energy sources at an affordable price". Energy security has many dimensions: long-term energy security mainly involves timely investments to supply energy in line with economic developments and sustainable environmental needs. Short-term energy security focuses on the ability of the energy system to react promptly to sudden changes within the supply-demand.

Concern related to physical unavailability of supply is more prevalent in energy markets in which networks and systems must be kept in constant balance, such as electricity and, to some extent, natural gas. This is particularly the case in instances where capacity constraints exist or where prices cannot function as an adjustment mechanism to balance supply and demand in the short term.

The world has plentiful energy resources, including those from fossil energies. In the long term, however, fossil-based energies are exhaustible and are heavily location-constrained. Geopolitics, the changeable economic outlook, the prevailing investment climate and a rapidly shifting technology landscape mean that the circumstances surrounding exploitation of fossil fuels are ever changing. At the same time, the world's RE resources are vast (see Figure 2-1) and, if the full technical potential of such resources is captured, would meet the world's energy needs many times over.

2.1.2 Climate change

The Intergovernmental Panel on Climate Change (IPCC) has concluded that, in the absence of fully committed and urgent action, climate change will have severe and irreversible impacts across the world. Avoiding dangerous climate change and its environmental consequences will require sustained and important reductions in greenhouse gas (GHG) emissions.

Energy production and use account for two-thirds of global GHG emissions generated by human activity. Therefore, transforming the energy sector is essential for addressing the climate challenge. Despite efforts to decarbonize the world's energy system, the past 30 years have seen little change in the share of fossil fuels in global energy supply, which totalled around 81% in 2013. Meanwhile, coal power accounted for the highest contribution to the energy mix in the past 40 years.

Since the Industrial Revolution, annual CO_2 emissions from fuel combustion have dramatically increased from nearly zero to over 32 Gt CO_2 in 2013, and yet since the early 1900s, the carbon intensity of the energy supply (the amount of emissions per unit of energy going into the system) has barely changed (see Figure 2-2). Between 1990 and 2013, a stable carbon intensity of supply combined with an increase in population (35%) and in per capita GDP (60%), leading to a dramatic increase in global CO_2 emissions of nearly 60%. The atmospheric concentration of these gases has increased steadily to 445 parts per million carbon-dioxide equivalent (ppm CO_2-eq) in 2014.

The global energy system is thus at a crossroads in the race against climate change. The recent UN Climate summit delivered an unprecedented response to this challenge. Countries from around

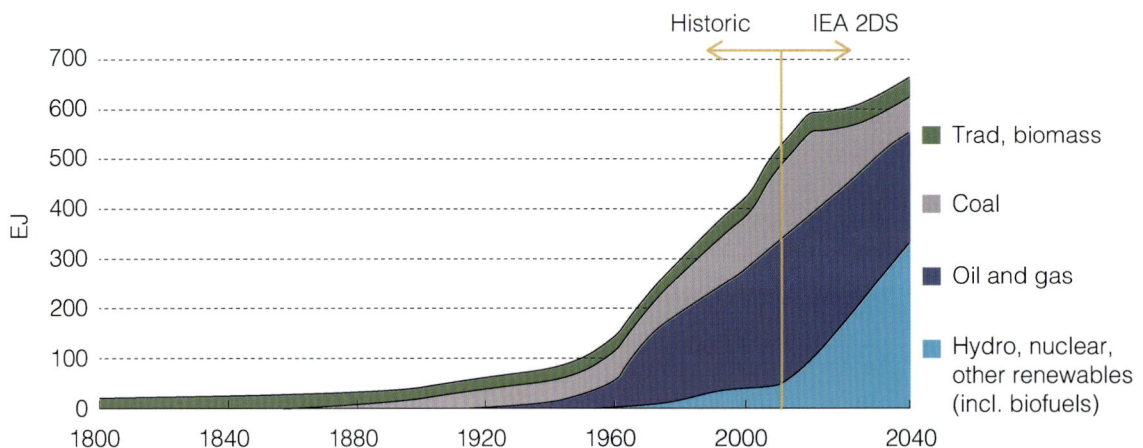

Figure 2-1 | Primary energy supply by source, historic 1800-2013, and IEA 2-degree scenario 2013-2050 (IEA)

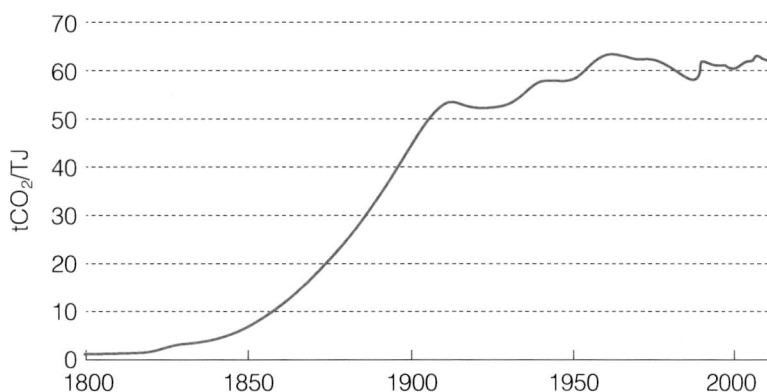

Figure 2-2 | Carbon intensity of global energy supply, 1800-2013 (IEA)

the world gathered in Paris for the 21st Conference of the Parties (COP21) to negotiate an international agreement and set a direction for combating climate change within the next decade and beyond – one that aims to reach global peaking of GHG emissions as soon as possible, with an ambition to limit the global average temperature rise to well below 2 °C and pursue efforts to limit the temperature increase to 1.5 °C. The international commitment to keep the increase in long-term average temperatures to within this target of temperature rise relative to pre-industrial levels will require substantial and sustained reductions in global emissions.

GHG remain in the atmosphere fort many years – what matters for climate change is the concentration of GHG that accumulates over a period of time. The world had emitted an estimated 1970 $GtCO_2$ by 2014. The IPCC estimated that the cumulative amount of CO_2 emitted between 1991 and 2100 would have to remain below approximately 3 000 Gt to maintain a 50% chance of keeping global warming below 2 °C. Taking into account estimated non-energy related emissions of GHG, around 880 Gt to 1 180 Gt could be emitted by the energy sector between now and 2100 – around 60% of what was emitted during the last century.

2.1.3 Environmental pollution

An estimated 6,5 million annual deaths are linked to air pollution, a number that will only increase unless the energy sector takes greater action to curb emissions. Premature deaths due to outdoor air pollution are projected to rise from 3 million today to 4,5 million by 2040, concentrated mainly in developing Asia. The IEA estimates that under a clean air scenario, premature deaths from outdoor pollution would decline by 1,7 million in 2040 – a scenario that would only require a 7% increase in total energy investment

2.2 The GEI concept

2.2.1 Why larger-scale interconnection?

The challenge of providing an affordable and secure supply of energy, and one that is sustainable and adequately mitigates the risk of dangerous climate change, requires unprecedented investments in new energy infrastructure and technology, and the large-scale retrofitting of existing energy delivery systems. Crucially, a future energy system that meets these goals will have to dramatically reduce its reliance on fossil fuels, improve the efficiency of supply and increase the share of renewable and clean energy sources. At the crossroads of this challenge is the progressive large-scale interconnection of power systems.

The key renewable resources are to a large degree constrained both in time and space. The best wind and solar resources are often located far from centres of energy demand; sites with the most extensive such resources (e.g. wind in Northern China or solar in the Southwestern US) are often located in remote regions far from the major demand centres. While technological progress in wind and solar photovoltaic (PV) is opening new deployment possibilities in less favourable resource areas, transmission expansion is often the only possible way to utilize most attractive resources. Hydropower, the largest clean energy power source today, is constrained by the geographic location of suitable natural resources, and the same is true for less deployed renewable technologies such as geothermal, wave or tidal power.

In the case of wind and solar, the output of such energies fluctuates depending on wind speed and solar irradiation at any given moment. Transmission interconnection is proving to be a valuable flexibility tool for facilitating the integration of variable renewable resources, as it allows the smoothing of generation profiles.

Similarly, hourly patterns of energy demand vary greatly from country to country, depending on time zones, behaviours or the structure of an economy. Demand patterns exhibit considerable variability due to differences in overall economic structure as well as in the spread of air conditioning and electric heating in various regions.

Interconnection allows for balancing of electricity demands across larger areas: linking winter peak demand regions with summer peak demand regions and separate regions in different time zones yields large benefits by smoothing daily peak/valley and seasonal loads. Similarly, there is a regional disparity between renewable production patterns and resource endowment. As a result, a

strong transmission interconnection can increase the flexibility of the power system and achieve measurable savings in peak capacity needs.

The trend towards extensive interconnection has been present in many countries. While continental-scale interconnected and frequency-harmonized systems have existed for decades, large-scale long-distance power flows have been limited (often focussing on connection of distant hydro resources), and interconnections have primarily served system security purposes. Interconnecting regions and continents on a much larger scale can bring significant benefits to any sustainable energy scenario. Within this context, achieving interconnection on a global scale could become a possible solution to many energy challenges.

2.2.2 What is GEI?

GEI would constitute the ultimate stage of a natural progression of power grids towards ever-greater interconnection: a globally interconnected power system, supported by Smart Grid infrastructure, and making optimal use of UHV technology to transmit power over great distances. Such large-scale power grids would form the backbone for the extensive deployment of clean energy, allowing for an appropriate allocation of power generation plants where resources are best.

Scenarios that would benefit from higher levels of interconnection and GEI would also contemplate much higher electricity demand than that of today, with greatly increased levels of electrification of industrial processes that have traditionally relied on fossil fuels, transport – particularly private transportation – and increased demand for electric heating, cooling and appliance energy use in the residential and commercial sectors.

The GEI concept is thus built on three pillars:

- A large-scale deployment of clean energy, particularly variable renewables, coupled with high levels of electrification

- The transmission of power over large distances, which necessitates UHV technology

- Smart Grid solutions leveraging intelligent monitoring and control at all voltage levels (see Figure 2-3)

2.2.3 Potential benefits of GEI

Achieving very high levels of interconnection across large geographical areas affords the creation of platforms for power exchange, with greater balancing of electricity demand and supply and generally increased utilization of power generation assets. On a global scale, this would represent a comprehensive platform for clean energy deployment and access to low carbon electricity and result in potential economic, social and environmental benefits:

- A global network could bring environmental benefits, as it would form the backbone for deployment of RE where such resources are optimal from the power plant perspective

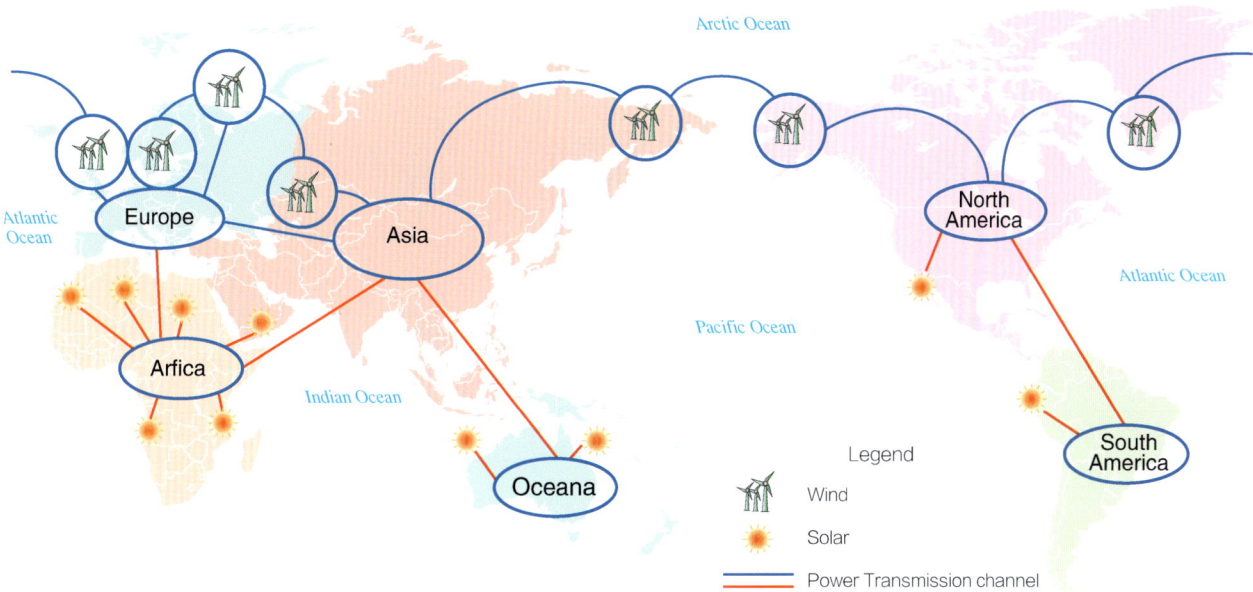

GEI = UHV Grid + Smart Grid + Clean Energy

Figure 2-3 | The GEI concept

- While cost trends between now and 2050 cannot be predicted, low carbon scenarios aimed at assessing the lowest cost of decarbonizing the global energy system have identified RE as the key pillar of decarbonization

- The large-scale deployment of transmission grids and low carbon power would bring social benefits to developing countries in the form of energy access to clean power and opportunities for local capacity building and employment

2.2.4 GEI vision

GEI would constitute an organic whole. The development of national grids would be coordinated with increased levels of interconnection in transnational and transcontinental grids. UHV transmission technology and technologies affording smart monitoring and control of electricity grids would form the backbone of such grids, laid out to facilitate connections to wind power bases in northern latitudes and the Arctic, solar energy bases in the equatorial regions as well as major RE bases and main load centres on all continents. An integrated view of concurrent electrification, generation deployment and transmission and distribution capacity, would split the future development of a globally interconnected energy network into three distinct phases at a high level:

- A first phase, in which alignment on the objective of increasing the degree of interconnection to levels much higher than those of today would be progressively reached by governments, system owners and operators, utilities and other stakeholders. During this phase domestic grids would continue to be upgraded and strengthened and national power systems would be progressively decarbonized

- A second phase, in which transnational interconnection would be promoted within each continent and large-scale clean energy bases would be developed (e.g. Northern European wind, Western China wind and solar, Northen Africa solar power)

- A third and final phase, in which more distant energy hubs would begin development of wind power in northern latitudes and the Arctic and solar power around the equator, and transcontinental interconnection would start to emerge

Section 3

Energy trends and market readiness for GEI

3.1 Global energy resources and energy demands

Total world primary energy demand has maintained an almost uninterrupted growth trend, with constant changes in the energy mix (see Figure 3-1). Each major transition from one dominant form of energy to the next has taken, on average, between 20 to 40 years to complete. Until the mid-nineteenth century, traditional biomass was the primary source of energy consumed globally. With the start of the Industrial Revolution, consumption of coal and its derivatives increased substantially as more energy services and end-uses were found for the fuel. A third major shift towards oil and gas occurred towards the middle of the twentieth century, and by the end of the 1970s the world was poised for another major transition. Since then, however, the share of oil demand in primary energy supply has peaked, while natural gas has experienced constant growth. Economic development in China has driven a rebound in coal consumption, albeit a minor one. More importantly, low carbon energy sources (hydro, nuclear and other RE sources) have risen greatly in prominence.

3.1.1 Energy resources

The world has plentiful energy resources, but the size of economic and technical potential varies greatly according to location and technical and economic conditions. Global energy resources primarily include fossil fuels (e.g. coal, oil, and natural gas), nuclear fissile energy (e.g. uranium and potentially thorium) and RE (e.g. hydro, wind, solar, biomass, geothermal or ocean energy).

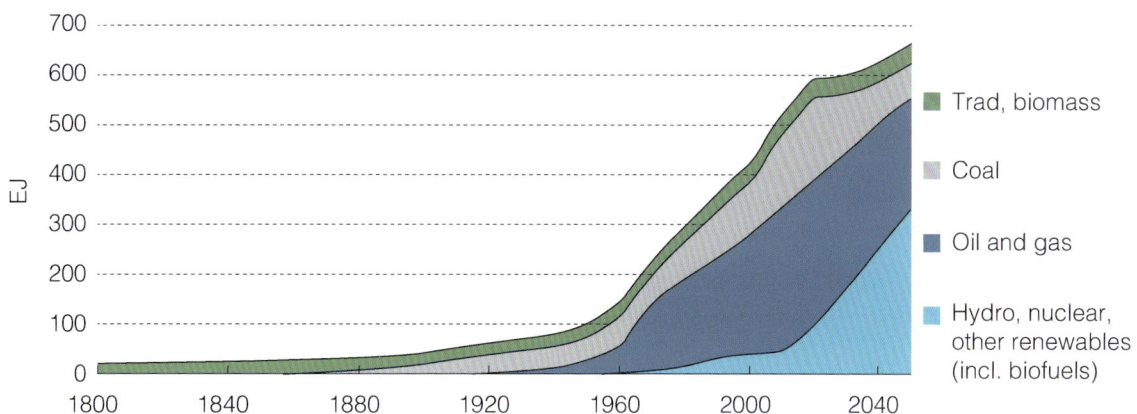

Figure 3-1 | Global primary energy supply mix, 1800-2013 (IEA)

3.1.1.1 Fossil energy and nuclear

The resource base from fossil energies is abundant – but fossil resources are unevenly dispersed and are not inexhaustible (see Figure 3-2). Globally, the remaining technically recoverable oil resources total approximately 6 100 billion barrels, 1 700 billion of which are categorized as "proven" (i.e. having a 90% chance of profitable extraction). At current rates of production, current proven reserves would be exhausted after 52 years while technically recoverable oil resources (a much more uncertain category) would last 185 years. Proven reserves for coal equate to 122 years of current production, while proven reserves of gas would sustain production for 61 years, and uranium reserves would last 120 years at 2012 consumption rates. As new technology develops, the size of the technically recoverable base for an exhaustible energy resource also expands.

Distribution of these fossil fuels is extremely unbalanced on a global basis: 95% of coal is distributed in Europe, the Eurasian continent, Asia-Pacific, and North America; 80% of oil is distributed in the Middle East, and in North, South, and Central America; and Europe, the Eurasian continent, and the Middle East are home to over 70% of natural gas reserves.

While the resource base is ample, much of the fossil fuel reserves – including an important share which is already part of the resource accounting of national and international oil companies – will have to remain unexploited if the CO_2 budgets are not to be exceeded. Figure 3-3 shows the maximum amount of current reserves that can be consumed in order to limit the planet to a certain temperature increase with a 50% probability, highlighting that consuming all current listed reserves would far exceed the threshold for a 3 °C increase.

3.1.1.2 Renewable energy (RE)

In total, the sun offers a considerable amount of power: about 885 million terawatt hours (TWh) reach the earth's surface in a year, that is 6 200 times the commercial primary energy consumed by humankind in 2008 and 4 200 times the energy that the world population would consume in 2035 according to the IEA Current Policies Scenario (see Figure 3-4). World wind resources, while various orders of magnitude smaller, have been demonstrated to exceed global electricity demand, and ample potential exists in most regions of

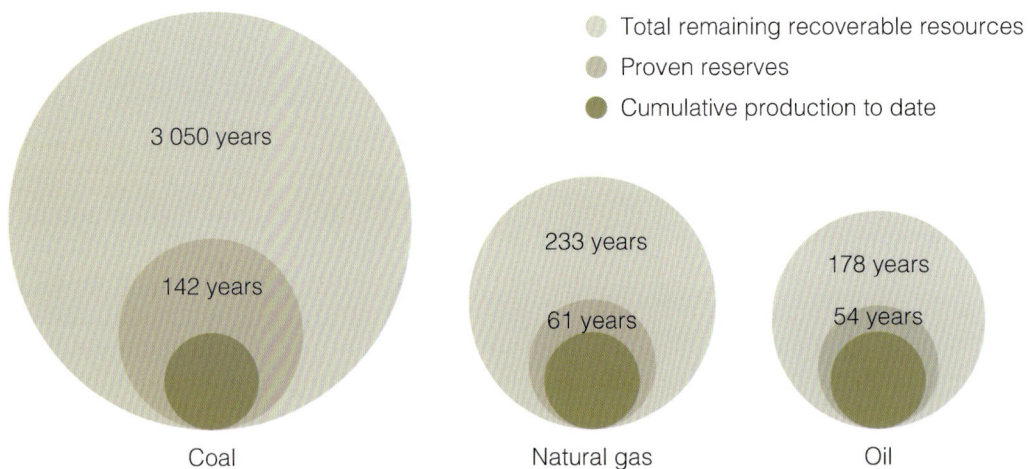

Figure 3-2 | Fossil fuel reserves time line

Comparison of listed reserves
to 50% probability pro–rata carbon budget

Peak warming (℃)
50% probability

3 356
2.5 319
2 269
1.5 131

1 541

762

● Potential listed reserves   ● Current listed reserves

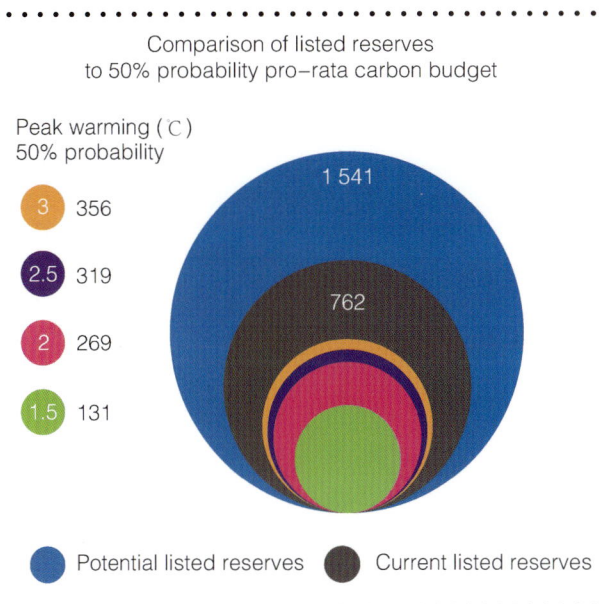

Figure 3-3 | 50% probability of reserves

the world to enable significant wind and hydro development. Using the standard IEA method of deriving primary energy equivalence (where electricity supply, in TWh, is translated directly to primary energy, in EJ), the IPCC 2007 estimate of onshore wind energy potential is 180 EJ/yr (50 000 TWh/yr), two and a half times greater than global electricity demand in 2014. The IEA has estimated global hydropower potential at more than 16 400 TWh/year, enough to cover two-thirds of global electricity demand.

Clean energy resources, however, are distributed very unevenly (see Figure 3-5). Hydro resources are distributed primarily in the drainage basins of Asia, South America, North America and Central Africa. Wind resources are distributed mainly in

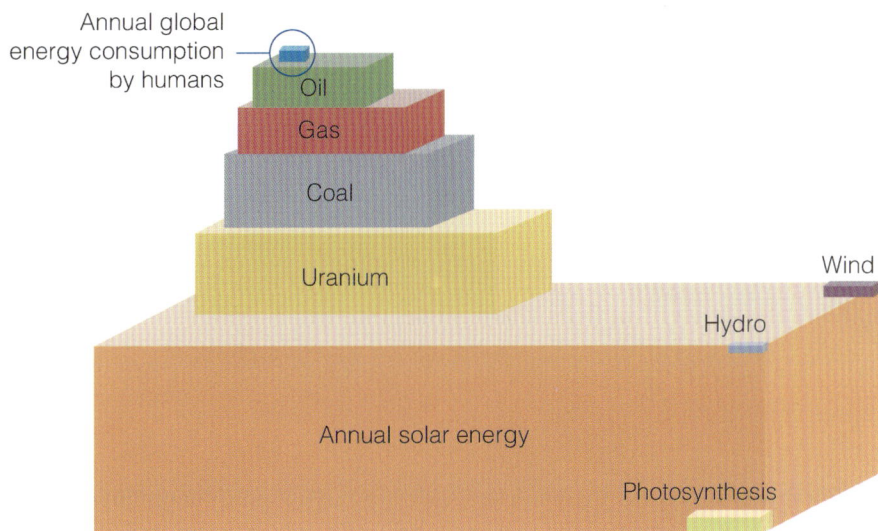

Annual global
energy consumption
by humans

Oil

Gas

Coal

Uranium

Wind

Hydro

Annual solar energy

Photosynthesis

Figure 3-4 | Annual global energy consumption by humans set against known resources (IEA 2012)

the Arctic, Central and Northern Asia, Northern Europe, Central North America, and East Africa. To a lesser extent, quality wind resources are also found in the near-shore regions of each continent. The highest quality solar energy resources are found primarily in North Africa, East Africa, the Middle East, Oceania, Central and South America and other regions near the equator. Additionally, areas of arid climate, such as the Gobi, Rajasthan and other deserts, are also endowed with quality solar resources. As previously highlighted, when concentrated in sparsely populated areas several hundreds to thousands of kilometres away from load centres, exploitation of RE on very large scales requires the ability to shift significant volumes of power over large distances, which would enable

the development of power generation capacities where resources are of the highest quality.

3.1.2 Energy demand

Over the last several decades, global energy consumption has grown at a much slower rate than GDP, primarily because of structural changes in the economy, energy efficiency improvements and fuel switching. Global energy intensity – defined as the amount of energy used to produce a unit of GDP at market exchange rates – fell by 32% between 1971 and 2012. Despite this partial decoupling of energy demand and economic growth, which has been particularly evident in the OECD, the two remain closely tied (see Figure 3-6).

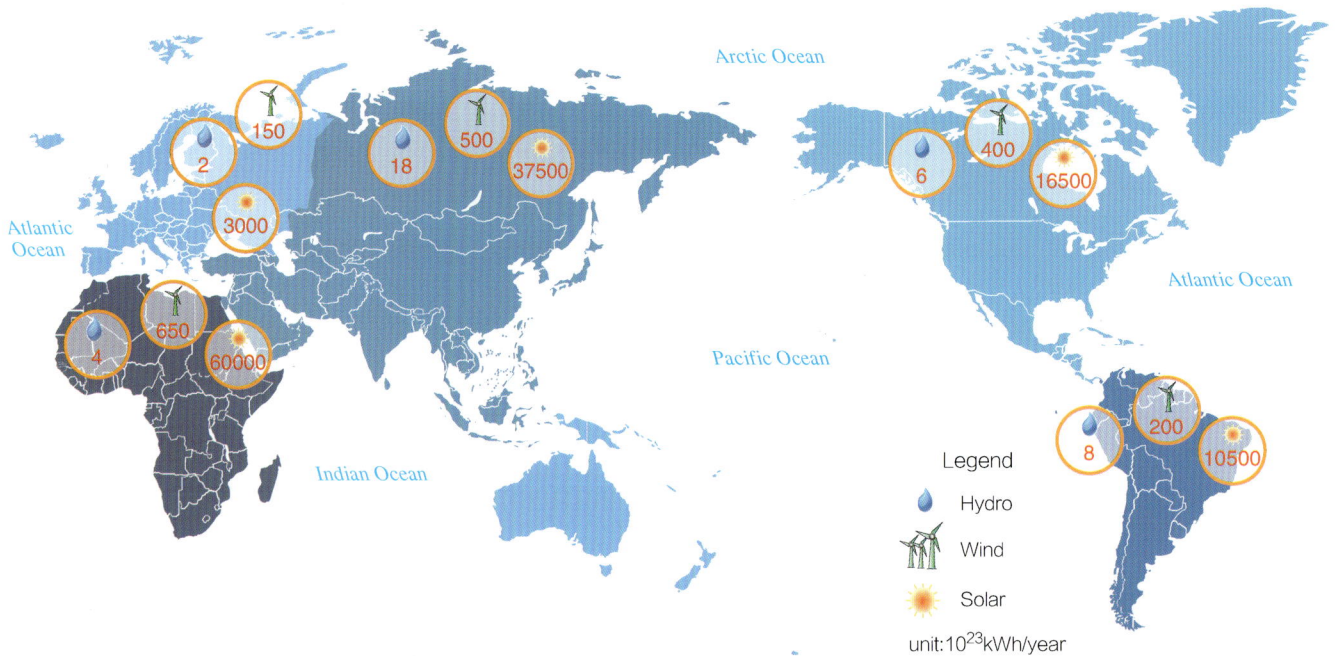

Figure 3-5 | Allocation of world clean energy

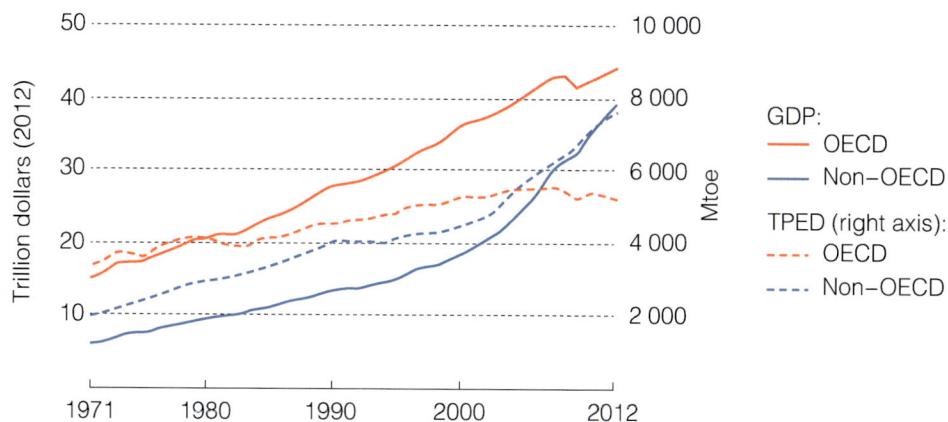

Figure 3-6 | Total volume and growth rate of global primary energy demand

The average rate of improvement, however, was much lower in 2000-2011 than in 1980-2000 (and energy intensity actually increased in 2009 and 2010) due to a shift in the balance of global economic activity to developing countries in Asia which have relatively high energy intensities. Projections are highly sensitive to assumptions about the rates and patterns of GDP growth.

The world's population will continue to grow from 6,92 billion in the same period to a projected 9,55 billion, while 1,3 billion people do not currently have access to clean energy. Rising energy demand across all energy carriers, particularly from new growth areas such as Africa, South Asia or Latin America, will be a mainstay of future energy systems.

3.1.2.1 Global energy demand

Primary energy demand worldwide is expected to continue growing, albeit at a steadily lower rate.

Electricity is already at the core of the global energy system and is projected to play an increasing role.

Almost 40% of global primary energy is currently used to generate electricity, yet electricity covers on average only 17% of all global final energy needs. Among all final energy carriers, per capita growth of electricity has been the strongest, more than doubling from 1 263 kilowatt hours per capita (kWh/cap) in 1974 to 2 933 kWh/cap in 2011. This trend is expected to continue to 2050. Generation from wind and solar technologies has grown annually at double-digit rates over the last ten years, but fossil fuels account for over 75% of net new electricity generation during the same time period.

Crucially, the electrification of new energy end-uses and sectors is expected to compensate for the decline in electricity intensity of OECD countries. Electrification of transport particularly private mobility, and heating and cooling, and maximizing the use of electricity in industrial processes, are driving electricity demand upwards in mainstream energy scenarios.

3.1.2.2 Regional electricity demand

Growth in electricity demand has been uneven across regions, in part reflecting the global economic recession or a shift away from increasing industrial development to a more service-oriented economy. Electricity system reliability has been questioned due to ageing infrastructure, while also being put to the test by deployment of renewables and increased intense weather patterns.

The share of developed economies in Europe and America in total global electricity demand will decline substantially, in contrast to a significantly higher share for Asia, Africa, and South America. In 1990, non-OECD countries accounted for only 35% of the world's total electricity. More recently, driven by the fast-growing electricity consumption among emerging economies, non-OECD countries accounted for 51% of total global consumption in 2010, a figure that rose to 53% in 2013.

3.2 Trends in cost reduction of key technologies for GEI

While renewable technologies are becoming increasingly competitive on a cost basis in a rising

number of regions and circumstances, public support remains necessary to facilitate their implementation in the vast majority of countries. Power generation from renewables grew by a record 128 gigawatts (GW) in 2014, accounting for nearly half of all new plants. Around 69% of all investment in new capacity went to RE sources. Over half of all power sector investments were accounted for by variable renewable generation technologies, namely wind and solar PV, with 14% of investments going towards hydro. Of the anticipated annual output of all capacity that came online in 2015, and assuming current load factors, new wind and solar plants would represent a fifth.

Costs for RE, particularly for solar PV and wind power, have fallen greatly over the last two decades. Technological progress, improved mechanisms and conditions for financing new projects, expansion to markets with good resources, and the consolidation of markets and build-up of local capacities have combined to reduce the cost per unit energy from renewable power sources, with further decreases forecast (see Figure 3-7).

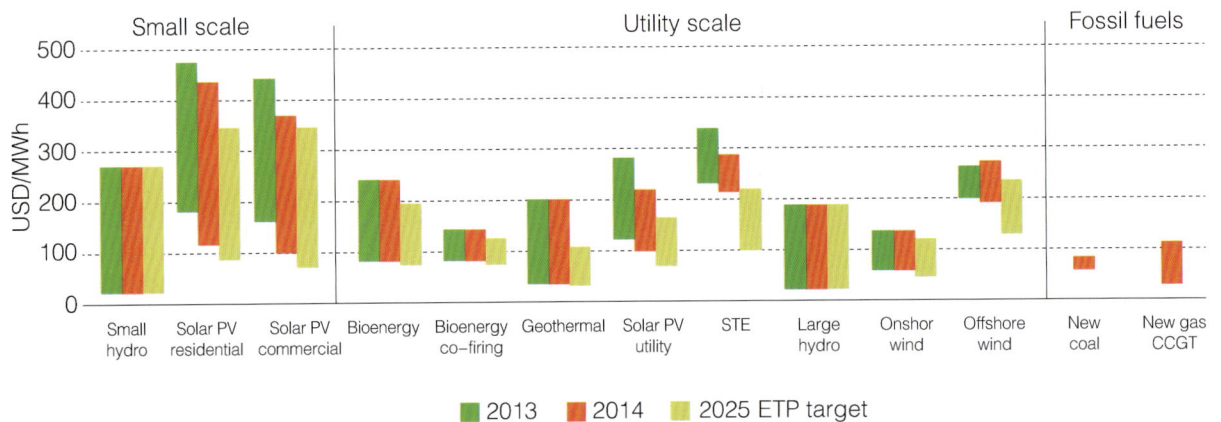

Figure 3-7 | Levelized cost of power generation in 2013, 2014 and 2025 target (IEA)

3.2.1 Market trends for wind power generation

The cost per kWh of wind power depends on various factors, including wind resources, investment costs, operation and maintenance costs, finance costs, as well as the ability of the conversion technology to turn wind output into electricity, generally measured as a capacity factor. Larger hub heights with larger swept areas result in higher capacity factors and a greater amount of electricity generated, all else being equal.

3.2.1.1 Onshore wind power generation

Onshore wind power is a mature technology with a global supply chain. Onshore technology has gradually evolved to maximize the electricity produced for every megawatt installed. Turbines have increased in height, with larger swept areas and often greater generating capacities. The result has been an increase in investment costs, but also a reduction in costs on a per unit energy basis due to the greater capacity factors achieved (see Figure 3-8).

New turbines with a greater swept area per megawatt have unlocked low- and medium-wind sites that previously were not viable to develop.

The trend responds to three factors. In some countries, such as Denmark and Germany, the relatively high penetration of wind power has reduced the availability of high quality wind sites. The reduction of incentives in some countries has squeezed profit margins for wind developers, adding pressure to maximize generation per megawatt (MW) installed. Finally, the trend away from uncompetitive feed-in tariff schemes and towards auctions and competitive tenders has increased competition.

An estimated 65% to 80% of the costs of wind power are accounted for by turbines. Costs associated with construction, grid connection and soft costs can also impact cost reduction trends. While competition, local production and market potential are major indicators of country-level turbine pricing, the drivers for other system costs are more complex. Table 3-1 shows the expected cost reductions in wind power out to 2020 in selected regions.

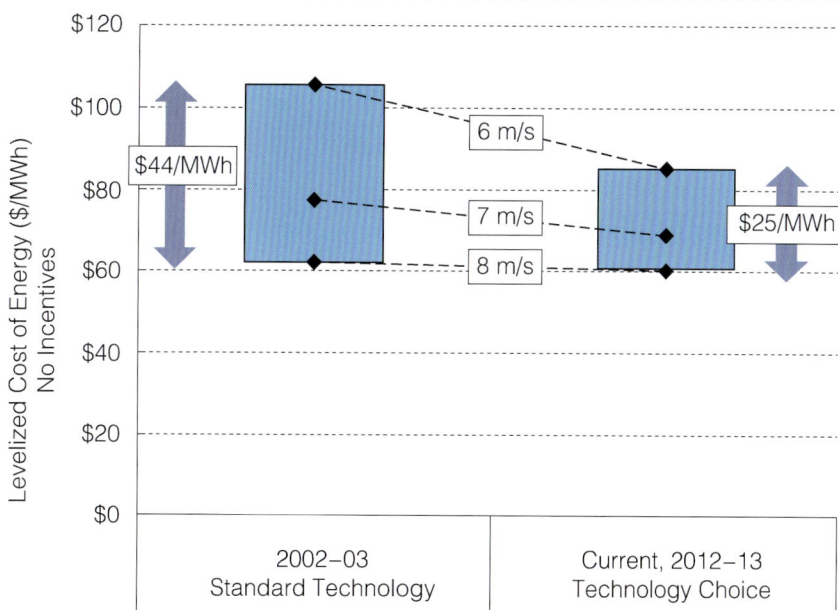

Figure 3-8 | Change trend of wind power cost under different wind [1]

Table 3-1 | Total investment costs per kW for onshore wind in selected countries (IEA)

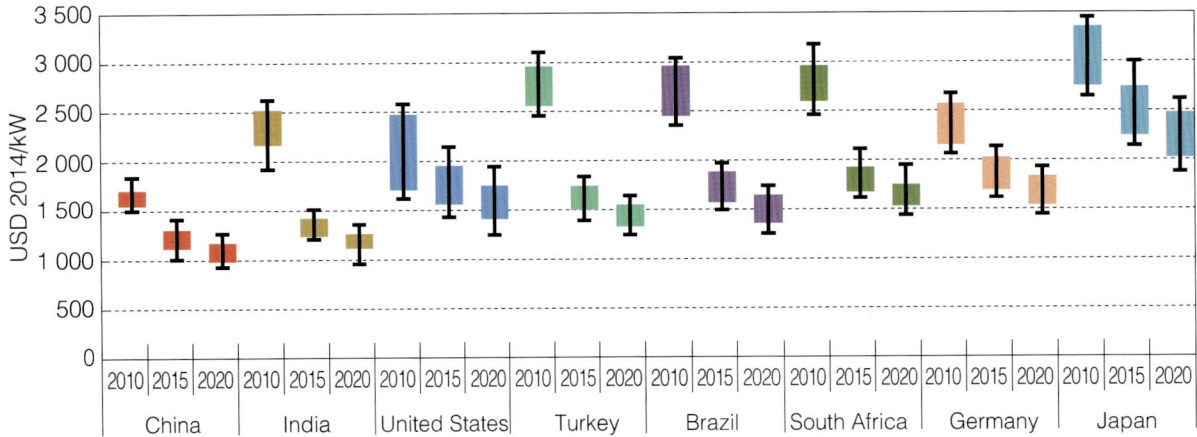

Globally, at the beginning of 2015, typical levelized cost of energy (LCOE) figures ranged from USD 60/MWh to USD 140/MWh. In the majority of countries having some deployment experience, LCOEs for onshore wind projects stand at USD 70-80/MWh. The lowest LCOEs are estimated in various large sites in Brazil and the US, where capacity factors can be close to 50% and developers were able to obtain low interest rates.

In 2014, LCOEs in China amounted to USD 64-84/MWh. In India, wind projects in general are marked by high financing costs and low capacity factors ranging from 17% to 23%, which results in relatively higher LCOEs even though systems costs are slightly higher than in China. In Germany, projects have LCOEs as low as USD 65/MWh in good sites, while typical costs range from USD 75-100/MWh.

3.2.1.2 Offshore wind power generation

The commissioning of large-scale projects in Europe and the commercialization of turbines with larger power capacity and higher rotor diameters have marked the trend in the offshore wind market over the last few years. The offshore wind supply chain has continued to evolve with further standardization efforts. The latest tender results in Denmark and the UK for projects expected to be commissioned within the period 2017-2020, and a large project pipeline in Germany, show the potential for a significant cost decrease over the medium term. Still, grid connection delays and the need for a long-term stable market and regulatory environment continue to constitute ongoing challenges to deployment.

Current system costs range from USD 4 000/kW to USD 5 250/kW. This cost range includes both onshore and offshore electrical infrastructure required to commission a project. Total investment costs are highly variable and project-specific. However, it is important to highlight the dynamics behind these costs. Going forward, offshore wind investment costs are expected to decrease with the deployment of larger power plants, increased competition among turbine manufacturers and providers of other supply chain elements, the standardization of some foundation structures, and more efficient operations and management (see Figure 3-9).

Turbines have the largest cost reduction potential, as they still account for the majority of investment

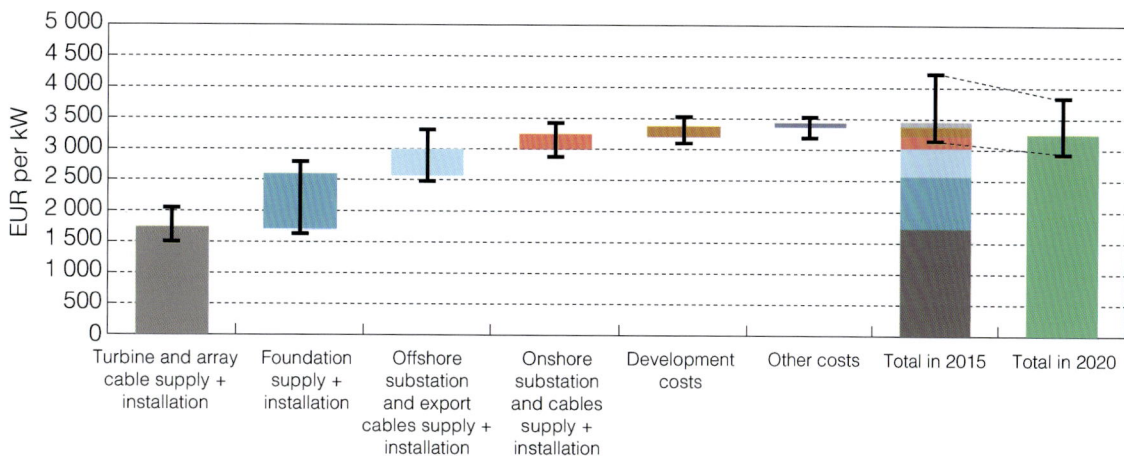

Figure 3-9 | European offshore wind farm investment cost components and trend (IEA)

costs, and increasing competition among offshore turbine manufacturers should reduce prices over the medium term. In addition, the increasing generator capacity of turbines is expected to lower construction costs significantly, as fewer foundations and array cables will be required. Floating offshore wind installations may offer innovative solutions in the years to come, including the use of vertical-axis turbines, a design that has been outpaced on shore but may have some advantages on floating platforms.

3.2.2 Market trends for solar power generation

3.2.2.1 Solar PV

By the end of 2014, the global total solar PV capacity reached 177 GW, with about 40 GW of capacity added in 2014 itself (see Figure 3-10). From 2008 to 2012, solar PV module prices were divided by five, and solar PV system prices divided by three in mature markets such as Italy due to sustained technology improvement and great economies of scale. In 2013 and 2014, module prices declined by 15%-18% annually in

markets such as Japan and Germany, however, they remained largely stable in China, with several months of higher prices. In early 2015, average module prices stood at USD 0,60-0,70 per watt, and differentials between markets have narrowed, though China still occupies the lower end of the price range. Increased domestic demand has been an important driver for stabilizing module prices in China, the source of almost half of global module shipments in 2014.

Technology improvement has been and will continue to act as an important driver for sustained investment cost reductions in solar PV systems (see Figure 3-11). Technology evolution will likely be marked by three broad trends:

- Incremental progress towards higher conversion efficiency, which would allow for smaller module sizes

- Lower materials usage

- Streamlined and more innovative manufacturing processes

Still, given uncertainty in trying to predict technology trends as well as separating the effects from industrial competition, some debate

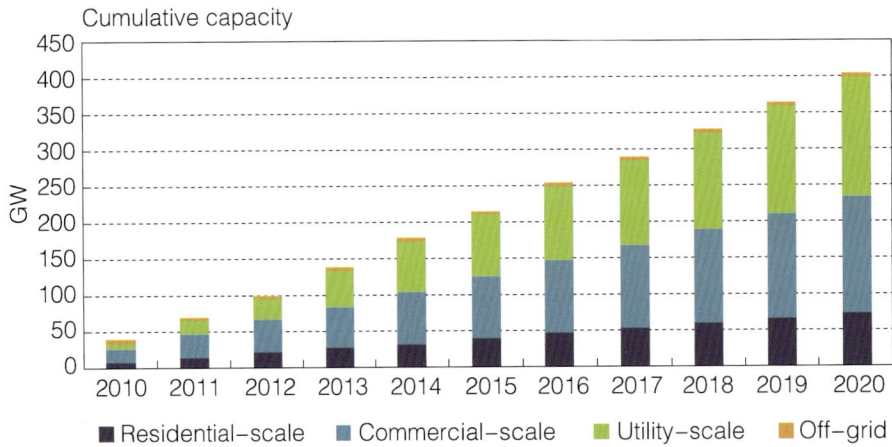

Cumulative capacity

Figure 3-10 | Global total solar PV capacity and trend, by sector (IEA)

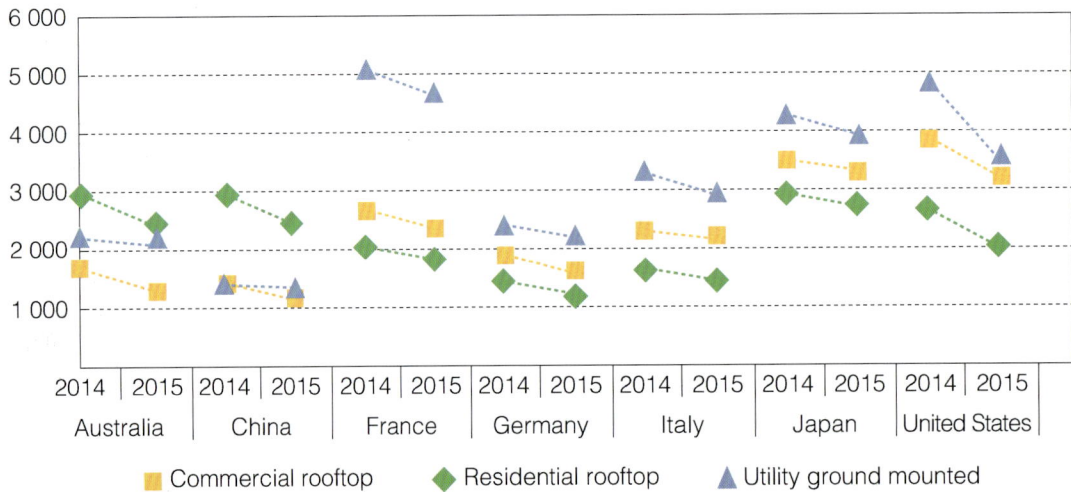

Figure 3-11 | System cost trend for PV technologies (IEA)

has emerged over the trajectory of the PV module learning curve going forward.

Even as module price decreases have somewhat slowed, balance of system (BOS) costs have experienced an accelerated decrease. In 2015, typical utility-scale solar PV prices were estimated to be as low as USD 1 300/kW in China and Germany. Commercial-scale solar PV prices were at USD 1 150/kW in China and USD 1 300 in Australia. Meanwhile, the lowest residential-scale systems still remained at levels of USD 2 000/kW and higher. In general, most new utility-scale projects in the world can currently be developed at investment costs of between USD 1 000-2 000/kW, depending on the market.

Going forward, solar PV investment costs are likely to decline due to a combination of continued global learning in module production and local improvements in soft costs. Average crystalline module prices are expected to reach around USD 0,50/W in real terms by 2020 (see Figure 3-12).

Beyond installed costs, the LCOE for PV systems depends greatly on the solar resource. Globally, LCOEs for typical utility-scale projects constructed in early 2015, without incentives, are estimated to vary from under USD 100/MWh to over USD 200/ MWh. Within this range, China and India are at the low end of the spectrum and Japan is at the high end. However, the estimated global reference suggests that weighted average deployment can take place at around USD 125/MWh. Distributed PV (i.e. small and rooftop scale), while exhibiting higher costs of 220/MWh in 2015, is expected to reach USD 160/MWh by 2020.

In the case of solar PV, and in general with non-dispatchable power sources, cost trends do not represent a full picture of competitiveness. A fuller assessment of its competitiveness versus that of other power sources would need to take into account the system value of solar PV, i.e. where the PV is deployed, when its electricity is produced, and how well this aligns with system needs and capacities both on the demand and the transmission sides.

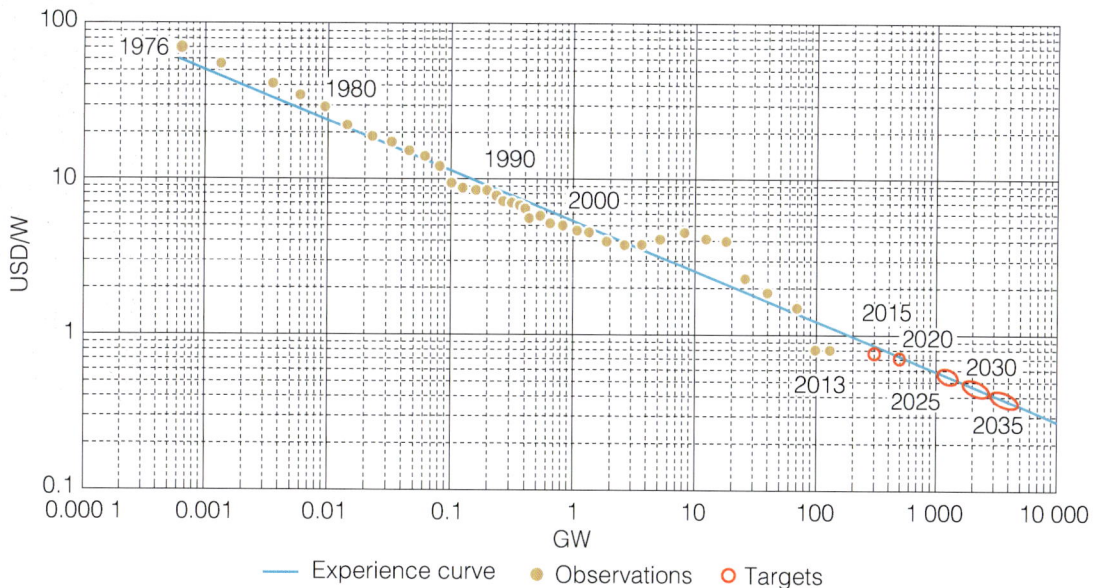

Figure 3-12 | Declining prices for crystalline modules (IEA)

3.2.2.2 Solar thermal power generation

Solar thermal energy (STE) from concentrated solar power (CSP) plants is a proven renewable technology that can provide firm peak, intermediate or base-load capacity thanks to thermal storage and/or a hybrid system (see Figure 3-13). By the end of 2015, total installed capacity in the world amounted to 4,94 GW. Of this, roughly 3,2 GW is without storage, while 1,8 GW includes thermal storage. Going forward, around 80% of the new capacity expected through 2020 should incorporate storage. However, a number of risks remain and the technology needs to move further down the cost curve to achieve a more rapid scale-up.

Storage and hybridization allow STE to have a generally higher value than PV for the system. Investment costs are characteristically high – for large plants (at least 50 MW) such costs amount to USD 4000/kW to USD 9000/kW. Over the medium term, the investment costs of STE plants are expected to decline with further deployment. For example, the solar field, whose size is linked to the amount of electric output, represents about half of the investment cost, and developers are

looking to reduce its size by increasing electric conversion efficiencies. Costs could be further decreased by scaling up thermal storage using molten salts. The IEA expects that by 2020, STE investment costs in the US could decline to around USD 3000-4000/kW with 6 h of storage and USD 4500-5500/kW for 12 h of storage. Figure 3-14 shows the current and expected trend out to 2020 in LCOE for STE. The LCOE varies greatly plant to plant and does not provide the full picture of the economic attractiveness of STE, which also depends on the value of the electricity generated.

3.2.3 Market trends for other geographically-constrained RE technologies

3.2.3.1 Ocean energy

Ocean energy remains a small part of the global power mix. There is however a significant resource and the number of demonstration projects underway indicate there could be a commercial scale-up in the medium term. In 2014, total ocean capacity stood at an estimated 0.53 GW, equivalent to a single large natural gas power

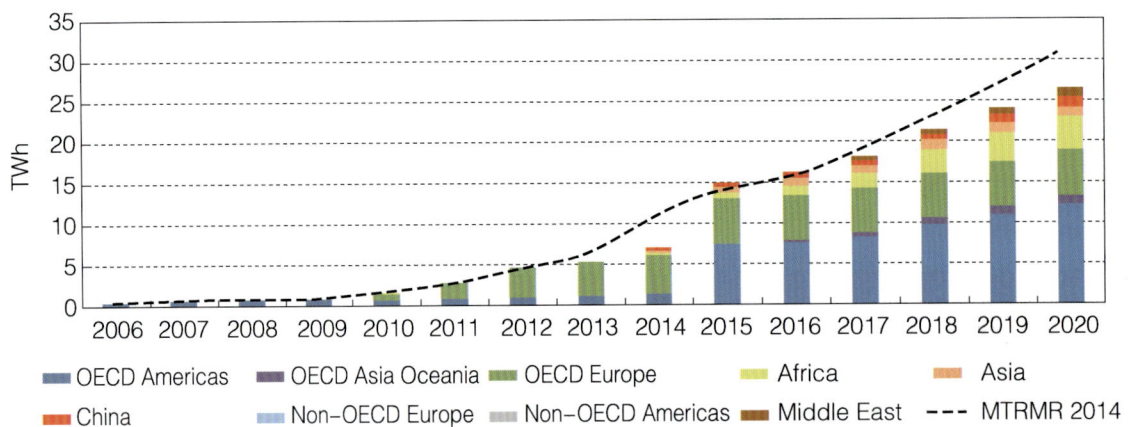

Figure 3-13 | Global total solar thermal power generation capacity and trend (IEA)

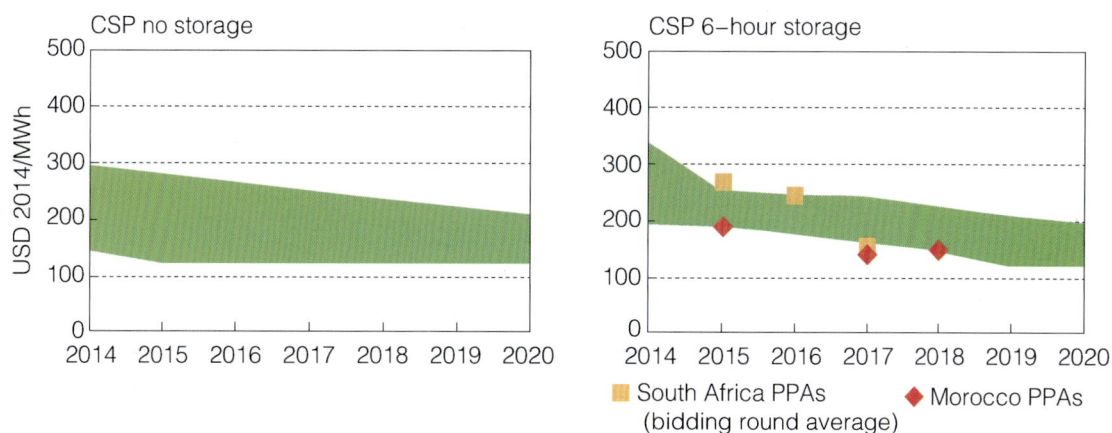

Figure 3-14 | Current and expected trend out to 2020 in LCOE for STE (IEA [2])

plant, including two large-scale tidal projects in France and Korea.

The IEA Technology Collaboration Programme on Ocean Energy Systems (IEA-OES) estimates total investment costs for a 3 MW wave energy plant at around USD 18 100/kW; however, costs could decrease by half to around USD 9 100/kW for a 75 MW plant. Investment costs for tidal projects of 10 MW are around USD 14 600/kW, but could decrease to USD 5 600/kW for larger projects of 90 MW.

3.2.3.2 Geothermal energy

The global geothermal resource is significant, and due to its dispatchability it is a highly attractive renewable generation technology option. Geothermal energy requires much exploration, extensive drilling and civil engineering works, which result in long lead times (i.e. 5-7 years).

Because of its characteristics, costs are very site-specific, with typical costs of a high-temperature plant at around USD 2 000/kW to USD 5 000/kW. Binary plants are slightly more costly at USD 2 400/kW to USD 5 600/kW. LCOEs for geothermal plants range from USD 35/MWh to USD 200/MWh,

a result of the high capacity factors reached in geothermal generation.

3.3 Practical experiences of power system interconnection around the world

Following the three-stepped approach towards greater interconnection across the globe highlighted in Section 2.2.4, this section examines practical experiences relevant to each of the three phases outlined.

3.3.1 Experiences with large-scale national transmission interconnection

3.3.1.1 China

Over the past decades, the scale of interconnection in the Chinese power grid has increased substantially, accompanied by a constant increase in voltage levels. Since the 1950s, the Chinese national grid has evolved from hundreds of isolated grids to approximately 30 provincial grids, and finally to large-scale regional grids. Currently, there are six synchronous grids in mainland China,

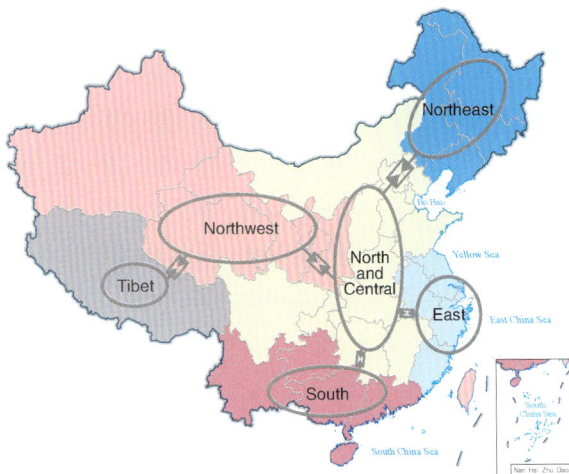

Figure 3-15 | Current status of grid interconnection in China (SGCC)

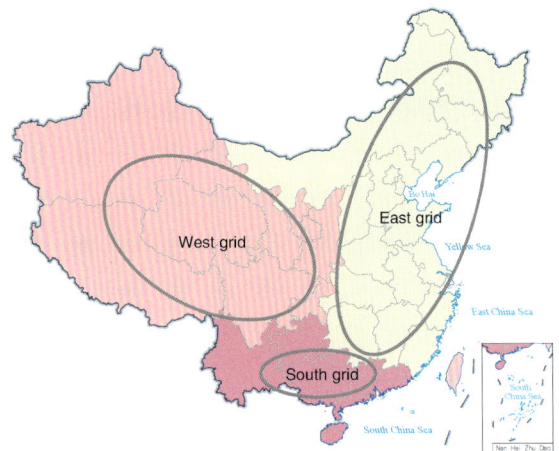

Figure 3-16 | Planned grid interconnection in China by 2020 (SGCC)

namely the North and Central grid – integrated into one synchronous grid in 2009 by the first 1 000 kV ultra-high-voltage alternating current (UHVAC) line –, the East grid, the Northeast grid, the Northwest grid, the Tibet grid, and the South grid. These grids are fully interconnected with HVDC links, as outlined in Figure 3-15.

With the number of planned and under construction UHV backbone transmission lines, these regional grids will be further consolidated in the future. In its new five-year grid development plan, State Grid Corporation of China (SGCC) proposed the formation of two synchronous grids by 2020, namely the East and West grids, as shown in Figure 3-16. The West grid will focus on the integration of a broad range of power bases, given Western China's rich resource endowment; the East grid will integrate major load centres. This clear two-region grid structure featuring a strong exporting region and a strong importing region is expected to support the cross-regional transmission of 88 GW of wind power, 20 GW of solar power and 60 GW of hydropower, helping the government to fulfil its decarbonization target.

3.3.1.2 Korea

Korea's electricity industry is dominated by the Korea Electric Power Corporation (KEPCO), which retains the nation-wide transmission and distribution grids (see Figure 3-17).

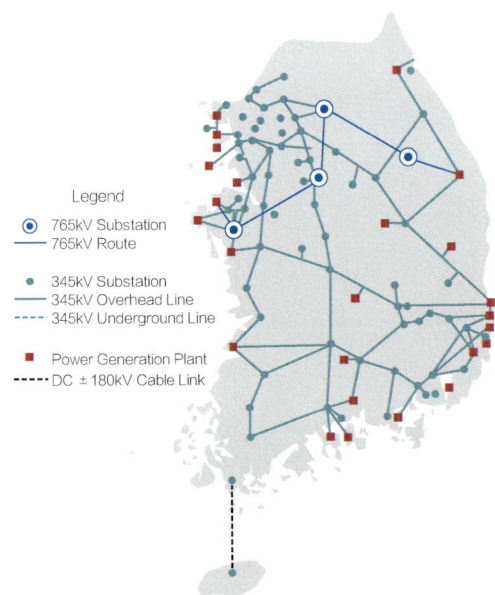

Figure 3-17 | National Power Grid of Korea (KEPCO)

KEPCO has pushed forward interconnection through UHV power transmission to address the serious supply imbalance between the high demand load centres in the Seoul metropolitan area and the power generation areas, concentrated in large-scale complexes. The commercial operation of the first UHV project in East Asia (a 765 kV transmission and substation project) began in 2002, using a range of advanced grid technologies with a low environmental footprint, including gas-insulated switchgear or steel towers with a low environmental impact. The Korean experience shows that upgrading and interconnecting the existing power grid with such UHV technologies allows for capacities 3,4 times greater than that of the prevailing transmission voltage of 345 kV. Land requirements are decreased by 22%, and transmission losses and construction costs are both reduced by a fifth (see Figure 3-18).

3.3.1.3 Japan

Figure 3-19 illustrates the domestic interconnected transmission network in Japan. As shown in the figure, excluding the Okinawa region there are nine regional networks, interconnected with each other via HVDC submarine cables, HVAC overhead lines, back-to-back systems and frequency converters.

There are two specific features in Japan's power system, relevant to the analysis of practical interconnection experiences worldwide.

First, power frequency differs between Eastern and Western Japan, set at 50 Hz and 60 Hz respectively. There are historic reasons for this difference: during the emergence of the electricity industry in Japan, the Tokyo area in the East adopted German-made generators, while Osaka in the West chose American-made ones. This

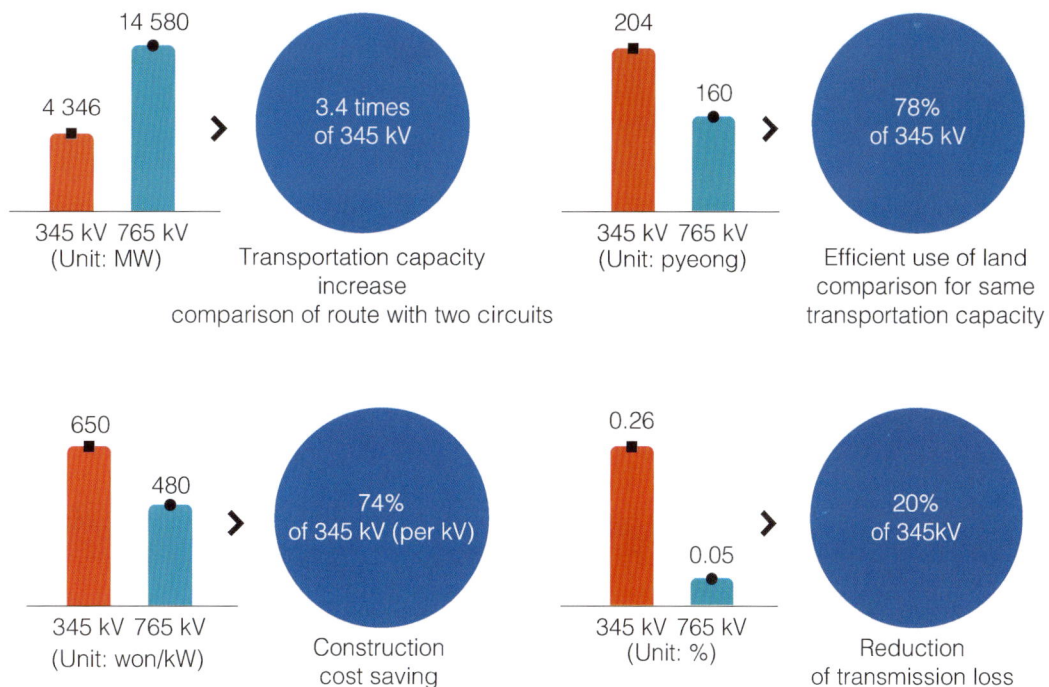

Figure 3-18 | Major benefits of the UHV transmission system in Korea (KEPCO)

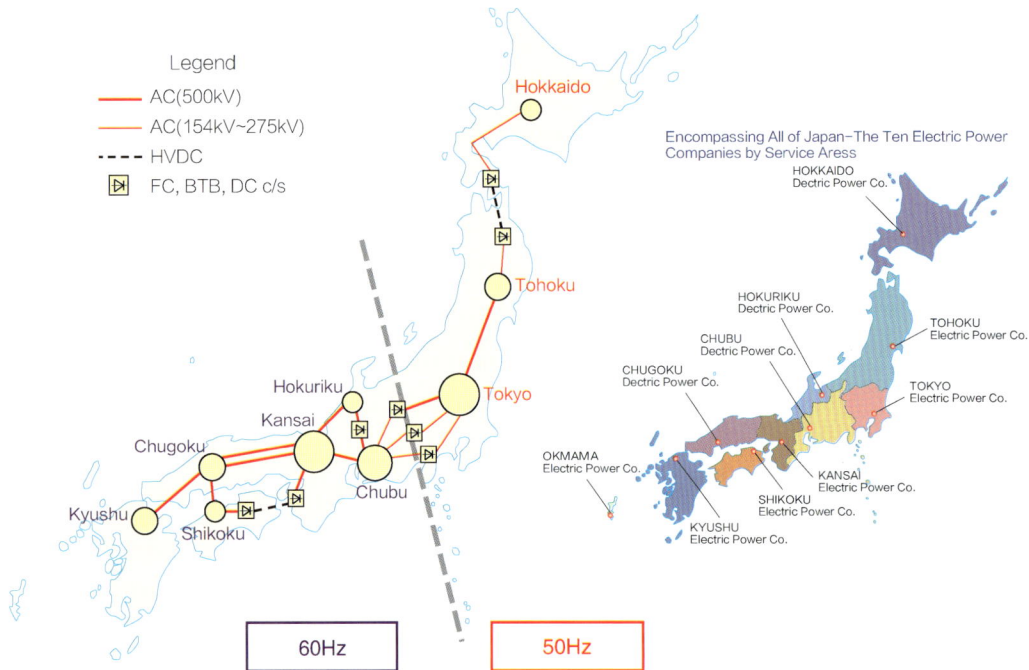

Figure 3-19 | Domestic interconnection of electricity transmission network in Japan (TEPCO)

frequency difference partitions Japan's national grid, requiring frequency converter facilities (FCFs) to exchange power between East and West. Three FCFs are currently in operation – with a total transmission capacity of 1,2 GW, the East-West Grid Connection is a bottleneck for power exchange.

Second, the nine individual utilities in operation in Japan have been individually responsible for securing adequate power sources for their own power demand and overseeing their own power system development and operation. In each region, supply and demand is strongly determined by the characteristics of local production and consumption. Interconnections have traditionally only been used for the purposes of transmitting electricity from distant power sources and emergency power system interventions. Therefore, almost all interconnection systems have only a minimum necessary minimum transmission capacity and have configurations suitable for those purposes.

In recent years however, Japan has been forced to rethink this conventional concept of network planning due to power supply deficiencies and imbalances in the Tohoku and Tokyo EPCO areas following the East Japan Earthquake in 2011, coupled to an increasing need for cross regional power exchange due to the full-scale liberalization of the electricity retail business in April 2016.

Figure 3-20 illustrates the enhancement plan for interconnections between Tokyo and Chubu EPCO via 900 MW HVDC transmission lines which will be commissioned in 2020.

3.3.1.4 India

The development of the Indian power grid can be divided into three stages:

- From 1947 to the 1960s, when state-level grids were progressively formed by interconnecting many isolated small grids

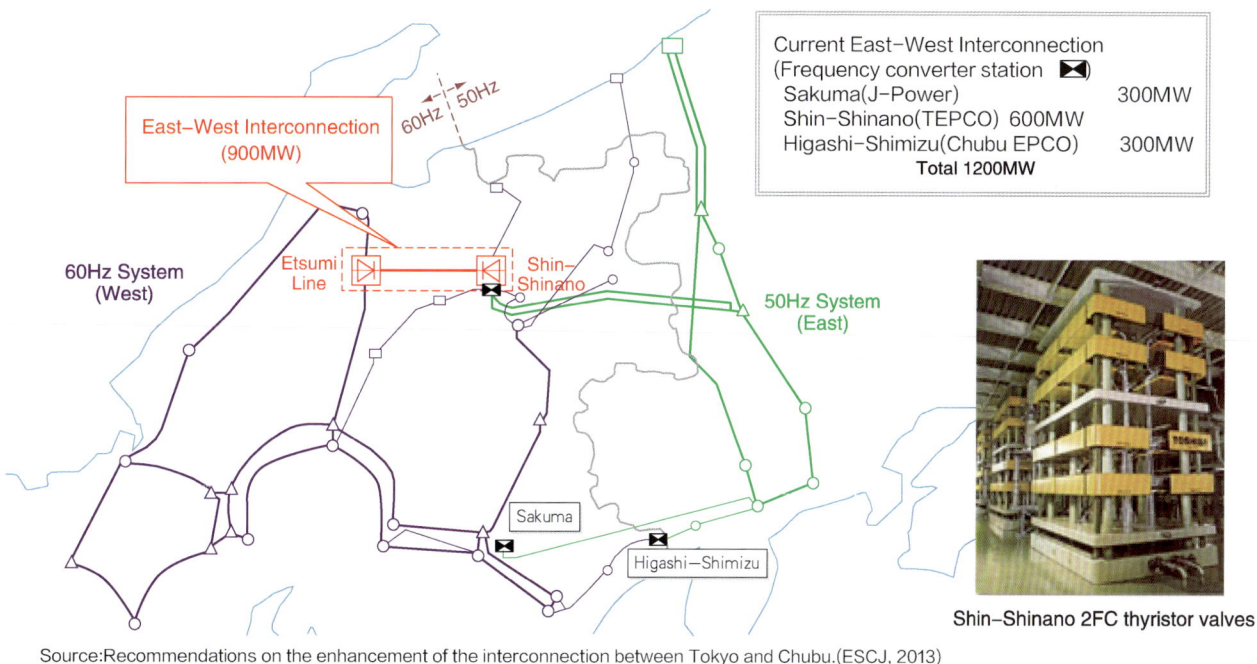

East–West Interconnection
(900MW)

Current East–West Interconnection
(Frequency converter station ▣)
Sakuma(J–Power)   300MW
Shin–Shinano(TEPCO) 600MW
Higashi–Shimizu(Chubu EPCO)   300MW
Total 1200MW

60Hz System
(West)

Etsumi
Line

Shin–
Shinano

50Hz System
(East)

60Hz | 50Hz

Sakuma

Higashi–Shimizu

Shin–Shinano 2FC thyristor valves

Source:Recommendations on the enhancement of the interconnection between Tokyo and Chubu.(ESCJ, 2013)

Figure 3-20 | Enhancement plan for east-west interconnection capacity by 900 MW HVDC

- From the 1960s to the end of the 1980s, during which five regional-level grids were formed by interconnecting state-level grids

- From the 1990s until the present time, when a national synchronous grid was created by interconnecting regional grids. The interconnection among the five regional grids in 2012 is shown in Figure 3-21

As in the Chinese case, the layout of the Indian power grid and its interconnections is driven by the uneven distribution of energy resources and load centres. The energy resources of India are mainly located in the North, Northeast and East of the country, while load centres are mainly located in the North, South and West. As a result, large amounts of power need to be transferred from East to West as well as from North to South. In the future, cross-regional grid interconnection in India will be improved through planned higher-voltage level transmission lines. India's 12th five-year grid plan contemplates at least two 400 kV AC or

765 kV AC or HVDC back-to-back links between regional grids by 2017. Also planned are ±800 kV UHVDC lines and 1 200 kV UHVAC lines to be built in the North and Northeast of the country. The first ±800 kV, 6 000 MW UHVDC line began operations on August 31, 2015, from Assam to Uttar Pradesh, and through West Bengal.

3.3.1.5 Brazil

Given its vast hydro resources, hydropower is the dominant form of generation in Brazil. Concurrent with the development of large-scale hydropower plants, cross-regional power grid interconnection in Brazil has accelerated. During the 1980s, four regional 500 kV backbone grids were formed, namely the North, Northeast, Southeast and South grids. At the end of the 1990s, a unified national synchronous grid was formed by interconnecting the four regional grids, through 765 kV, 500 kV and 345 kV links. There are also two ±600 kV HVDC lines in operation to transmit the power generated

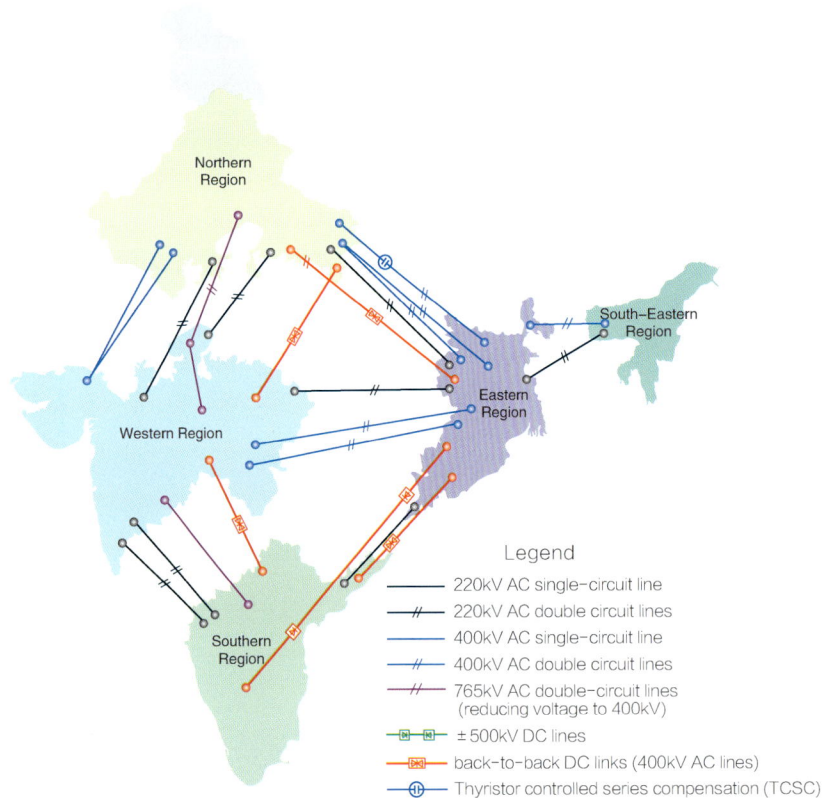

Figure 3-21 | Grid interconnection in India in 2012 (Government of India, Ministry of Power [3])

by the Itaipu hydropower plant. Brazil plans to continue to develop hydropower, especially in the Northwest and North of the country. Current plans would require further enhancement of cross-regional grid interconnection within Brazil. An illustration of the present and planned grid interconnection in Brazil is given by Figure 3-22. A ±800 kV UHVDC line is now under construction for transmission of the power generated by the 11 GW Belo Monte hydropower plant.

3.3.2 Practical experiences of regional interconnection

3.3.2.1 Asia

A number of interconnections exist in Asia which highlight potential pathways towards greater regional interconnection.

In Northeast Asia, the Chinese grid is now connected with the Russian grid by means of one 110 kV AC, two 220 kV AC and one ±500 kV back-to-back DC links. There are also two 220 kV AC lines delivering power from Inner Mongolia in China to Mongolia. Two further interconnections are planned before 2020: a ±800 kV/8 000 MW/ 1 830 km DC project delivering power between Russia and China, and a ±660 kV/ 4 000 MW/1 220 km DC project delivering power from Mongolia to China.

In Central Asia interconnections now exist between Kazakhstan and Russia through three 500 kV AC lines, one of them having been operated at the ultra-high voltage of 1 150 kV. A 500 kV AC loop has been formed between Kazakhstan, Kyrgyzstan, Tajikistan and Uzbekistan. Turkmenistan is also connected with Uzbekistan and Iran. A number of

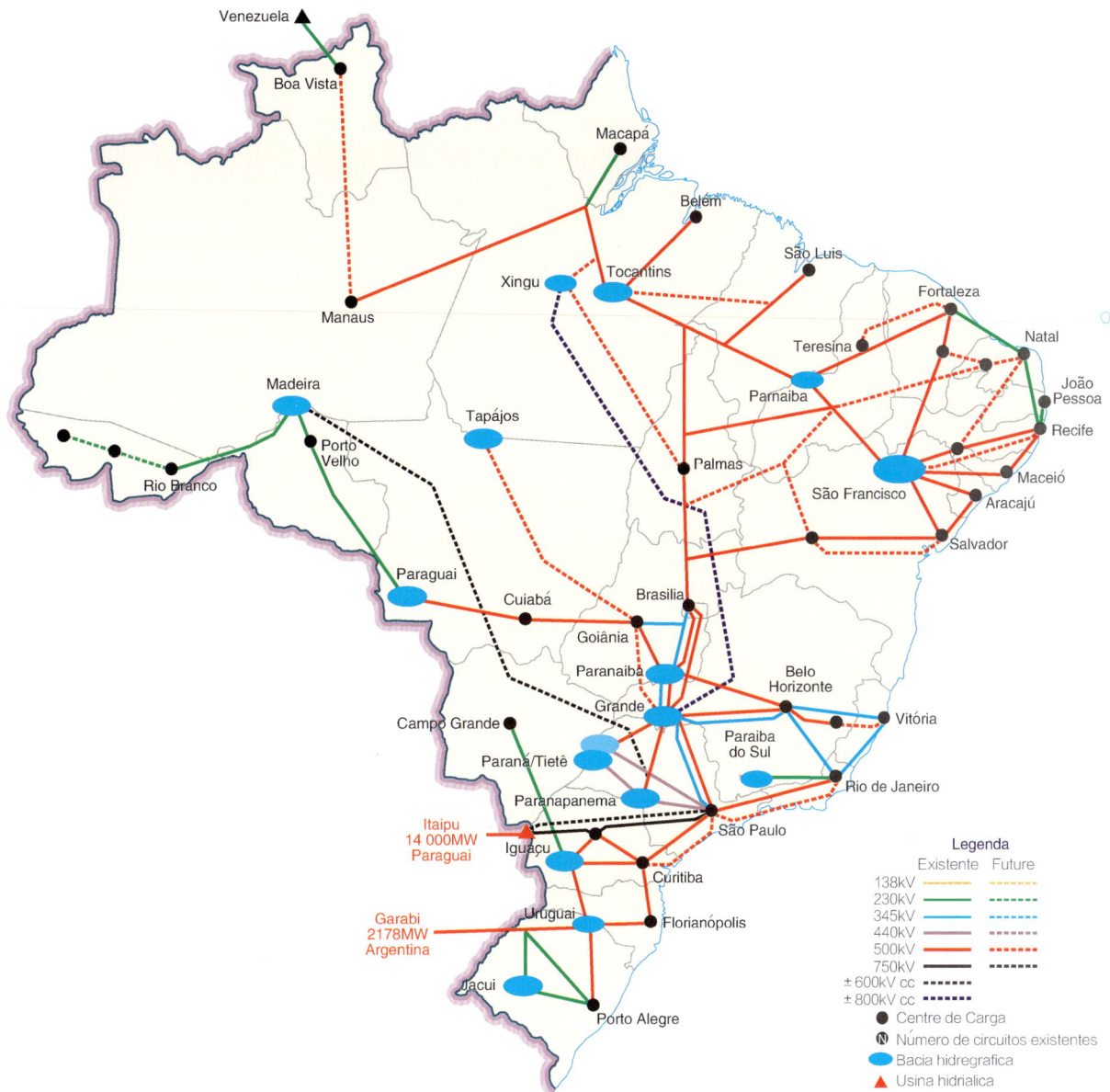

Figure 3-22 | Present and planned grid interconnection in Brazil (ONS [4])

500 kV links are under construction to enhance grid interconnection among the five Central Asian countries as well as Iran and Afghanistan. Figure 3-23 shows the existing and planned interconnection of Central Asian grids.

In West Asia, two synchronous grids have been formed through transnational grid interconnections. The first is the North Middle East Peninsula and Iran grid, which consists of

the Iraq, Syria, Jordan, Lebanon and Iran grids, connected by 400 kV and/or 220 kV AC lines. This grid is also interconnected to the North with grids of Turkey, Armenia and Azerbaijan, and to the West with the grid of Egypt. The second is the Gulf Grid, an interconnection between Saudi Arabia, Kuwait, Bahrain, Qatar, the United Arab Emirates and Oman (see Figure 3-24). In 2015, the Gulf Cooperation Council proposed to enlarge the Gulf

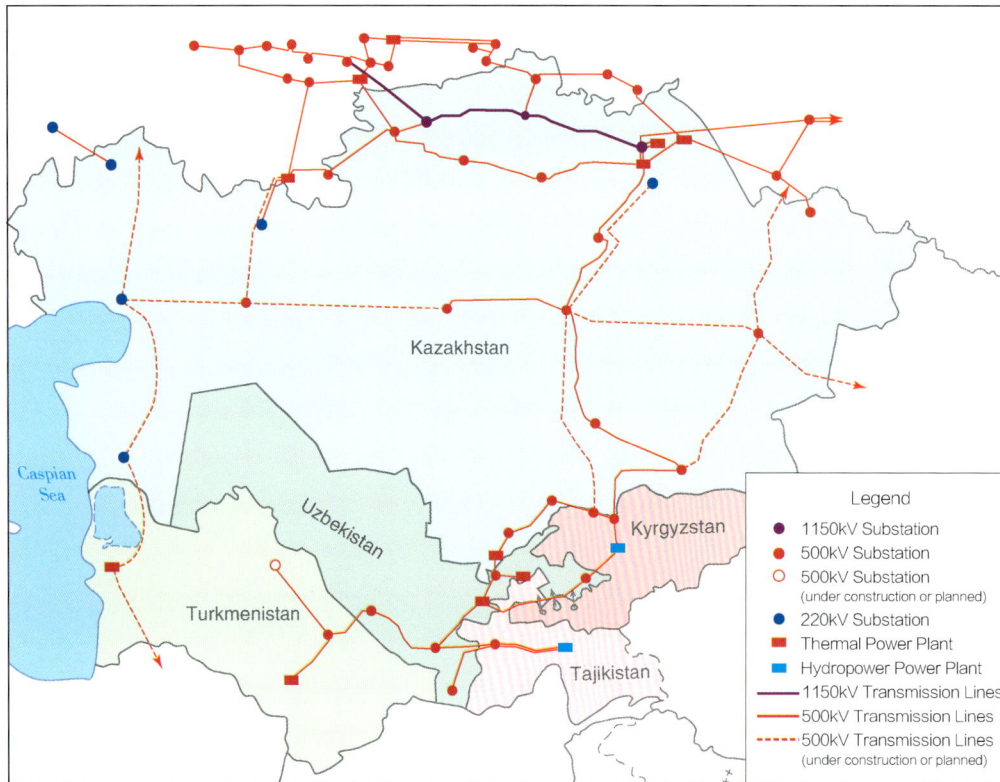

Figure 3-23 | Grid interconnection in Central Asia (GENI [5])

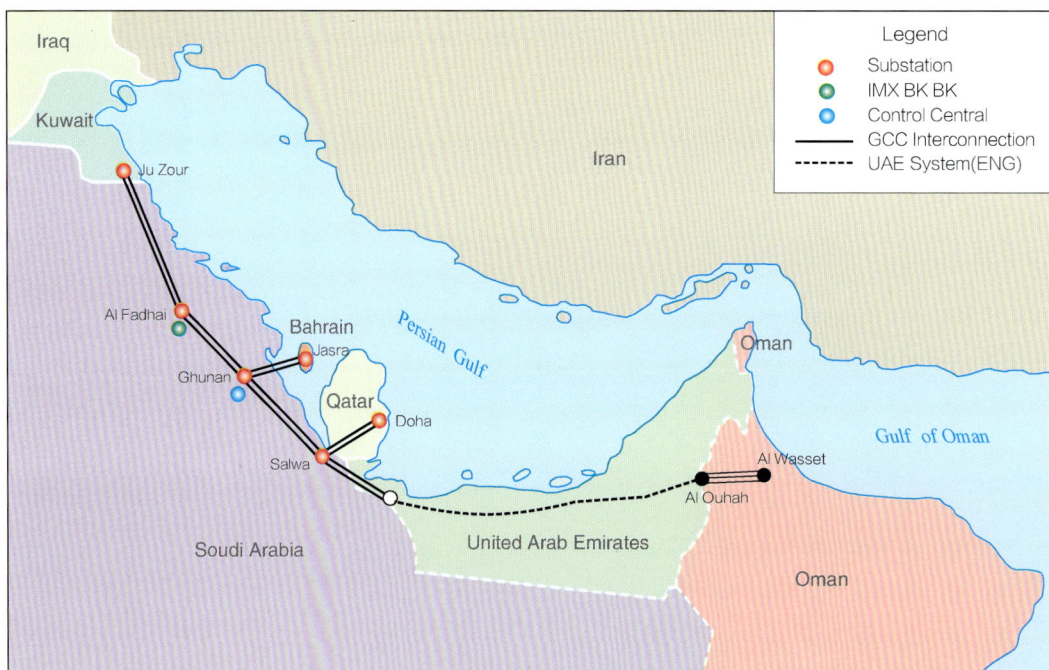

Figure 3-24 | The Gulf Grid (Gulf Cooperation Council Interconnection Authority)

Grid through interconnection with surrounding Middle Eastern and Northern Africa grids.

In South Asia, the Indian grid is now connected with Bangladesh by a ±400 kV back-to-back DC link, with Nepal by a 132 kV AC link and with Bhutan by three links. The Asian Development Bank has proposed an India-centred grid interconnection enhancement plan for South Asia, connecting India to Bhutan, Nepal, Sri Lanka, Bangladesh and Pakistan, as well as India to Central Asia, as shown in Figure 3-25.

In Southeast Asia, the Chinese grid is now connected with the Vietnamese grid by three 220 kV and two 110 kV AC lines. One 500 kV and one 220 kV AC point-to-grid connection from China to Burma have also been established. The grids of countries in the Indochinese Peninsula have already been interconnected by a dozen 500 kV, 220 kV, 110 kV AC links and by one ±330 kV DC link. According to the Association of Southeast Asian Nations (ASEAN) power grid development plan proposed by the Heads of ASEAN Power Utilities/Authorities (HAPUA), 16 AC

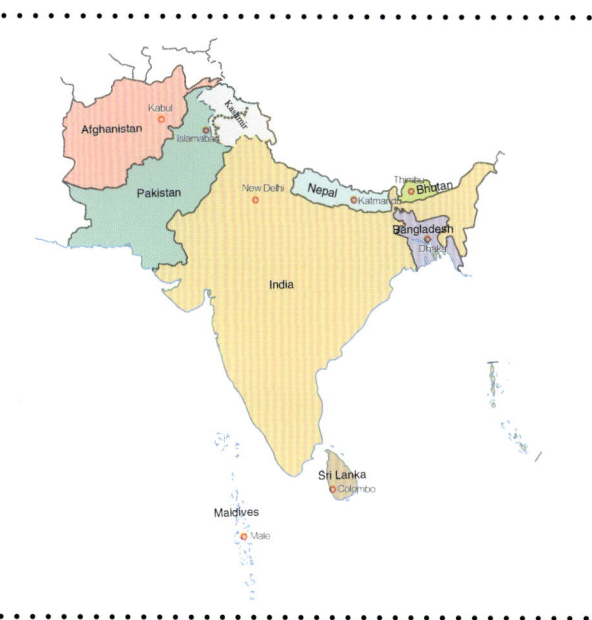

Figure 3-25 | Grid interconnection plan in South Asia (Nepal Energy Forum [6])

and DC projects will be built by 2025 to enhance grid interconnection among ASEAN countries (see Figure 3-26).

3.3.2.2 Europe, Russia and beyond

In Europe, interconnectors between countries have created a large synchronous frequency area extending into the eastern parts of the continent at a frequency of 50 Hz (see Figure 3-27). Interconnections of power grids among European countries started in the 1950s. The Western European interconnection first took shape and was then synchronously interconnected with Central European grids in 1996 [7]. Current interconnector capacity amounts to 11% of installed generation capacity across European countries. Today, as shown in Figure 3-27, the European power system mainly comprises five transnationally-interconnected synchronous grids in continental Europe, Northern Europe, the Baltic Sea countries, the UK and Ireland, as well as two independent power systems in Iceland and Cyprus. Grid interconnection and electricity market integration has enabled a high level of power exchange among the member states. In 2013, a total of 387,3 TWh was exchanged, representing 12% of total power consumption.

However, regional differences continue to exist. In the Baltic States, for example, there is a significant need for interconnectors to increase security of supply and reduce the market power of generators. In order to promote more cooperation among TSOs, the European Network of Transmission System Operators for Electricity (ENTSO-E) was founded in 2008 through integration of the former European Transmission System Operators association (ETSO) and five TSO organizations (ATSOI, BALTSO, Nordel, UCTE, and UKTSOA), covering 41 TSOs from 34 European countries [8].

Figure 3-26 | ASEAN Grid interconnection enhancement plan (EPRI)

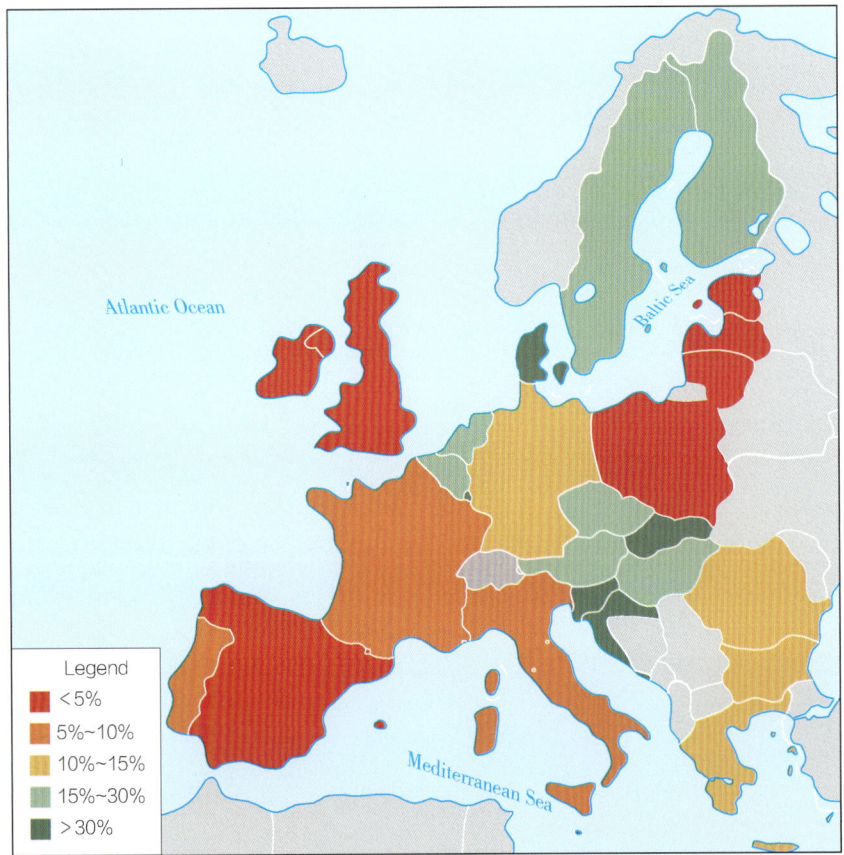

Figure 3-27 | Power exchange in Europe by 2020 (IEA)

A better interconnected European energy grid would bring notable market benefits to European citizens, as consumers could save between an estimated EUR 12 billion and EUR 40 billion annually by 2030. Such a grid is also crucial for accommodating the high level of RE required by the European Union's (EU) decarbonization policy. In 2014, the European Council discussed implementing a 15% goal for interconnection between member states in the EU. While this goal would bring visibility to the issue, the costs and benefits of interconnectors need to be thoroughly assessed, not only from an investment perspective, but also for public acceptability and understanding, which are required for transmission lines to be actually built. Public acceptance necessitates a thorough cost benefit analysis to demonstrate the positives of a project.

Russia and the EU are seeking to integrate the Integrated Power System/Unified Power System (IPS/UPS) and ENTSO-E grids, creating a synchronous super grid that would span 13 time zones. The formation of the IPS/UPS interconnection is now the world's largest synchronous grid in terms of geographical coverage, spanning eight time zones, and linking the grids in Russia, Azerbaijan, Belarus, Georgia, Kazakhstan, Kyrgyzstan, Moldova, Mongolia and Ukraine, among other countries. It is asynchronously connected with the Finnish power grid through back-to-back DC links, and is synchronously connected with the Baltic grid via AC links.

3.3.2.3 America

In North America, the greatest growth in interconnection was triggered by the development of large-scale hydropower as early as during the 1930s and was further advanced in the period of the 1950s-1980s with voltage level upgrades to meet the rapidly growing power demand. The North American grid has evolved into four major synchronous systems, namely the Western Interconnection, the Eastern Interconnection, the Texas (ERCOT) Interconnection and the Quebec Interconnection, together spanning Canada, the US and North Mexico, as shown in Figure 3-28 [7]. These interconnections are generally back-to-back DC links designed mainly for emergency backup purposes. Their power exchange capacity is limited and the power exchanged under normal operation conditions is negligible [9]. The different interconnections are not synchronized, precluding the use of AC interconnectors and limiting the level of physical interconnector capacity to DC lines. To date, only a few DC lines of about 2 GW of interconnector capacity exist between the Western and Eastern Interconnections, and one interconnector of 2,6 GW exists between Eastern and Texas Interconnections.

The mutual isolation of these various transmission regions and the lack of transmission capacity have been identified as potential barriers for the US in its attempt to achieve its aggressive renewable energy goals as well as to improve the reliability and efficiency of the entire US power system. Vast amounts of rich wind energy resources are located in the Midwest, the Great Plains and Texas, and are open for development on a large scale and for transmission to load centres located in both the East and West Coasts. The Tres Amigas SuperStation was proposed in 2008 to integrate the Western, Eastern and Texas Interconnections through a single nexus and to act as a renewable energy hub, and initial steps towards implementation have begun in 2016 (see Figure 3-29) [10].

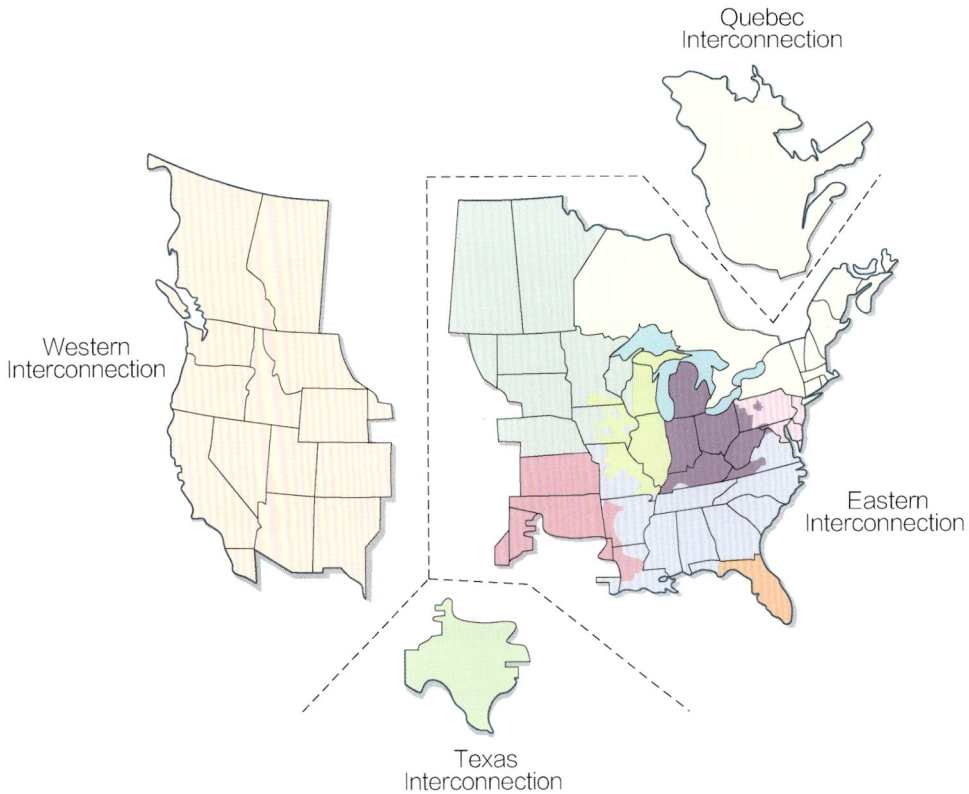

Figure 3-28 | Current North American interconnections [7]

Three Become One

The Tres Amigas superstation, now under construction outside Clovis, N.M., aims to interconnect the three main power grids of North America. Once finished, it will be able to move up to 20 gigawatts of electricity in any direction.

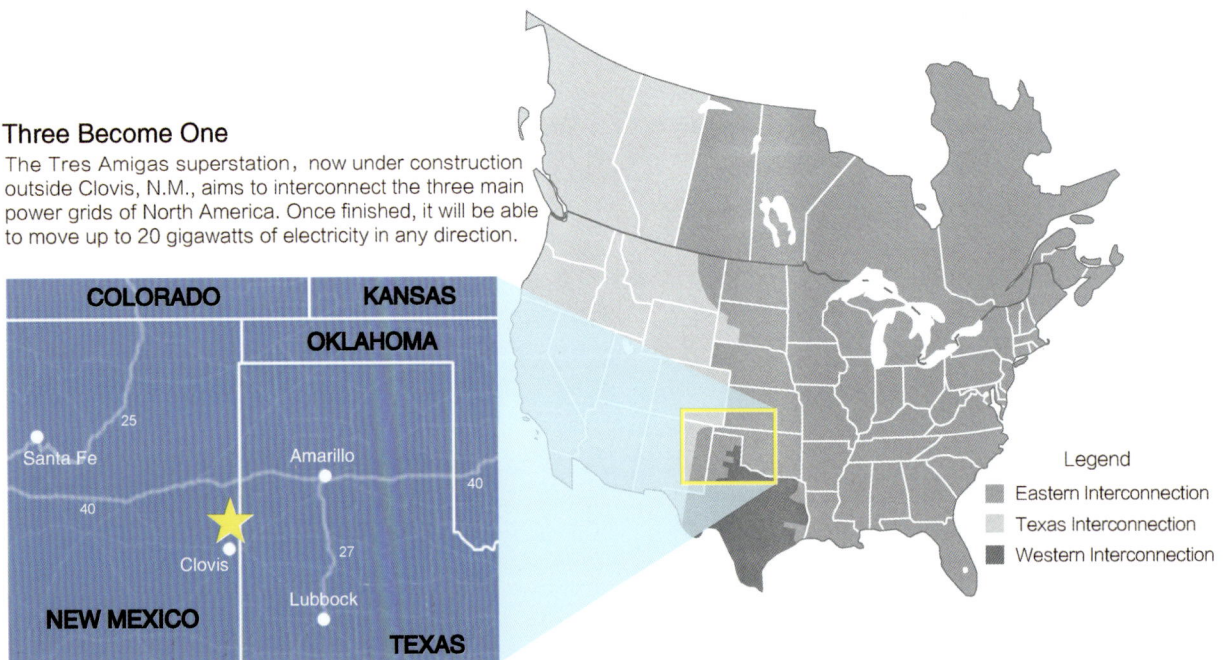

Figure 3-29 | Location of the Tres Amigas SuperStation (NERC, [10])

In South America, the existing, under construction or planned grid interconnections are mainly concentrated in two geographical areas, as shown in Figure 3-30. The northern section includes Colombia, Ecuador and Venezuela and the southern section Argentina, Brazil, Paraguay, and Uruguay. A grid interconnection between Columbia, Ecuador, and Peru is projected to be completed in 2017. The interconnection is planned then to be extended southward to reach Bolivia and Chile, as part of a larger programme to integrate the electric systems of the five Andean Community nations by 2020 [7].

In Central America, the grids of Costa Rica, Guatemala, Honduras, Nicaragua, Panama and Salvador, are interconnected through a chain of transmission lines, as shown in Figure 3-31, composed of 15 substations and 1 800 km long, 230 kV transnational lines [7].

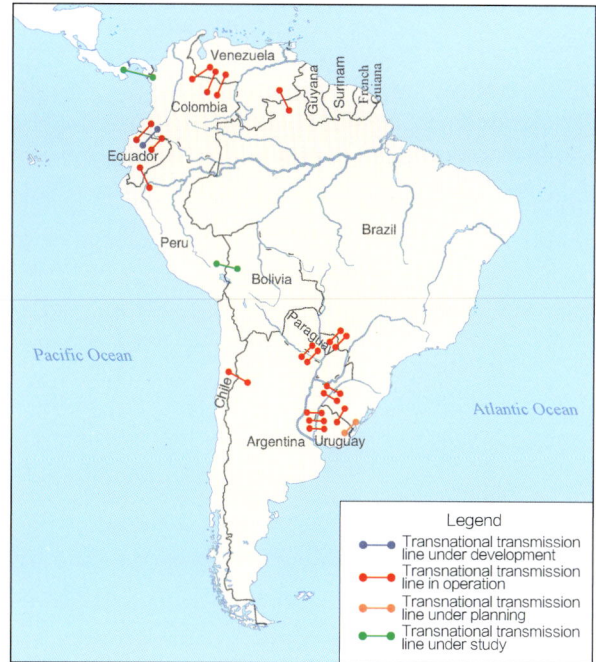

Figure 3-30 | South America Interconnection [7]

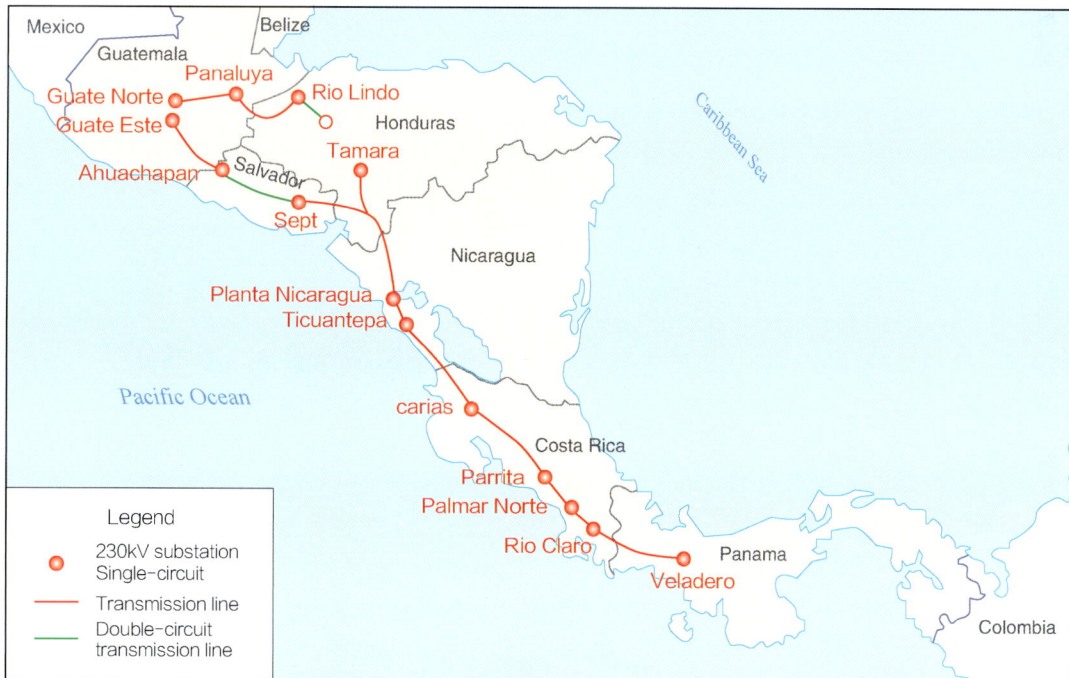

Figure 3-31 | Central America Interconnection [7]

3.3.2.4 Africa

Since its inception in 1995, the Southern African Power Pool (SAPP) has been actively promoting transnational grid interconnections. The alliance comprises 12 members, including Angola, Botswana, the Democratic Republic of Congo, Lesotho, Malawi, Mozambique, Namibia, South Africa, Swaziland, Tanzania, Zambia, and Zimbabwe. Nine of these countries, not including Angola, Malawi and Tanzania, have developed grid interconnections through 400 kV, 275 kV, 220 kV, and 132 kV AC links. Planned grid interconnection projects in South Africa fall into two main classes. One involves the interconnection among Angola, Malawi, Tanzania and other member countries. The other involves central transmission channels, including a Zimbabwe–Zambia–Botswana–Namibia interconnection, a transmission corridor in central Zimbabwe, and transmission projects in Zambia [7].

African countries are also planning to form a pan-African power grid in 2020 by interconnecting the Southern, Western, Central and Northern African grids.

3.3.3 Transnational interconnection initiatives

Adopting a longer-term perspective, transnational power grid interconnection of larger areas has been studied, with several initiatives created, pre-feasibility studies carried out and specific plans proposed. These include the European Super Grid, the Desertec project, the Medgrid project, and the Gobitec and Asian Super Grid projects. Such projects would fall under the later stage of the GEI concept.

3.3.3.1 The European Super Grid

A range of European super grids have been assessed, generally including the interconnection of European countries with neighbouring North African and Middle Eastern countries and eventually with Caspian countries through UHVDC technology [11]. While a fully transparent cost-benefit analysis showing the attractiveness of such a grid relative to alternatives remains to be carried out, it would allow at a high level for the large-scale utilization of offshore wind power in the coastal regions of Northern Europe and rich amounts of solar resource in the South [where high direct normal irradiance (DNI) could also allow for the exploitation of CSP], as well as transmission of power from these bases to load centres around Europe using the rich hydro resources for system balancing (see Figure 3-32).

3.3.3.2 The Desertec project

The focus of the Desertec project is on harnessing solar power from the deserts of North Africa and the Middle East to provide these regions with both clean power and fresh water through sea water desalination, and to eventually export large volumes of electricity to Europe (see Figure 3-33). While renewed interest in the project has recently resurfaced, desert power remains in its infancy.

3.3.3.3 The Medgrid project

The Medgrid project was launched in 2010 by a Consortium of more than 20 utilities, manufacturers and investors, largely from European and North African countries circling the Mediterranean Sea. Medgrid's objective is the development of 20 GW of renewable energy, largely from solar power, with 5 GW dedicated to exporting power to Europe. Although the Medgrid Consortium ceased operation in January 2016, a number of grid interconnection planning studies had been conducted, including the design of three transmission corridors between North Africa

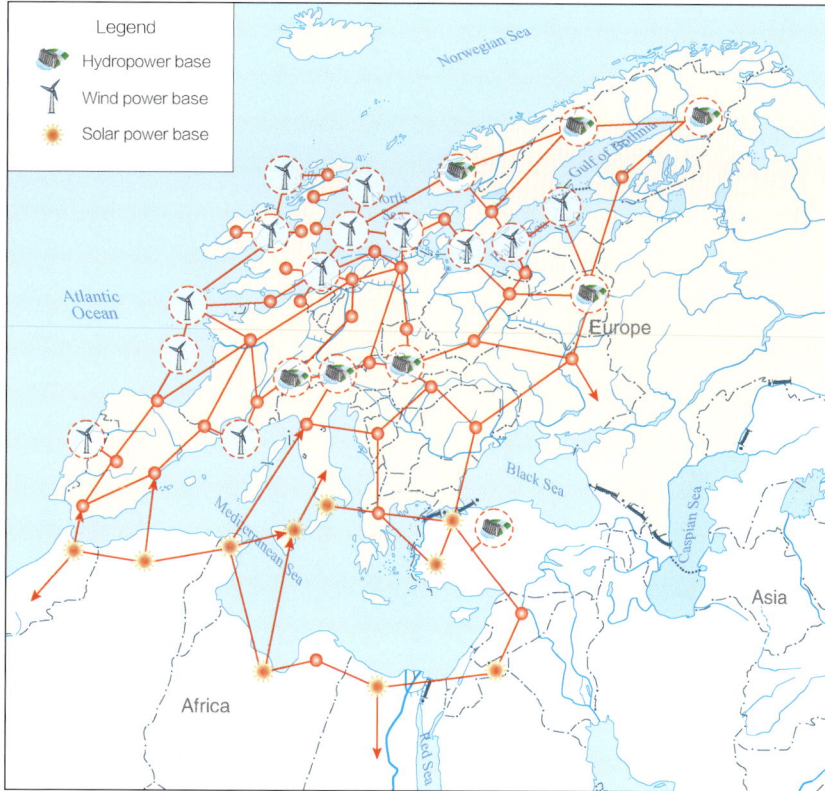

Figure 3-32 | Ilustration of the European Super Grid concept (Friends of the Supergrid)

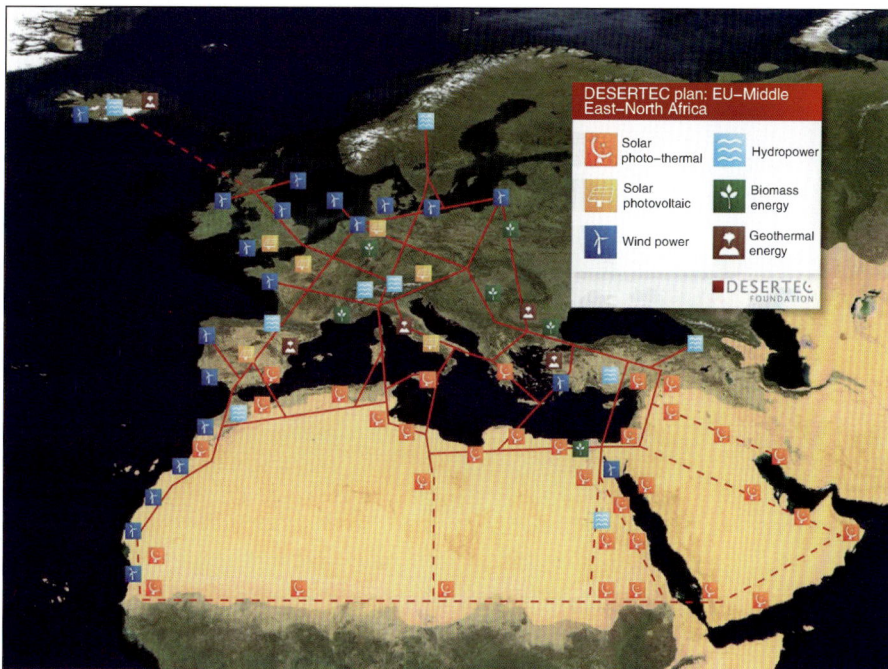

Figure 3-33 | An illustration of the Desertec concept (Desertec Foundation)

and Europe (see Figure 3-34) and completion of pre-feasibility studies on the western and central corridors.

3.3.3.4 The Gobitec and the Asian Super Grid projects

First proposed in 1998, the Gobitec project and the Asian Super Grid (ASG) project aim to exploit the vast renewable energy resources of the Gobi and Taklamakan deserts and of the Russian Far East, for the purpose of transmitting large volumes of power to Northeast Asian load centres in China, South Korea and Japan. These projects have been discussed and studied since 1998. A vision of the ASG was provided in a 2014 report [12] authored by research and government institutions from Mongolia, Japan, Russia and South Korea (see Figure 3-35) [12].

Using UHVDC transmission as a backbone, the ASG would interconnect wind and solar power bases in the Gobi desert and hydropower plants in Irkutsk, Russia with load centres in Beijing, Shanghai, Seoul and Tokyo. Despite the significant political, legal, institutional and financial challenges involved, organizations such as the Asian Development Bank and the SGCC are now supporting further studies.

3.4 Economic feasibility of GEI

As stated earlier in this White Paper, generally speaking, power system interconnection between

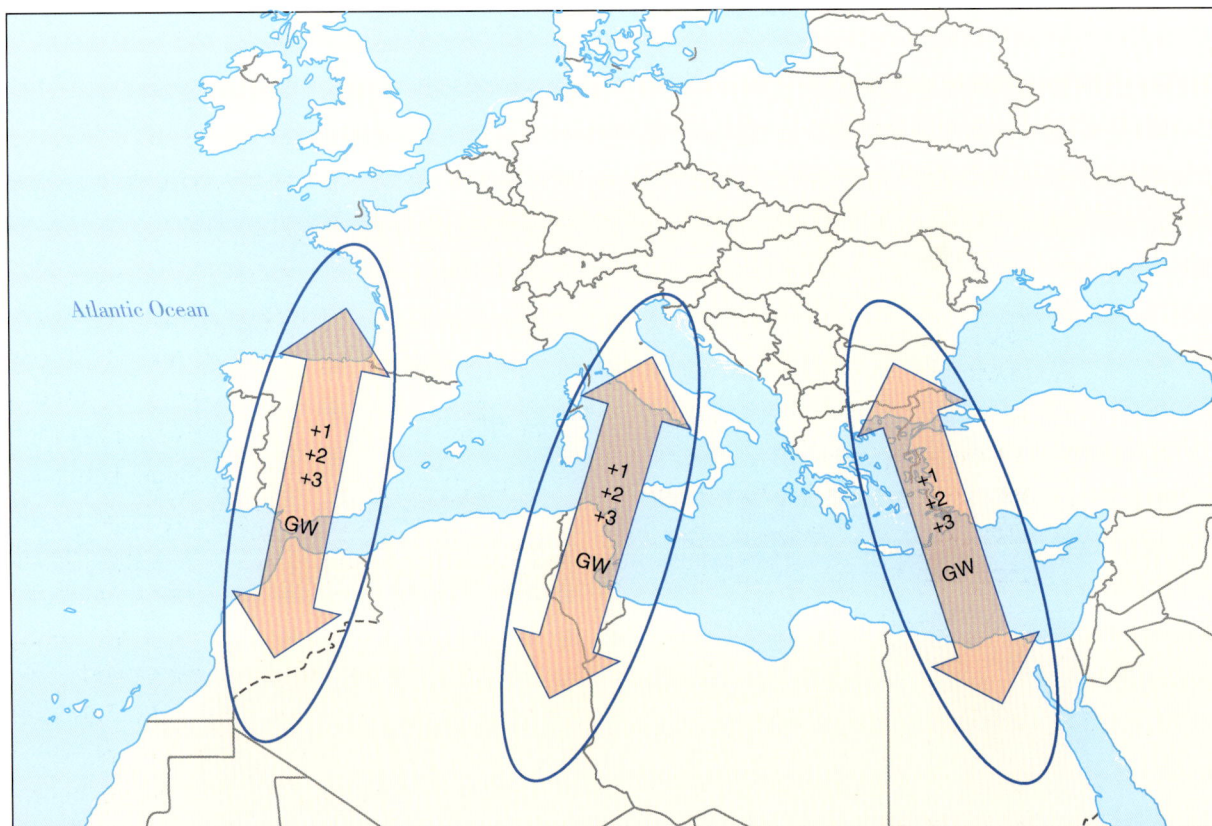

Figure 3-34 | Potential transmission corridors between North Africa and Europe (Medgrid)

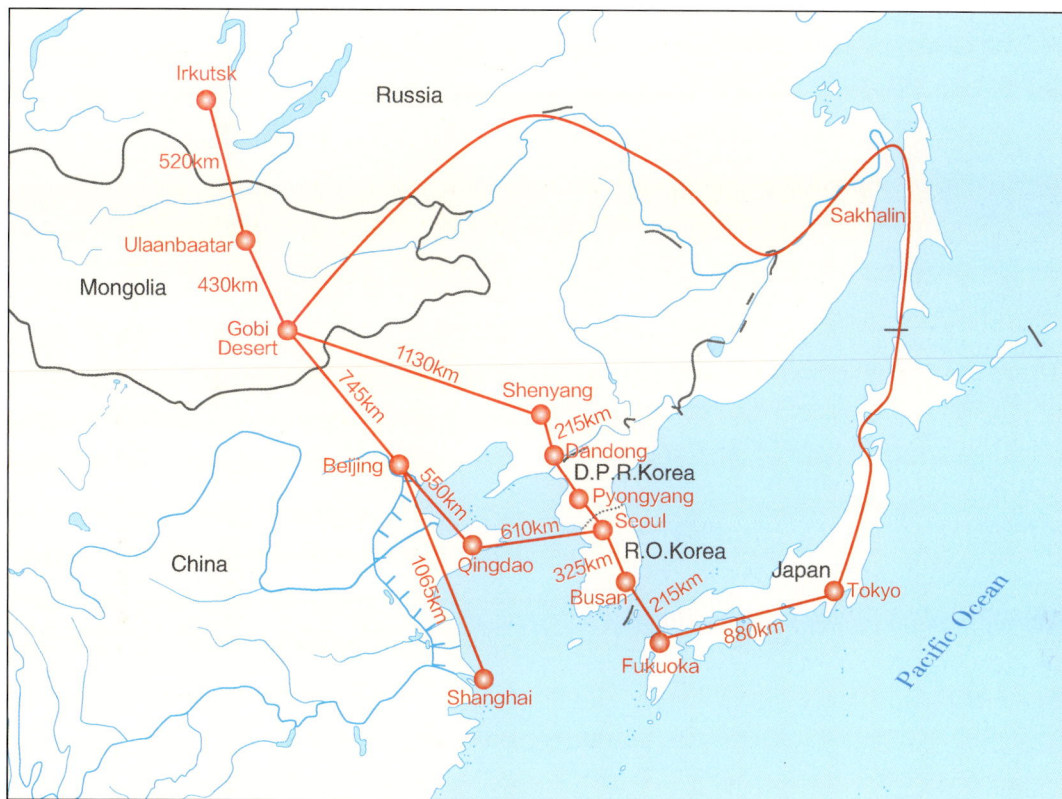

Figure 3-35 | A vision of the Asian Super Grid [12]

countries can be an attractive proposition to enhance system security and reliability, aid in balancing and ensuring resource adequacy, increase asset utilization and reduce costs, and facilitate the decarbonization of power systems. The need for careful assessment of the costs and benefits a ssociated with new transmission lines requires the application of a rigorous approach to cost-benefit analysis (CBA). With the interconnection of larger areas, as envisaged in GEI, proposals have become more complex from a regulatory, political and economic standpoint.

The economic benefits targeted in an interconnection proposal may include, among others, shared reserves, higher reliability and supply security, enhanced competition, production and operational cost savings, capacity savings due to capacity requirements, recovery of (partly) stranded investments, environmental impact

reductions, such as lower carbon emissions, and lower congestion costs.

Balancing the benefits referred to above are the direct costs of the proposal, including investment costs related to the assets injected, and indirect costs, including the social and environmental costs generated by the transmission investment. An important change that interconnection brings relates to the price differentials between two regions, which might have differing benefits and cost sharing issues. The interconnection might bring benefits to generators in a region with a lower price, as the larger interconnected region will command higher electricity prices. This might in turn crowd some generators in the region with a higher electricity price. Provided there is sufficient network capacity, this supply change will lead to the alignment of prices between the regions. Consumers will benefit or be penalized accordingly, in the opposite direction. Ultimately, only when the benefits accrued by realizing the interconnection outweigh the costs will the undertaking be economically justified.

Two principles are fundamental for new network investments:

- Net benefit assessments, comprising both benefits and costs, should generally recognize full-scale market impacts of new investments

- Ex ante investment cost allocation commensurate with identified beneficiaries can mitigate financing uncertainties and enhance project acceptance

The inclusion of CBA in the planning framework can facilitate transparency and consultation among all market players, which is likely to result in mutually acceptable assumptions on important factors that trigger future costs and benefits. The coordinated development of such assumptions on future conditions is essential, as any investment planning can only be based upon expected developments. Such assumptions should also be accompanied by risk assessments, as uncertainties in the assumptions can alter benefits. Risks can generally be regarded as price risks and/or quantity risks for all relevant assumptions such as demand, fuel sources or supply capacities. The projection of benefits into the distant future increases the level of uncertainty, as is the case with GEI. Applying such a long-term planning time frame over such large areas will inevitably increase planning uncertainties, creating the risk of under- or overestimated benefits. The inclusion of adequate measures to assess long-term benefits and risks in economic planning principles is necessary.

Section 4

Enabling technologies for GEI

A series of enabling technologies are required for the levels of electricity interconnection envisaged in the GEI concept. These technologies are examined in this section. The description of enabling grid technologies sets the stage for the discussion of standardization needs in Section 5.

4.1 Transmission technologies

4.1.1 UHV transmission technologies

4.1.1.1 UHVAC transmission

UHVAC is one of two key options for transmitting power over vast distances, and refers to AC transmission technologies with rated voltage of 1 000 kV and above. UHVAC is already a mature technology today, having begun development as early as the 1960s in parallel in the former Soviet Union, the US, Japan and Italy [7]. The world's first UHVAC project, the 495 km-long Ekibastuz to Kokchetav line, began trial operations in 1985. In China, research into UHVAC started in 1986. In 2006, SGCC began implementation of a 1 000 kV UHVAC pilot project, a 640 km-long single-circuit line linking the North China grid with the Central China grid, commissioned in 2009 and re-inforced in 2011 to reach a power transmission capacity of 5 GW [13]. Lessons learned from the pilot led to the commissioning of two other 1 000 kV UHVAC projects in East China, with four others under construction.

Relative to lower voltage level AC transmission technology, UHVAC can transmit higher volumes of power over much longer distances at lower unit losses, footprint and costs. A brief comparison between the technicalan deconomic features of 1 000 kV and 500 kV AC transmission is provided in Figure 4-1 [14].

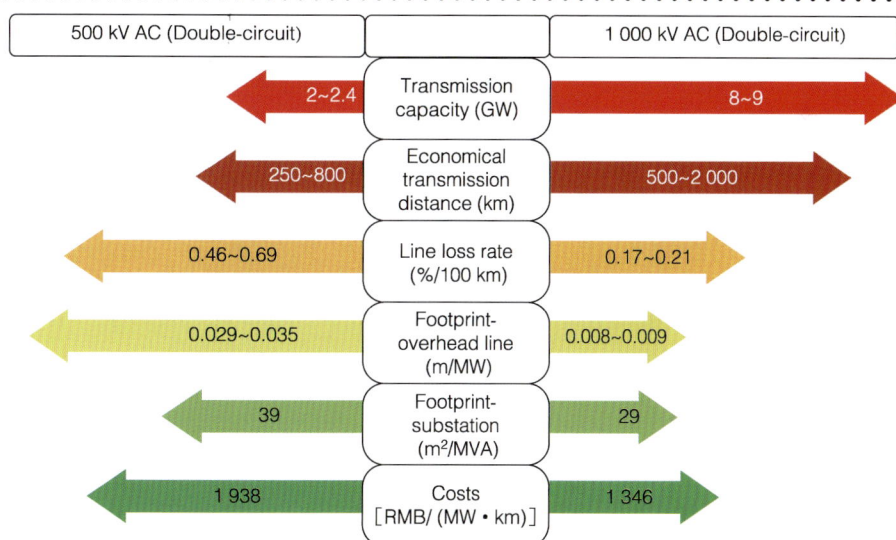

500 kV AC (Double-circuit)		1 000 kV AC (Double-circuit)
2~2.4	Transmission capacity (GW)	8~9
250~800	Economical transmission distance (km)	500~2 000
0.46~0.69	Line loss rate (%/100 km)	0.17~0.21
0.029~0.035	Footprint-overhead line (m/MW)	0.008~0.009
39	Footprint-substation (m²/MVA)	29
1 938	Costs [RMB/ (MW · km)]	1 346

Figure 4-1 | Feature comparison between 500 kV and 1 000 kV AC transmission (SGCC)

4.1.1.2 UHVDC transmission

UHVDC is the second option for shifting large volumes of electrical energy over long distances, and refers to DC transmission technologies with a rated voltage of ±800 kV and above. Currently one variety of the technology, line-commutated converter-based high-voltage DC (LCC-HVDC), also known as current-source converter based HVDC (CSC-HVDC) can reach ultra-high voltage levels. LCC-HVDC technology is a mature technology, having been deployed commercially for the first time in 1954. It is currently the option for long-distance, large-capacity, point-to-point power transmission as well as for connecting AC grids with different system frequencies. Relative to classical AC transmission, it affords advantages such as reduced losses, lower costs, smaller footprint, or better controllability. In large emerging countries such as Brazil, China, India, and South Africa, where much power infrastructure remains to be built and there is a need for very large-capacity power transmission over very long distances,

UHVDC transmission has been planned or deployed to a high degree in recent years.

The majority of UHVDC projects currently in operation and under construction around the world are being developed in China. Their main purpose is to transmit power generated in Northern and Western China to load centres in Central China and along the Chinese coast. SGCC currently operates four ±800 kV UHVDC projects, with five others under construction, while China Southern Power Grid (CSPG) manages two ±800 kV UHVDC projects already in operation, and one under construction. The transmission distance of these ±800 kV UHVDC projects ranges from 1 100 km to 2 400 km. In January 2016, SGCC began construction of the world's first ±1 100 kV UHVDC project, with a transmission distance of 3 324 km and a rated power of 12 GW.

A brief comparison of technical and economic features between UHVDC and ±500 kV HVDC transmission technology is provided in Figure 4-2 [14]. Over long distances, UHVDC can

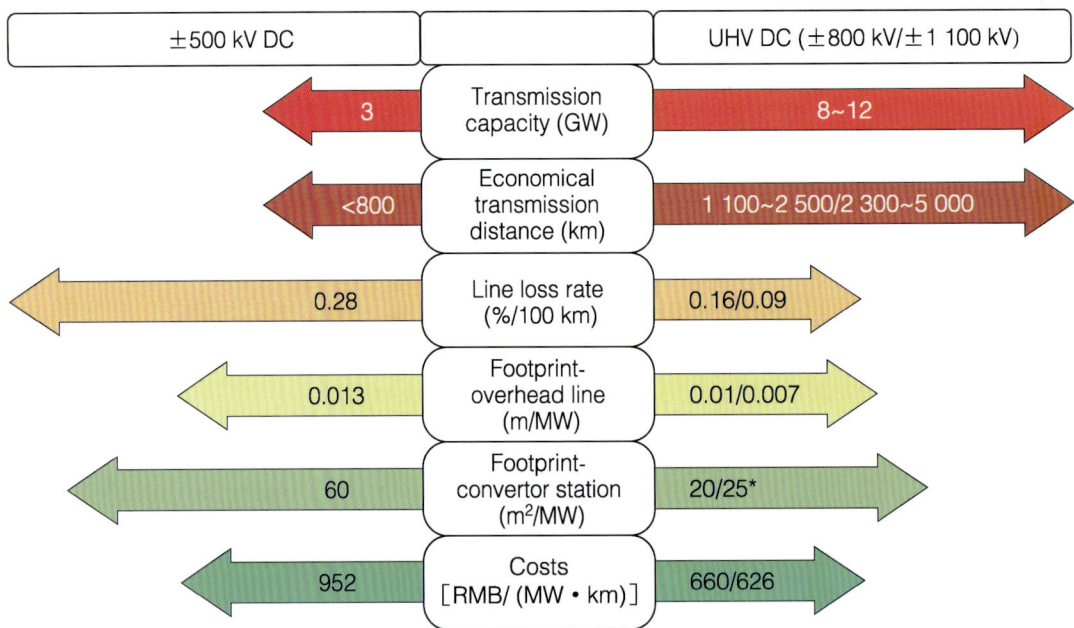

* The convertor station is connected to the AC system in two voltage levels.

Figure 4-2 | Feature comparison between 500 kV and 1 000 kV AC transmission (SGCC)

transmit much larger amounts of power at lower transmission losses, with reduced footprint and costs, when compared to lower voltage HVDC. Crucially, with current ±800 kV and ±1 100 kV UHVDC technology, transmitting power can become economical at distances of 2 500 km and 5 000 km respectively.

4.1.1.3 UHV transmission for GEI

Current UHV transmission technology can already be deployed to build the backbone grids for large-scale interconnected regional and transnational power grids, and eventually for GEI. As portrayed in Table 4-1 [7], distances between some major global energy bases and load centres range from 2 000 km to 5 000 km, within the transmission distance that can be economically feasible for UHV. UHVAC or UHVDC assets at different voltages could be deployed for different purposes and different transmission distances. For example, UHVAC grids would preferably be used to collect power on the supply side, or to deliver power on the demand side, while UHVDC could be used for point-to-point power transmission. Beyond the 5 000 km mark, power could potentially be transmitted using ±1 500 kV UHVDC technology, currently in the demonstration phase.

4.1.2 Flexible AC/DC transmission

4.1.2.1 Flexible AC transmission

Based on advanced, large-capacity power electronics components and innovative control strategies, various flexible AC transmission systems (FACTSs) have been developed since the 1990s. These have greatly improved the controllability, flexibility, stability and capacity of AC transmission. FACTS are also helpful in variable RE integration for voltage and power flow control.

4.1.2.2 VSC HVDC and HVDC grids

Voltage-source converter-based HVDC (VSC-HVDC) and HVDC grids are a fundamental component of modern power system interconnections, and would form a key pillar of future regional and transnational grids. Unlike conventional LCC-HVDC (CSC-HVDC), which uses semi-controllable valves, VSC-HVDC, a newer alternative first commercialized in 1997 [15], uses fully controllable valves. Compared to LCC-HVDC, these characteristics offer the following advantages:

- VSC-HVDC permits quick control of both active and reactive power independently, and even black starts. Therefore it does not rely on

Table 4-1 | Distance from selected major renewable resource bases to load centres [7]

From	To	Distance (km)
Arctic Kara Sea (wind power)	North China	4 400
Bering Strait (wind power)	N. China, Japan, S. Korea	5 000
Bering Strait (wind power)	West US	4 000
Arctic Greenland (wind power)	North UK	2 100
Arctic Greenland (wind power)	Quebec Canada	2 000
North Africa (solar power)	Europe	<2 000
Middle East (solar power)	West India	4 000

the strength of the AC system to which it is connected and can provide dynamic reactive power and voltage support for the AC system rather than consuming a large amount of reactive power. This feature is also desirable for integrating remote renewable generation, especially for offshore wind power integration.

- It simplifies the design of equipment on both sides of the connection, namely the converter transformers, and reduces the complexity and size of converter stations. See Figure 4-3 and Figure 4-4 for configurations of LCC- and VSC-HVDC converter stations.

- Power flows are easy to reverse, and they are not susceptible to commutation failures. This makes the technology suitable for forming multi-terminal HVDC (MTDC) and HVDC grids, which is difficult or impractical with conventional LCC-HVDC technologies.

Dozens of VSC-HVDC projects are in operation, in construction or in the planning stage, mainly in Europe, China and the US. They are implemented for different purposes, including grid interconnection, offshore wind power integration, as well as power supply to offshore oil or gas platforms and to large cities. Key examples include the ±320 kV/2 x 1 000 MW link between France and Spain, the ±500 kV/2 x 600 MW link between Italy and France, a number of links delivering North Sea offshore wind power to Northern Europe, the ±200 kV/400 MW Transbay project in the US, and the ±320 kV/1 000 MW real bi-polar project commissioned in Xiamen, China in 2015 [8],[16],[17],[18].

The voltage and power ratings of VSC-HVDC are still relatively low as compared to LCC-HVDC due to the limited availability and high cost of valves and cables. Currently available maximum voltage and power ratings for VSC-HVDC are 500 kV and 2 GW [19], but they are expected to increase steadily.

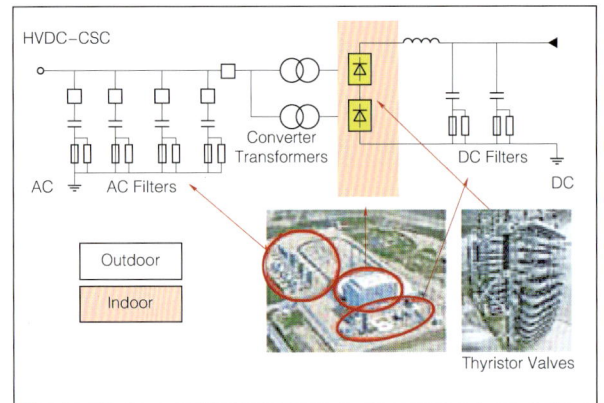

Figure 4-3 | Configuration of a conventional LCC-HVDC converter station [20]

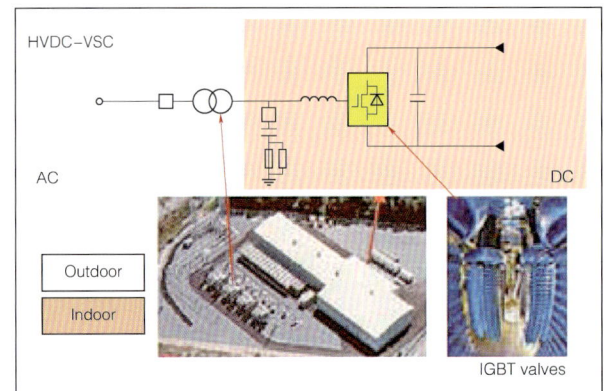

Figure 4-4 | Configuration of a VSC-HVDC converter station [20]

HVDC grids are a key element of large-scale, regional and eventually global energy interconnection. Building on the improvements of VSC-HVDC technologies, HVDC grids have been envisioned and intensively studied [21]. A HVDC grid consists of at least three converter stations and includes at least one mesh formed by transmission lines. It may also include a HVDC switching station to enable grid reconfiguration. The technical feasibility of HVDC grids has been established, although challenges remain, including adequate protection, control and grid simulation, and may be in many cases more cost-effective than point-to-point HVDC schemes for integrating disperse variable RE sources. In practice, HVDC grids can be formed by gradually expanding MTDC schemes, i.e. HVDC schemes with more than two converters connected together [17].

In Europe, the Super Grid, Desertec and Medgrid concepts and initiatives proposed for integrating North Sea offshore wind power and North African and Mediterranean solar power into the European grids, all rely on the implementation of HVDC grids. In the US, a submarine interconnector from New Jersey to Maryland and Delaware connecting multiple offshore wind farms has also been proposed [17]. Finally, in China the world's first and second VSC-MTDC projects have been commissioned, namely the three-terminal Nan'ao offshore wind power integration project commissioned in 2013 in the Southern coastal Guangdong Province [22], and the 5-terminal Zhoushan Islands interconnection project (see Figure 4-5) commissioned in 2014 in the Eastern coastal Zhejiang Province [23]. HVDC grids for

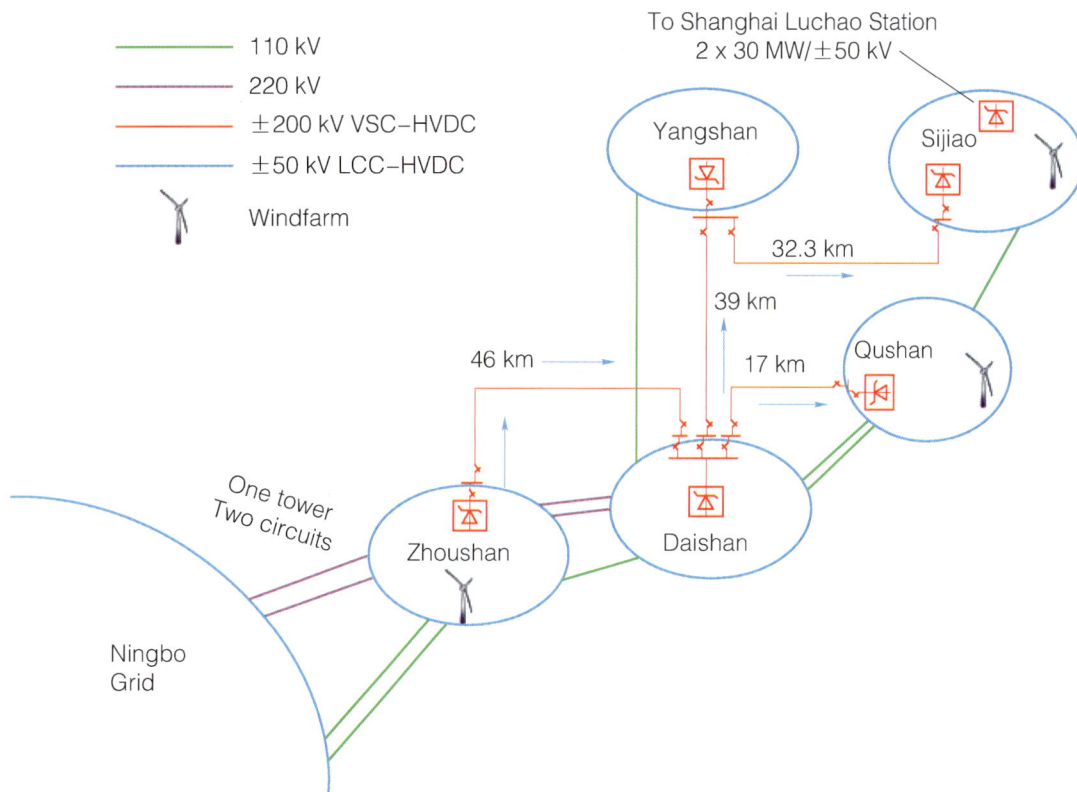

Figure 4-5 | Configuration of the Zhoushan MTDC [23]

integration of RE sources in wide areas of West and North China are also under study [24].

Continued development of VSC-HVDC and HVDC grid technologies will make large-scale grid interconnection and regional, transcontinental and global energy interconnection more feasible and efficient in integrating RE bases spanning large geographical areas.

4.1.3   Other emerging technologies

4.1.3.1 Half-wavelength AC transmission

Half-wavelength AC transmission (HWACT) is a promising technology under development for long-distance, high-capacity power transmission. Its name refers to three-phase AC transmission over a distance close to half of the length of a power frequency wave, which is 3 000 km for 50 Hz and 2 500 km for 60 Hz [25]. The concept of HWACT was first proposed in the 1940s by former Soviet Union scholars for transmitting thermal power in Kazakhstan and hydropower in Siberia to western load centres. During the first decade of the 21st Century interest in HWACT has been renewed and CIGRE working group A3.13 has been set up to carry out feasibility studies.

UHV-HWACT can be a practical and economical alternative to UHVDC for large-capacity power transmission over distances of 3 000 km or multiples of 3 000 km (in the case of 50 Hz system frequencies), and demonstrations of this technology are under way. Such technologies can play a key role in transnational, transcontinental grid interconnection and ultimately the realization of GEI [25].

4.1.3.2 High-temperature superconducting transmission

High-temperature superconducting (HTS) transmission refers to power transmission over high-temperature (defined as–180°C and above) superconducting cables. Theoretically, HTS trans-

mission can offer vast advantages over classical power transmission, including the following features [26] that are very desirable for large-scale interconnection and GEI:

- Very large transmission capacity: a ±800 kV HTS UHVDC line can transmit 16~80 GW, i.e. about 2~10 times that of a current conventional UHVDC

- Very low power losses: about 25%~50% of the loss of conventional cables

- Lower spatial footprint and lighter weight, as well as flexibility in changing transmission capacity by regulating temperature and limiting fault current through phase changing

Despite its technical advantages, progress in HTS physics and materials is required before HTS transmission can be used in practical power transmission projects and play a role in power system interconnection and GEI in the long term. Intensive research, development and demonstration of HTS cables, first focused on AC cables then shifting towards DC cables, have been carried out since the 1990s, mainly in the US, Europe, Japan, South Korea and China [26]. The length and voltage and power ratings of these cables are still very low. For AC cables, the length ranges from 30 m to 1 000 m, with voltage rating ranging from 10 kV to 138 kV. For DC cables, the length ranges from 200 m to 2 500 m and voltage rating ranges from ±1,3 kV to ±80 kV.

4.2   Smart Grid technologies

4.2.1   Large grid operation and control technologies

Beyond physical power system assets and technologies, transmitting power over regions and continents, in areas as large as those envisaged within the GEI concept requires advances in the operation, monitoring and control of large grids.

4.2.1.1 Control and protection of large-scale grids

Traditionally, power system monitoring and control has been mainly based on supervisory control and data acquisition/energy management system (SCADA/EMS) systems and protection has relied on local measurements to detect faults and abnormal states. SCADA/EMS systems allow measurements of voltage, frequency, power and status of circuit breakers/switches to be collected by field terminal units (FTUs) and sent to control centres, where the necessary technical properties can be calculated through state estimation. A major drawback of SCADA/EMS systems is that the gathered data is not time-synchronized, meaning that state estimations may differ between measurements.

Supported by satellite navigation systems, phasor measurement units (PMUs) can directly record timely synchronized voltage magnitudes and phase angle measurements of buses and send them to control centres, which enables the transition from "state estimation" to "state measurements" [27]. Many applications have been developed based on PMU networks, which are called wide area monitoring systems (WAMSs) [28], including wide-area visualization, oscillation detection and damping control, generator model and parameter validation, island detection, voltage instability monitoring, post-event analysis, or wide-area protection, among others applications, which have significantly improved the control and protection level of large grids. Future PMU/WAMS application trends include developing high-precision PMUs, switching from offline to online and from monitoring to control, and combining PMU/WAMS technology with big data technology [29]. In the context of GEI, PMU/WAMS technology is expected to play a fundamental role (see Figure 4-6).

Based on technology innovations such as online fault monitoring and diagnosis, new types of relay protection and wide-area backup protection, fault recovery strategy optimization and smart reconfiguration, power grids of the future could possess a strong security, stability and self-recovery capability in the face of different operating

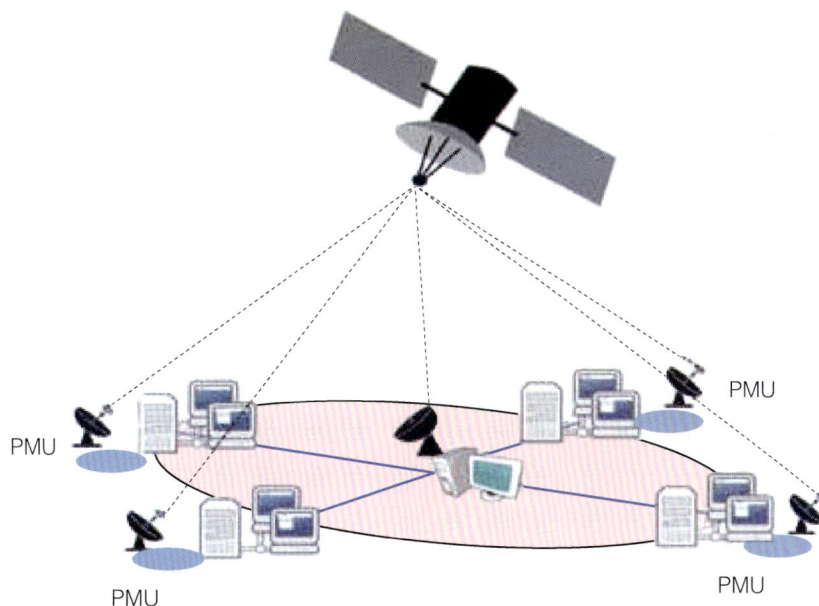

Figure 4-6 | Illustration of a PMU/WAMS system

environments and different types of faults. These technologies can greatly improve the defense capability of large grids against cascading faults, extreme weather conditions, and harmful external elements. With the development of ICT and control theory, grid operation and control is gradually moving in the direction of forecasting, pre-warning and automatic fault recovery. Highly automated operational control, expected to materialize in the medium-term, can support day-ahead forecasts for renewable power generation within a small (i.e. 5%) margin of error and help achieve a low cost integration of renewables, traditional energy and loads [7].

4.2.1.2 Large grid simulation and analysis

Since it is impossible to run experiments involving disturbances or faults on an actual running power grid, simulation and the analysis of simulation results are indispensable to explore the characteristics of a given power grid. With the continuous upgrade of algorithms, models and computer hardware and software, simulation has played a key role in guaranteeing the secure and stable operation of power grids as their technology has evolved over time.

The growth of the grid scale that comes with large-scale interconnection imposes ever-higher requirements on the timeliness of grid operation analysis and decision-making. In the early days, power system analysis was based on offline simulations due to the constraints of computer technology. However, with the progress of ICT technology, an increasing number of simulations can be performed online, which has enabled online dynamic security assessment and pre-warning. Through online transient stability analyses, one can not only assess the current level of grid security, but also help the power system dispatchers develop preventive control

strategies to improve grid security. Real-time[1] and even faster-than-real-time simulations have also been achieved for grids of a certain scale, which will further improve the operation and control level of large grids.

In the context of large-scale interconnection and GEI, the complexity of power system operation would be tremendously increased, which imposes much higher requirements on the precision, speed and efficiency of simulation and analysis. There is a need to improve simulation capacities using super-computing and hybrid electromechanical and electromagnetic transients simulation technologies to support the analysis of power systems with millions of buses. Accurate models of high penetrations of renewable generation plants, DC transmission and new types of grid control and protection elements need to be established. Hybrid digital and analogue simulation is also required, so that physical control and protection devices can be connected to digitalized system models in a hardware-in-the-loop manner in cases where accurate modelling is difficult (see Figure 4-7). In addition, management and sharing of global equipment and network data is necessary to support both centralized and distributed simulation and analysis.

4.2.2 Information and communication technologies (ICT)

The ambitious vision of a GEI network – which would equate to a global super-smart high-voltage grid – requires the deployment of sophisticated next generation ICT technology based on the most modern standards.

The operation of such an intelligent, complex technical network would require the efficient convergence of operational and commercial data/

---

1 A "real-time" simulation means that the time used in simulating a system event equals the time that the physical event lasts in the real world.

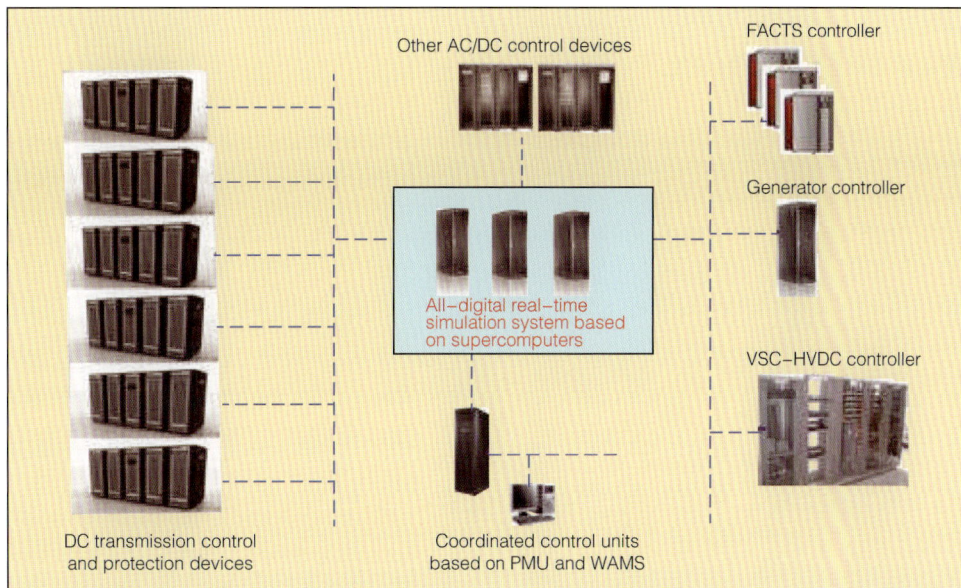

Figure 4-7 | Architecture of a hybrid digital and analogue simulation platform (SGCC)

processes to enable critical decisions and business transactions in real-time. This necessitates a new kind of technical platform that bridges the historic "Chinese Wall" between OT and IT systems in order to provide a platform adequate for transactions over such large areas.

This IT/OT integration platform will also be the technical application basis for comprehensive information systems that are necessary to manage the core processes of planning, operation and maintenance of the grid, metering, billing and settlement of energy flows and related services, and continuous process analysis in real-time to immediately identify technical and commercial issues such as technical losses, fraud, outage risks, etc.

This platform would also include automated data exchange between involved partner companies based on common market standards and processes, and orchestrating of an extended asset information and business network to optimize the collaboration with suppliers and market partners.

4.2.3 The need for an IT/OT integration platform

Existing IT landscapes are today made up of dozens if not hundreds of sometimes integrated, but in many cases also completely separated systems such as business and business intelligence (BI) systems, energy portfolio management and trading systems and operational systems such as SCADA, geographical information system (GIS), and network information systems and data historians. With the rapid increase in volume and granularity of data coming from the GEI Smart Grid, it is becoming more important for the affected TSOs to reduce the number of times this data is replicated in order to improve their analytical ability. It will not be economically feasible to continue replicating these big data volumes from one siloed system to another in a consistent way. In addition, most analytical and business processes will provide better results and deeper insights if they leverage an up-to-date, comprehensive and consistent data set.

In addition to the rising data volume, the time span between the moments when the data is measured and when it has to be made available to support business processes is growing shorter and shorter, and in many cases (near) real-time data will be required.

At a high level this leads to three important functions a TSO platform has to perform in the context of GEI:

- Handle both a steeply increasing volume of data and many different data types

- Combine data from various different sources and enable the integration of business and operational systems (IT/OT integration)

- Make the data available in (near) real-time

The following business processes represent examples of required functions for a TSO platform in the context of the GEI. These examples highlight some of the key requirements involved but by no means constitute an exhaustive list of all the business processes that have to be supported now.

- **Grid analytics** support near real-time analysis of the grid to improve grid stability and effectiveness and prevent outages. This requires correlation analysis, for example to understand under what circumstances specific equipment such as a transformer is overloaded, and forecasting capabilities to predict peak loads. The analytic results are required to trigger manual interactions or the intervention of other systems that actively control the grid assets.

  This process heavily relies on sensor and event data from the grid, however meter data is also required. The grid analytics solution provides most benefit if the data and analysis is available in near real-time, i.e. within a couple of minutes or even seconds after receiving the data, to enable rapid actions.

- **Predictive maintenance** estimates when a failure or decrease in efficiency of an asset is to be expected and triggers maintenance actions accordingly. This is based on meter and sensor data as well as on historic values. In general, predictive maintenance is of interest for grids and power plants, but especially for assets in remote locations such as offshore wind power plants and secluded transmission facilities.

  Data requirements are similar to those of the grid infrastructure analytics process, however data would not be required in real-time but rather on a daily basis. Unstructured data, for example texts from work orders or customer messages, can support this process as well.

- **Leakage management** supports processes such as fraud management and an early detection of technical losses. It contributes to determining where losses occur and whether fraud could be the cause and acts as a starting point for follow-up processes. It also has a safety aspect.

  In addition to meter, asset and GIS data, forecasted consumption data, event data and customer data from the customer relationship management (CRM) and billing system are required to support these processes. Unstructured data, for example from social media platforms, can also be leveraged to detect possible fraud. While a daily data upload would be sufficient for fraud management, detection of technical losses benefits from real-time data.

- **Energy settlement** aggregates metered data for a group of delivery points over a certain time period as a basis for the commercial settlement of transmission services. This information can then be sent via market messages to each of the participants in the operational area for further processing.

The above-mentioned business processes and the respective applications would benefit from a single platform that provides a unified data repository as well as generic tools and functions. The reason behind this is that business processes would then operate on comprehensive, consistent and actual data, thus reducing the need for data replication. Applications would benefit from generic functions that do not have to be redeveloped repeatedly in each siloed application. Moreover integration between different applications would be simplified, as less data exchange and fewer interfaces would be required.

The overall total costs of such a platform, including applications on top of it that reuse many generic functions, is expected to be much lower than the total costs of a system landscape involving several different products, each with its own data tables, tools and technology. Costs would be lower, for example due to the reduced effort needed to replicate data, cleanse it and keep data consistent.

To fulfil all these requirements, a TSO platform would need to support the business processes outlined above and to provide functions in support of heterogeneous applications.

Such a platform therefore would need to be able to:

- rapidly upload different types of data in high volumes;

- process different kind of data from various sources, including data from meters and sensors, event data and geographical data, as well as prices, weather data and more;

- enable data uploads at different frequencies, from monthly to sub-daily (down to real-time);

- handle data that comes in any granularity from monthly values down to minutes or even seconds;

- handle equidistant time intervals and non-equidistant (discrete) values;

- handle unstructured data.

Beyond uploading and storing the data, the platform would also need to be able to:

- validate, estimate and edit data;

- store versions of the data if it is changed;

- support auditability, for example when reports have to be delivered due to regulatory rules;

- store data for periods longer than one year and support data aging.

In addition the platform would need to support generic functions that can then be used by all applications residing on the platform. These include:

- Calculation tools, for example to calculate consumptions out of raw data, replacement values, or energy consumption or generation costs

- An aggregation engine to aggregate data from several points of the network, for example all delivery points, that belong to one holding company, or all meters linked to one transformer. The data would be used for analysis and pattern recognition in business processes such as grid infrastructure analytics or fraud management

- Forecasting algorithms for maintenance and replacement strategies for assets

- Data mining tools to support data analysis, for example in predictive maintenance

- Complex event processing, as required in many business processes, for example outage management; the platform does not need to support the entire business process, but rather make analytic results available for respective systems

- Interfaces to external systems and data gathering from external data suppliers or from other GEI participants

To cope with those requirements, operators of large-scale energy networks and GEI would require an IT/OT integration platform, including a portfolio of products tightly optimized to work together to solve today's data management challenges. Such management elements include data processing across massive volumes of data storage, high velocity streaming data, automated data movement, and data visualization and further processing. These challenges include the ability to handle master data, information governance and information modelling. Today's requirements also involve supporting the vast variety of data types, including structured data, semi-structured (or text-based) data, as well as unstructured big-data such as image, audio and video. The combination of Hadoop® Distributed File System and Hadoop® MapReduce framework is emerging as a standard for very large unstructured data-pre-processing and processing.

The IT/OT platform will need to address all these data management challenges from the ground up, with proven ability to scale. It has to include capabilities that provide organizations with a robust, yet flexible environment for managing their data needs, including online transactional processing, data processing and analysis, data modelling and movement, information governance as well as a unified administration and monitoring tools. Among other elements, the portfolio or products inside the IT/OT platform need to include:

- An in-memory computing platform that provides in-memory online transaction processing (OLTP) and analytical capabilities with the ability to embed code libraries and advanced and statistical algorithms close to the data

- Classical database technology to augment and complement in-memory requirements for better economics and price/performance requirements, especially critical as more customers scale into Petabyte class data volumes. It features a native MapReduce framework and provides integration techniques with Hadoop® for big-data analytics

- Event streaming processing capabilities for high speed streaming data analysis and filtering for ultra-low latency applications enabling continuous intelligence

- Extended data security components with most progressive security protocols and data encryption capabilities to safeguard mission-critical technical data and to avoid any intrusion

In addition to that, the IT/OT integration platform will need to provide tools for data modelling and data movement and a development framework for partners and customers who can build their own applications on the same platform.

All components of the IT/OT integration platform will have to be open for integration with third party tools, for example to support business intelligence, information management, or infrastructure management.

The realization of such a platform requires the merging of commercial enterprise resource planning (ERP) systems with technical applications such as meter data management (MDM), SCADA and document management system (DMS). Figure 4-8 illustrates the conceptual architecture of such an IT/OT platform as envisioned by SAP. The data integration of SAP's commercial MDM application with the technical head-end system (HES) from a partner on a common, cloud-ready in-memory capable platform (the SAP HANA Cloud Platform) connects business transactions with technical mass data in real-time and enables the introduction of fundamentally new processes, such as real-time forecasting of transmission loads, etc.

4.2.4 Advanced planning, operation and maintenance of the grid with Asset Intelligence Networks

The effective and secure management of technical assets has been a core requirement of the energy

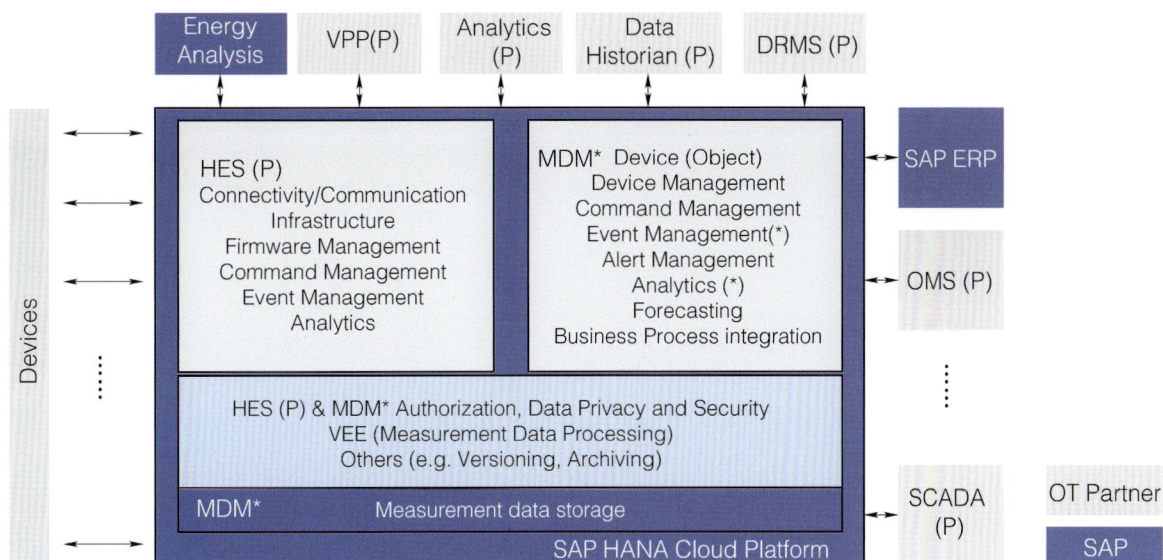

Figure 4-8 | The concept of an integrated IT/OT Platform (SAP)

industry since the beginning. Hence there are various proven IT solutions on the market which very effectively support the planning, operation and maintenance of power grids.

However, some of the specific needs of a TSO who would operate within a complex GEI framework require more intelligent and interconnected asset management processes. A key requirement for a sustainable GEI will be the standardization of asset management processes around the world to leverage best practices and to enable the international collaboration of TSOs ensuring the reliable transmission of energy across country borders. The importance of those Standards has already been described comprehensively in the IEC Whitepaper *Strategic asset management of power networks*.

Today, the industry has not yet fully integrated the asset management chain. There is little consistent definition of model information, and every original equipment manufacturer (OEM) and operator typically uploads the same data manually – possibly introducing errors and delays

that make the data incorrect. Lack of complete, consistent, consumable equipment data hampers future purchasing and maintenance decisions. Business processes for asset management are rarely integrated across enterprise boundaries, a deficiency which helps keep everyone in the dark. But the realization of a GEI will only succeed with a collaborative, efficient management of technical assets and processes based on common Standards. This requires the introduction of an integrated Asset Intelligence Network (AIN).

The transition to the digital economy and the increasing adoption of new technologies such as IoT and cloud-based networks provide an opportunity to automate data exchange and enable a simplified collaboration model among involved stakeholders via asset management networks. An AIN, as conceptualized in Figure 4-9, could answer the above described challenges by providing a secure cloud platform that serves as a central clearing house and communications hub for all stakeholders in GEI asset management.

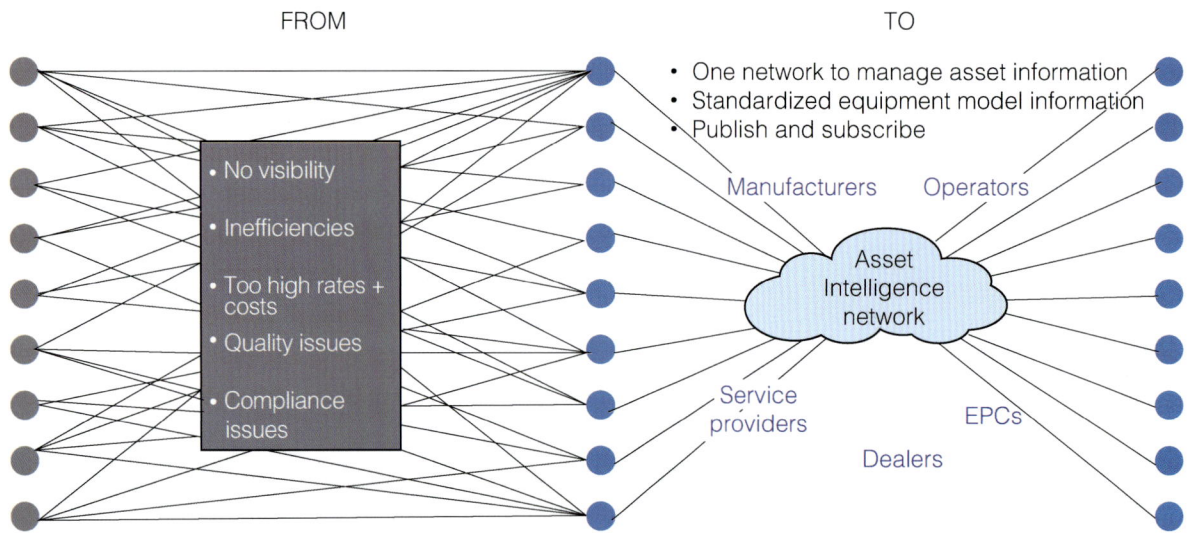

Figure 4-9 | The concept of an AIN connects assets and businesses everywhere in one seamless network (SAP)

Such an AIN will bring business partners together in a common environment to facilitate the next wave of collaboration among organizations within the asset management ecosystem, i.e. operators, OEMs, EPCs, and service providers. It is a single cloud-based IoT linking all the equipment in an ecosystem. A host of applications runs on this collaborative platform to simplify maintenance and enhance cooperation for complex tasks. Built-in analysis inspires innovation for managing assets as a service or redesigning them based on performance (see Table 4-2).

The equipment in the AIN should be based on standardized models (e.g. on API 610 datasheet for pumps) furnished by OEMs or third-party content providers. These datasheets for models will provide technical attributes about equipment and content, such as recommended maintenance strategies, standard job instructions, bills of materials, spare parts lists, drawings, etc. Manufacturers will only have to provide the datasheet once, and it will then be available for consumption by all approved business partners. Moreover, operators

will have a single site from which to retrieve consistent datasheets from multiple manufacturers ready for use in their environmental assessment and management (EAM) environments.

The AIN could provide a number of benefits to all involved GEI stakeholders (see Figure 4-10).

4.2.4.1 Global job catalogue, visual work instructions, and task lists

The AIN enables operators to build a global library of recommended maintenance strategies, maintenance plans, standard jobs and safety instructions for use in their work management system. OEMs will publish recommended maintenance strategies, maintenance plans and standard jobs as part of the model information.

4.2.4.2 Business context for predictive maintenance

The AIN provides the business context for predictive maintenance and service, whether

Table 4-2 | The vast potential of an AIN

Category	Value	Capability	Arena
Effective asset management processes	Increased revenues from faster project commissioning	Operators and contractors can source and validate missing asset information from the network	Standardized equipment management
	Reduced capital expenditure	Engineering teams can investigate alternatives and tighten production expenses	Collaborative network services
	Improved asset availability	Stakeholders can reduce asset downtime collaborating with OEMs and using updated information and predictive maintenance	Maintenance process execution Collaborative network services
	Reduced spare-parts inventory	Warehouses can reduce obsolete and excess inventory for B- and C-class spares per network updates	Maintenance process execution Standardized equipment management
	Lower maintenance costs	Operators can optimize maintenance activities through closer collaboration with OEMs and service providers	Maintenance process execution Collaborative network services
User productivity	Reduced effort locating and updating asset information	All members have access to updated information already integrated with enterprise systems	Standardized equipment management Collaborative network services
	Shorter maintenance wrench time	Field workers always have up-to-date task-time instructions and spare part details	Maintenance process execution Collaborative network services

an operator, manufacturer or service provider is monitoring and maintaining equipment. This will significantly improve the interaction between TSO and manufacturer by alerting the operator and manufacturer about imminent failure.

4.2.4.3 Performance improvements

The AIN provides the platform for OEMs, service providers and operators to increase collaboration on improving machine design to reduce failures, lower operating costs, improve ease of maintenance and ultimately increase profits. This is enabled by the flow of information about how the machine is being used, where it is installed, what failures have occurred, what service bulletins have applied, etc. and failure mode and effects analysis (FMEA) from the operator.

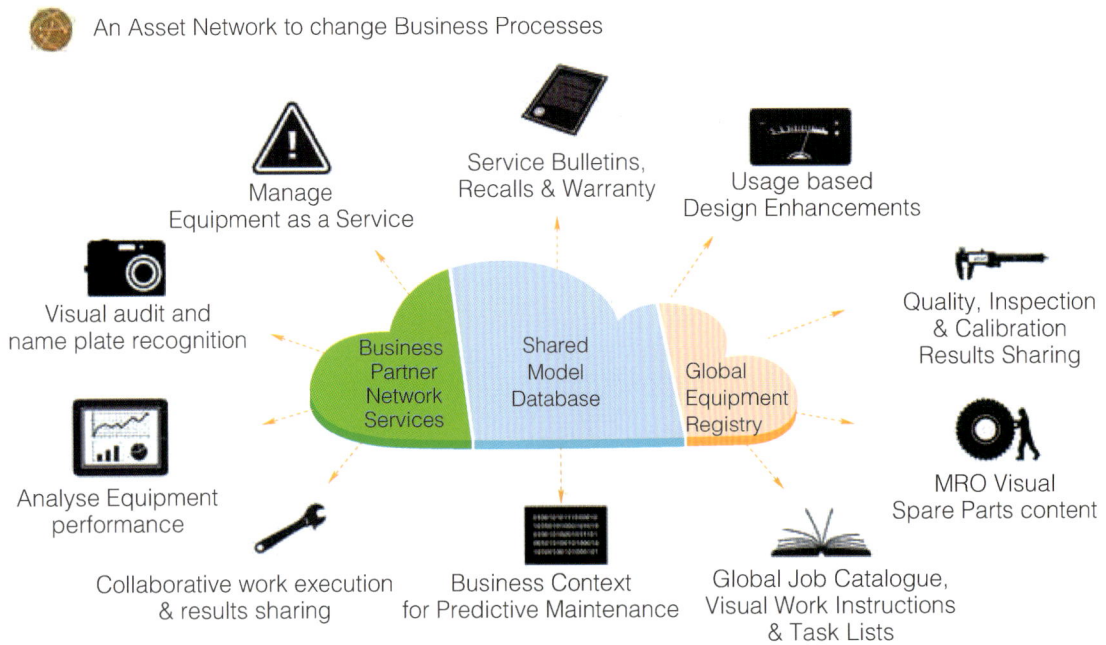

An Asset Network to change Business Processes

Figure 4-10 | Benefits of an AIN (SAP)

4.2.4.4 Integrated work planning and execution

The AIN facilitates collaborative maintenance activity between operators and service providers. Certain complex activities might need to be broken down into sequential steps, of which some are carried out by asset operators and more specialized ones by the service provider.

4.2.4.5 Manage equipment as a service

Operators want to minimize their capital expenditure and risks, whereas OEMs want to bundle value-added services with products. This convergence of requirements, along with new technologies such as the IoT and collaborative networks, is resulting in the new business model of managing equipment as a service.

4.2.4.6 Analyze equipment performance

The AIN helps operators drive asset improvement programmes by benchmarking reliability metrics from different operator sites that can be analyzed to identify best practice for operation and maintenance around the world. Depending on the requirements of the different parties supplying and consuming information, the information could be anonymized.

4.2.4.7 Marketplace of intelligence

Companies are capturing more and more information about their machines. And more advanced algorithms are possible to analyze data and make predictions and prognoses to improve machine performance. Is it still feasible or desirable that operators do all of this data processing themselves? Can manufacturers, service providers or even individuals provide more of this "intelligence" in a competitive marketplace where the best provider wins? An AIN could provide a marketplace where business partners can connect with other third parties to competitively source the best intelligence for their machines. With a solid foundation of asset information in the network, a new class of potential enterprise scale solutions becomes possible.

4.2.4.8 Quality, inspection, and calibration results sharing

The AIN facilitates sharing of quality, inspection, certification, and calibration results. Statutory authorities and independent assurance companies, e.g. Lloyds Register, DNV GL, and TüV, will have access (provided they are given the necessary authorization) to view up-to-date information on whether statutory inspections have been performed on time with the relevant inspection results. Another example is obtaining the results and reports of condition-based maintenance tasks, such as oil analysis of engines, which are typically sent to an external laboratory for analysis.

4.2.5 Metering, billing and settlement of energy flows and related services

Like any other transmission grid, a GEI would operate in a commercial framework that bills the recipient and/or the remitter of the transmitted energy for the transmission service. This requires the availability of specific customer information systems, which are able to manage typical industry-specific processes, including orchestration of meter data reading processes, acquisition and management of large amounts of meter reading data in time series (load profiles), performant and reliable charging of transmission services, etc.

There are several solutions on the market which can satisfactorily fulfil those business requirements. However, due to the increasing importance of settlement rules based on most granular data (e.g. prices based on minute intervals) and the related data growth, the ideal solution should be able to process information in real-time. This requires the usage of modern, in-memory-based applications, which allow much faster processing times for complex calculations with mass data. Such systems combine the transactional and analytical data processing in one database and eliminate typical time-consuming batch processes. Moreover, they allow sophisticated operation reporting activities in real-time based on most recent data.

4.2.6 GEI market communication platform

The GEI will operate as a network with many national TSOs. In order to ensure the reliable and sustainable transmission process across country or even continental borders, a highly automated data exchange process based on internationally agreed communication formats is mandatory. Typical data exchange processes include nomination of transmission capacities, transmission forecasts and schedules, exchange of technical data to support cross-border ancillary services, exchange of asset and operational data to optimize collaborative asset management processes, measurements as input for settlement of transmission services, or billing of transmission charges.

Various market communication standards are already available for TSOs that should be considered as a basis for the extended GEI market communication.

For example, the European Network of Transmission System Operators for Electricity (ENTSOE-E) maintains an Electronic Data Interchange (EDI) Library which contains all the documents and definitions approved by ENTSO-E for the harmonization and implementation of standardized electronic data interchanges.

In the context of a potential GEI market model, it should be discussed whether a centrally operated GEI market communication hub could help to increase the efficiency of the GEI processes. This could be a cloud-based service provided by an "IEC-like" organization, which centrally orchestrates the communication flows and the intercompany data exchange between all GEI participants. The necessary IT technologies for such platform are available and are already productive in various clearinghouse projects.

Section 5

Standardization for GEI

Standardization is of central importance and, at the same time, represents one of the biggest challenges for the success of GEI, which demands an unprecedented degree of system integration across sovereign borders, technical domain borders, hierarchical borders and equipment life cycle phases. To achieve this success, consensus-based Standards and Specifications will form an indispensable basis upon which to build.

Existing but also future consensus-based Standards will create a firm basis for technical procurement, support communication through standardized terminology and concepts, ensure interoperability, certify fitness for use, and determine market relevance. Drawing up GEI concepts at an early stage by a consensus-based standardization process and through close cooperation between researchers, industry, regulators and the standardization bodies is one of the central requirements for success of the multi-phased implementation of GEI.

To succeed, these principles should be consistent with existing standards that support the core GEI technologies, i.e. UHV, clean energy, and Smart Grids. Not only will this facilitate subsequent promotion and application of equipment, interfaces and technology, but it will also create conditions for building international-level interconnections among energy grids and related equipment.

5.1 Present situation

Standards currently exist that cover the foundational technical domains of GEI, representing UHV, clean energy and Smart Grid. These Standards are required for incorporating multiple technologies into parts of a very complicated, large-scale power and energy system that will interconnect not only physical infrastructures across large areas but also the supporting ICT systems. The Standards involved are related to many technical committees inside IEC and to other coordinating organizations outside IEC. The following is a list of current IEC technical committees (TCs) and subcommittees (SCs) handling specific activities that support GEI:

5.1.1 Transmission

- TC 7: Overhead electrical conductors
- TC 14: Power transformers
- SC 17A: Switching devices
- TC 20: Electric cables
- TC 28: Insulation co-ordination
- TC 36: Insulators
- TC 115: High Voltage Direct Current (HVDC) transmission for DC voltages above 100 kV
- TC 122: UHV AC transmission systems
- ACTAD: Advisory Committee on Electricity Transmission and Distribution

5.1.2 Clean energy – renewable generation and energy storage

- TC 4: Hydraulic turbines
- SC 8A: Grid integration of Renewable Energy generation
- TC 21: Secondary cells and batteries
- TC 82: Solar photovoltaic energy systems

- TC 88: Wind energy generation systems

- TC 114: Marine energy – Wave, tidal and other water current converters

- TC 117: Solar thermal electric plants

- TC 120: Electrical Energy Storage (EES) Systems

5.1.3 Smart Grids

- TC 8: Systems aspects for electrical energy supply

- TC 13: Electrical energy measurement and control

- TC 22: Power electronic systems and equipment

- TC 57: Power systems management and associated information exchange

- TC 64: Electrical installations and protection against electric shock

- TC 77: Electromagnetic compatibility

- PC 118: Smart Grid user interface

- SyC Smart Energy

- ISO/IEC JTC 1: Information technology

- CISPR: International Special Committee on Radio Interference

5.2 Future standardization needs

Development of global energy systems for GEI will provide a worldwide platform that enables new technologies to be used optimally for maximum performance and reliability. For example, the prospects for wind power are very positive: the IEA forecasts that installed onshore and offshore capacity will exceed 1 300 GW in 2040, with onshore capacity making up 85% of the total, against 98% in 2011. This expansion will require additional International Standards to cover new areas. The very nature of the RE technologies means that standardization requires a dedicated effort to keep pace with developments in the various fields.

Also, Smart Grids and energy storage are more than ever to be unified with electricity generation and distribution systems, regional energy hubs and long-range ultra-high voltage lines.

The biggest market trend for UHVAC is towards long-distance bulk power transmission and interconnection with existing power systems. There is also a trend towards building strong power reception grids to receive more large-scale power feed-in. The grid changes are driven by rapidly growing power consumption in load centres of emerging countries and by structural changes from coal, gas and nuclear power generation towards full renewable power generation involving wind, solar, large hydro and other energies at distant generation locations. With increasing renewable power generation, mainly from wind, large hydro and solar, electrical energy will be competitive with oil, gas and coal sources, but it will need new AC transportation systems to cope with projected needs.

With the growth of load demand and the imbalance between energy demand and supply, power plants are needed which will be located far from load centres (e.g. large hydropower and pit-mouth fossil-fired power stations), and clean and renewable distributed generation (e.g. wind power and solar power) will be introduced extensively. The former are characterized by large capacity and long distance and will enjoy remarkable advantages when employing HVDC transmission technology.

Construction of HVDC transmission systems in severe environmental conditions, such as building converter stations and DC transmission lines at a very high altitude (3 000 ~ 5 300 m), are posing higher requirements for the HVDC transmission technology.

Smart Grid implementation has already started and will continue to be implemented in the form of an "evolution" of successive projects over several decades.

It is now necessary to manage the integration of new equipment that has a lower life span than traditional network assets: three to five years for consumer electronics and telecommunications, compared to 40 plus years for lines, cables, and transformers.

The Smart Grid represents a technical challenge that goes far beyond the simple addition of an information technology infrastructure on top of an electrotechnical infrastructure. Each device that is connected to a Smart Grid is simultaneously an electrotechnical device and an intelligent node. Today's "connection" standards need to address both aspects concurrently.

Adopting advanced monitoring and control technologies is a key objective for future Smart Grids.

In order to support these future standardization needs for GEI, some important general considerations for standards are given below.

5.2.1 Systems standards

While smart energy activities will confront new issues and questions for GEI, new tools between standards developing organizations (SDOs) and stakeholders, such as creating use case repositories and system level standards, must be launched to bridge gaps between organizations working in totally different areas. Drafting of systems level standards will require understanding the interrelationship between other components from a physical/electrical point of view, as well as the flow of information with the grid network and changes in system behaviour.

From a conformity assessment perspective, understanding is also required of how the life of a standard evolves as changes occur at the component surroundings levels. Most importantly, system level standardization thinking for GEI is the understanding of the interrelation between the many systems-of-systems and the growing equipment assets that make up the GEI system.

In the IEC, a Systems Committee (SyC) Smart Energy has been set up to provide systems level standardization, coordination and guidance in the areas of Smart Grid and Smart Energy, including interactions with heat and gas. Key International Standards such as IEC 61850 have been introduced to ensure device and communication compatibility in substations, while IEC 61970 has been developed to define application programme interfaces for energy management systems. SyC Smart Energy has just begun its outreach to various internal and external stakeholders, but much work remains to be coordinated.

5.2.2 Management standards

Open data and data sharing facilitate data analytics and simulation, which provide the basis for planning, scheduling, operation and control. The large efficiency gains from integration and interoperability, however, are only realized if all the stakeholders collaborate effectively and agree to share data or information. Data aspects shall become a key issue in GEI, including data analytics, data utilization, data privacy and cyber security. The lack of exchange of fundamental data on customers, infrastructures and operations is one of the most important barriers highlighted by stakeholders. Specifications for data sharing and standards on data format are both needed. On the other hand, a series of management specifications or guidelines are also needed to guarantee the coordination in planning, trading and operation among all the participants.

Although many regional and national organizations, such as NERC, Nordel, UCTE, ENTSO-E and NGET, have their own reliability criteria, it is necessary to coordinate such criteria for the GEI.

For example, specifications are necessary for coordinating the control and protection strategy of interconnecting links and grid connection codes.

5.2.3 Standards for information exchange

Control, protection and scheduling for GEI depends upon effective information exchange based on appropriate ICT architectures. Therefore the Smart Grid core International Standards, IEC 61850, IEC 61968 and IEC 61970, are also very important but must be studied further to see if they can accommodate GEI, or whether it will be necessary to develop new Standards and to revise current ones. Cyber security is another major challenge for GEI, for which corresponding standards are required, and many consortia as well as ISO/IEC JTC 1 will need to re-evaluate this aspect.

5.2.4 Standards for new materials and equipment

As presented throughout this White Paper, for the implementation of GEI, energy would be globally interconnected via the Smart Grid, with UHV networks constituting the backbone and clean energy the main resource. Consideration should be given to new areas of standardization based on new material discoveries or environmental challenges that will further enable a GEI network to be installed.

For example, huge energy bases in the North Pole region and the equatorial belt area will deliver RE such as wind, solar and marine energy to customers worldwide. Higher voltage level UHV technologies will be a prerequisite for transmitting this large capacity power across long distances and to remote sites. Since the UHV transmission systems must adapt to such extreme environmental operating conditions, new energy conducting materials may need to be engineered and new reliability guidelines developed for this purpose.

Furthermore, with the rollout of the Smart Grid and microgrids, a development which implies that electrical storage will be installed at customer sites, extra RE is expected to be transferred to gas or stored in the form of hydrogen gas, thereby necessitating standards for energy transfer and energy storage technologies. The market for small and dispersed EES is also expected to grow substantially. EES will be used not only for single applications but for several objectives simultaneously by integrating the multiple dispersed storage sites that will be required by GEI.

In most cases, standardization plays a stabilizing role by pursuing research activities on which real market opportunities are built.

Section 6

Conclusion and recommendations

The GEI is an ambitious concept, integrating a large-scale deployment of clean energy led by variable renewables: a Smart Grid with various levels of interoperability and with IT and OT integration capabilities currently not deployed on an adequate scale, the large-scale deployment of advanced technologies for transmitting power over vast distances and forming high-capacity and high-voltage networks, and electrification of a large number of energy services involving new equipment.

Many of the building blocks of large-scale energy networks and an eventual GEI are available today. Large-scale RE is a reality, and achievements in UHV power transmission are redrawing the boundaries of how much power can be cost-effectively transmitted and across what distances. Technologies on the horizon, described in Section 4, will only expand this frontier further. Meanwhile, the vast potential for ICT and smart technologies in power systems has only begun to be tapped.

While the required technologies themselves are largely available or are in the pipeline, the challenge for large-scale, transcontinental or global energy interconnection is one of implementation, in which barriers and challenges will need to be overcome as the process unfolds. As such, the analysis in this White Paper provides a number of key recommendations for both evaluating and implementing large-scale interconnection and GEI.

6.1 Recommendations addressed to policy-makers and regulators

- **Policy-makers and regulators should consider the need to develop tools and methodologies to assess the costs and benefits of large-scale, regional, trans-continental and eventually global energy interconnections.** Interconnections are generally assessed on a case-by-case basis by the countries involved. Even under the relatively long planning time frames of TSOs, projects as ambitious as large-scale regional and transcontinental networks might fall below the planning horizon necessary to encourage assessment of the full range of benefits. Section 3 has presented practical experiences of regional energy interconnection, which provide confidence concerning the benefits that can be accrued when a longer-term system perspective is adopted between a large number of actors.

- **While large-scale deployment of renewables should continue to be encouraged, emphasis needs to shift to the joint planning of transmission and generation assets.** Regulators and governments should recognize the need to plan all power system elements jointly. Assessments of this aspect can reveal the advantages, for example of building long links to distant resources, reinforcing grids to pave the way for an accelerated deployment of energy generation in a given area or better designing incentives for deployment of new capacities.

- **Policy-makers and regulators should establish fora for discussion of large-scale grid interconnection initiatives.** While a large number of convening groups for industry stakeholders, governments or regulators already exist, organizations for discussing large-scale planning of grids are highly regional. Local TSO organizations have progressively coalesced into fora spanning larger geographical areas. A next natural step would be the establishment of international fora to share interconnection experiences around the world and establish dialogue concerning new opportunities.

6.2 Recommendations addressed toward meeting industrial needs

- **Studies should be carried out concerning the market readiness and economic feasibility of establishing remote bases for renewable energy, namely in far northern latitudes, in the arctic or along the equator.** While technologies have been deployed in extreme conditions, the human and implementation challenges involved in deploying generation and transmission assets on a large scale in these intense climatic conditions remain to be determined.

- **Scaling of equipment will pose challenges to industry so there will be a need for prior coordination and joint participation in demonstration efforts (e.g. development of technology), in order to avoid the first missteps on the Smart Grid.** It is clear that Smart Grid technology is a good investment but deploying the new technology is relatively expensive. The lesson learned will be to avoid the "big bang" approach in favour of a pilot demonstration-based approach. This

suggests that full-scale deployment of GEI will be phased and allow further occasions for industry to generate investment.

- **Joint planning by relevant agencies, regional bodies and TSOs should be promoted and encouraged.** Taking advantage of each country's achievements in energy technologies, strategic planning, market establishment, policy innovation and cooperative research, and making good use of these best practices throughout the world, could significantly enhance the "know-how" of all stakeholders.

- **A coordinated and collaborative approach to code drafting and code implementation is needed to ensure that the activity of systems operators is compliant with the network codes.** In the context of the GEI market model, it should be discussed whether a centrally operated GEI market communication hub could help to increase the efficiency of the GEI processes. This could involve a cloud-based service provided by an "IEC-like" organization, which centrally orchestrates the communication flows and intercompany data exchange between all GEI participants.

6.3 Recommendations addressed to the IEC and its committees

- **The IEC Market Strategy Board (MSB) should consider new internal avenues that will allow the IEC to provide faster responses to industry.** In light of the large number of stakeholders who would have an interest in GEI, the MSB should enhance its outreach to industry through the activity of its project teams. The latter should survey the needs surrounding revolutionary GEI-related technologies.

- **It is recommended that the IEC Standardization Management Board (SMB) form an Advisory Committee on GEI to help prioritize needs in this area and to coordinate development of standardization efforts in response to these needs.** Specifically the AC should consider internal coordination for development of an architectural framework clarifying the GEI concept and the rules of interoperability and integration. This would involve identifying the gaps between the requirements for GEI and the existing interoperability Standards developed in the affected technical committees.

- **The IEC should consider expanding opportunities to affiliate countries in the equatorial regions for full participation in the development of International Standards for GEI.** As the equatorial regions of the globe will generate and contribute significant amounts of solar and wind energy to the GEI network, the IEC should encourage IEC Affiliate National Electrotechnical Committees (NECs) with Affiliate Plus status to be actively engaged in the Standards process for solar and wind. It is recognized that the IEC Affiliate Country Programme has been a pioneer in bringing the benefits and advantages of involvement in the IEC to many countries throughout the world, not only through the benefits afforded by the Programme, but also via measures such as opening participation in its Conformity Assessment Systems to developing countries Such Affiliates will directly benefit from the investment necessary for bringing large-scale renewables online, thus helping to bring social benefits in the form of energy access to clean power and opportunities for local capacity building and employment.

Bibliography

[1] WISER, R., LANTZ, E., HAND, M., et al., *IEA Wind Task 26: The Past and Future Cost of Wind Energy*, IEA Wind, May, 2012.

[2] International Energy Agency, *Medium-Term Renewable Energy Market Report 2015*, [Online]. Available: www.iea.org/bookshop/708-Medium-Term_Renewable_Energy_Market_Report_2015. [Accessed 19 September 2016].

[3] *Report of the enquiry committee on grid disturbance in Northern Region on 30th July 2012 and in Northern, Eastern and North-Eastern Region on 31th July 2012*, [Online]. Available: powermin.nic.in/ sites/default/files/uploads/GRID_ENQ_REP_16_8_12.pdf. [Accessed 19 September 2016].

[4] Operador nacional do Sistema Eléctrico (ONS), *Mapas do SIN*, [Online]. Available: www.ons.org.br/ conheca_sistema/mapas_sin.aspx. [Accessed 19 September 2016].

[5] Global Energy Network Institute (GENI), *The Water-Energy Nexus in the Amu Darya River Basin: The Need for Sustainable Solutions to a Regional Problem*, [Online]. Available: www.geni.org/ globalenergy/research/water-energy-nexus-amudarya-river/Water-Energy Nexus-AmuDarya-River-RD.pdf. [Accessed 19 September 2016].

[6] Nepal Energy Forum, *Pros and cons of regional electricity grid*, [Online]. Available: www. nepalenergyforum.com/pros-and-cons-of-regional-electricity-grid. [Accessed 19 September 2016].

[7] LIU, Z., *Global Energy Interconnection*, Elsevier, 2015.

[8] BONPARD, E., FULLI, G., ARDELEAN, M., MASERA, M., *Evolution, Opportunities, and Critical Issues for Pan-European Transmission*, IEEE Power and Energy Magazine, Vol. 12, no. 2, pp. 40-50, 2014.

[9] ZHANG, Yi, ZHANG, Yang, *Overview of the Practice of Renewable Generation Integration and Transmission Planning in North America*, Energy Technology and Economics, Vol. 23, no. 8, pp. 1-7, 23, 2011.

[10] KUMAGAI, J., *The U.S. may finally get a unified power grid*, IEEE Spectrum, Vol. 53, Issue 1, pp. 35-36, January 2016.

[11] ANDREWS, D., *Why Do We Need The Supergrid, What Is Its Scope And What Will It Achieve?*, A Claverton Energy Reseach Institute Presentation, 19 June 2009.

[12] MANO, S., OVGOR, B., SAMADOV, Z., et al., *Gobitec and Asian Super Grid for Renewable Energies in Northeast Asia*, Spotinov print Ltd., 2014.

[13] IEC, *Grid integration of large-capacity Renewable Energy sources and use of large-capacity Electrical Energy Storage*, White Paper, 2012.

[14] HUI, L., *Research on the Economics of Ultra-High Voltage and Global Energy Interconnection*, Presentation, Sino-Europe Workshop on Technology and Equipment of Global Energy Interconnection, Berlin, 10-11 December 2015.

[15] ADAPA, R., *HVDC Technology: The State of the Art*, IEEE Power and Energy Magazine, Vol. 10, no. 6, pp. 18-29, 2012.

[16]   MAJUMDER R., BARTZSCH, C., KOHNSTAM, P., et al., *High-voltage DC on the New Power Transmission Highway*, IEEE Power and Energy Magazine, Vol. 10, no. 6, pp. 39-49, 2012.

[17]   ANDERSEN, B. R., *HVDC Grids – Overview of CIGRE Activities and Personal Views*, CIGRE, 2014, [Online]. Available: www.e-cigre.org/.../ELT_275_2(2).pdf. [Accessed 19 September 2016].

[18]   YUE, B., MEI, N., LIU, S.-Y., et al., *Overview of HVDC Flexible*, China Electric Power (Technology Edition), no. 5, pp. 43-47, 2014 [in Chinese].

[19]   CHEN, G., HAO, M., XU Z., et al., *Review of High Voltage Direct Current Cables*, CSEE Journal of Power and Energy Systems, Vol. 1, no. 2, pp. 9-21, 2015.

[20]   BAHRMAN, M. P., JOHNSON, B. K., *The ABCs of HVDC Transmission Technologies*, IEEE Power and Energy Magazine, Vol. 5, no. 2, pp. 32-44, 2007.

[21]   LUNDBERG, P., CALLAVIK, M., BAHRMAN, M., SANDEBERG, P., *High-Voltage DC Converters and Cable Technologies for Offshore Renewable Integration and DC Grid Expansion*, IEEE Power and Energy Magazine, Vol. 10, no. 6, pp. 31-38, 2012.

[22]   RAO, H., *Architecture of Nan'ao Multi-terminal VSC-HVDC System and Its Multifunctional Control*, CSEE Journal of Power and Energy Systems, Vol. 1, no. 1, pp. 9-18, 2015.

[23]   TANG, G., HE, Z., HUI, P., et al., *Basic Topology and Key Devices of the Five-Terminal DC Grid*, CSEE Journal of Power and Energy Systems, Vol. 1, no. 2, pp. 22-35, 2015.

[24]   YAO L., WU., J., WANG, Z., et al., *Pattern Analysis of Future HVDC Grid Development*, Proceedings of the CSEE, Vol. 34, no. 34, pp. 6007-6012, 2014.

[25]   XUMING, L., *Technology Research and Application Prospect of Half-wavelength Alternating Current Transmission*, Smart Grid, Vol. 3, no. 12, pp. 1091-1096, 2015 [in Chinese].

[26]   LIYE, X., LIANGZHEN, L., *Status Quo and Trends of Superconducting Power Transmission Technology*, Transactions Of China Electrotechnical Society, Vol. 30, no.7, pp. 1-9, 2015 [in Chinese].

[27]   SOONEE, S. K., AGRAWAL, V. K., AGARWAL, P. K., et al., *The view from the wide side: wide-area monitoring systems in India*, IEEE Power and Energy Magazine, Vol. 13, no. 5, pp. 49-59, 2015.

[28]   NUTHALAPATI, S., PHADKE, A. G., *Managing the grid using synchrophasor technology*, IEEE Power and Energy Magazine, Vol. 13, no. 5, pp. 10-12, 2015.

[29]   LU, C., SHI, B., WU, X., SUN, H., *Advancing China's smart: phasor measurement units in wide-area management system*, IEEE Power and Energy Magazine, Vol. 13, no. 5, pp. 60-71, 2015.